ORANGE COUNTY VIRGINIA FAMILIES

Volume III

Contents of this volume contain the second half of Browning's Extracts, a typewritten loose-leaf book kept by J. W. Browning, county clerk of Orange County, Virginia, from 1930 to 1936. Much of this data was taken from loose papers and supplemented by items not recorded and are believed to be the only source for this valuable information. The list of King's Attorneys, Surveyors, Churchwardens, Justices, Sheriffs, Ministers, Magistrates, are valuable for those seeking memberships in patriotic organizations. Brief sketches of many Orange County Families that are connected by marriage include the Ballards, Brockmans, Cattertons, Dowells, Salmons, Rhodes, Chapmans, Collins, Ellis', Humes, Macons, Masons, Montagues, Quisenberrys, Simms, Terretts, Towles, Clarks, Smoots, and Willis of Orange. Bible records of Graves, Shotwell, Edwards, Salmon, Mahannes, Marshall and Durrett.

Compiled by:
William Everett Brockman

Southern Historical Press, Inc.
Greenville, South Carolina

This volume was reproduced from
An 1957 edition located in the
Publisher's Private Library
Greenville, South Carolina

Please direct all correspondence and orders to:

www.southernhistoricalpress.com
or
SOUTHERN HISTORICAL PRESS, Inc.
PO Box 1267
Greenville, SC 29602-1267
southernhistoricalpress@gmail.com

Originally published: Minneapolis, MN, 1957

ISBN #0-89308-795-5

Printed in the United States of America

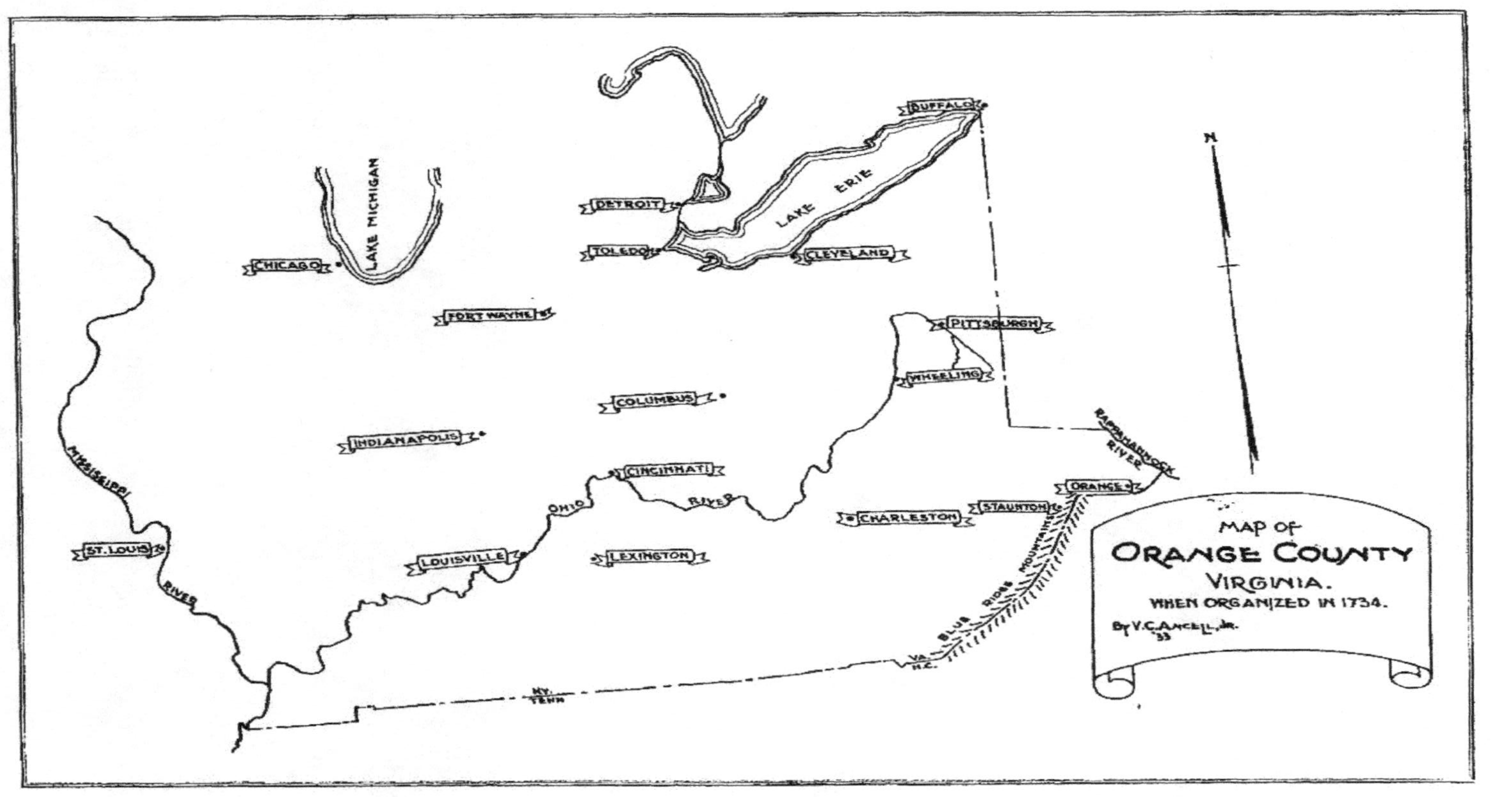
MAP OF
ORANGE COUNTY
VIRGINIA.
WHEN ORGANIZED IN 1734.
BY V. C. ANCELL, JR.
'33
N
LAKE MICHIGAN
LAKE ERIE
CHICAGO
DETROIT
TOLEDO
CLEVELAND
BUFFALO
FORT WAYNE
PITTSBURGH
WHEELING
COLUMBUS
INDIANAPOLIS
CINCINNATI
OHIO
RIVER
CHARLESTON
STAUNTON
ORANGE
RAPPAHANNOCK
RIVER
ST. LOUIS
MISSISSIPPI
RIVER
LOUISVILLE
LEXINGTON
BLUE RIDGE MOUNTAINS
VA.
N.C.
KY.
TENN.

ORANGE COUNTY VIRGINIA FAMILIES VOLUME III

The publication of any genealogy or historical treatise brings much correspondence and leads to research so that gradually a vast amount of information is collected from private sources. Unless this data is made available it becomes lost and posterity is deprived of its usefulness. Many of the names mentioned in this third edition of Orange County Virginia Families are living and have been living in other counties east and west and south of Orange. However when one considers the indefinite county lines that existed for a half century and that Orange County once extended west to the Mississippi River and north to the Great Lakes and that most of the settlers of Orange were from the lower counties, then it is not incorrect to include all of Virginia north of the James River, as having some connection with the county of Orange. The early settlers camped on the water and followed the streams west and gradually crossed the Blue Ridge, and others went Southwest to the Carolinas and the far South. Those living in Essex found in many cases that after 1734 they were in Orange, and those in New Kent after 1758 were residents of Albermarle and Louisa, and from Henrico, Goochland and southern Albermarle were populated. The ruthless destruction of records in some of the lower counties during the Revolutionary and War between the states has added confusion to research and it is said that the shortage of paper for loading muskets necessitated the use of county records and it is satisfying that so much does remain. For those in search of private records, I have found the attic and the upstairs over old coach houses or garages the favorite source. The much sought after Captain William Simms Bible was located by myself and a relative in the attic at Aspen Grove, Albermarle, and the Bible of Ambrose Brockman in the upstairs garage at the home of Sampson Jones in Kentucky. Other instances exist and in so many cases the families having these records give little thought to their value but when discovered they cling to them as if they were secret documents and are reluctant to allow their careful examination. In one home in Orange County all of the Sheriff's records were found in an old desk but they should be turned over to the county clerk. Many of the old families receive requests for family data with coldness and give the impression that their private rights are being invaded, since they are satisfied and rest on the laurels that have been passed down to them by their fathers. With much pride they refer to Crown Grants, Land Patents, as if some great honor was being bestowed on their forefathers, and of course this is one way that the English Kings had of paying off their debts for political support just as a politician may now be given a cabinet post for "services rendered" either in the form of money or influence. Many of the large grants in Virginia came through rulers such as the two Charles, Cromwell, James the 1st, but those who were on the losing side found themselves in the West Indies and many finally made their way to the States as head-rights and had to work out their freedom to pay their "importer" for advancing their passage money. In one case a dear lady denied that she had a certain Bible and when I finally gained access to it I found that one member of the family several generations back, had "taken his life by his own hand", just as the father had written it in the Bible. My practice has been to forget such things and in cases of mental derangement where guardians have been appointed, I have not found room enough to fit it into the copy. If it were possible to collect and arrange the mass of information that is submitted by applicants for membership in the organizations such as the D.A.R., truly there would be a valuable source of information that would fill many books. Somehow this data is considered secret and it took me three years and two trips to the East Coast to dig up information that was all the time in one of the "secret" files of a library in Washington. The librarians as such have been most cooperative and in many cases have made their records available on Holidays and off-hours. To these and others my thanks and appreciation.

W E Brockman
October 1959

A REVIEW OF ORANGE COUNTY FAMILIES VOL. II. BY W. E. ROCKMAN, 1956.

By Kathrine Cox Gottschalk. (1959)
650 East Capitol St., N.E., Washington 3, D.C.

This splendid compilation of Court Records from the books in Orange County, Virginia (Court House) is very valuable to any one interested in research in this county or the areas cut off from the jurisdiction of the original formation of the Court of Orange County. These were the counties of Culpeper in 1749 and Madison in 1793 and the vast sections taken from Orange County when the great influx of settlers poured in down the Shenandoah Valley to the south even to North Carolina. This made it necessary to organize Courts convenient for these settlers to record their transactions. Augusta County was thus formed in 1745. It extended from what is the present boundary between Rockingham and Shenandoah County. The area above or northward and westward from a line drawn on westward from this boundary line was organized as Frederick County. (1743)

The earliest records of this western Area were usually recorded in the very early books of Orange County. On pages 50-51-52-53-54-55-56-57, beginning at the seventh line of this book you will find a 'List of IMPORTATIONS to Orange County, Va." These were the declarations made from the new comers to the Valley of Virginia, that is of Augusta and Frederick Co., Va. in order to obtain their headrights, and title to the fifty acres, due them. Later you will find them on the newly formed Courts of Augusta and Frederick and the counties formed from that jurisdictional area.

Then again on pages 135 et seq. the lists of tithables in the several districts beginning in 1735 is valuable in learning the locations for residence of Orange County at that time.

The long list of marriages has a duplication in assembling some of the pages in this section and in a few other places some names are not quite rightly spelled. This misspelling occurs on the transcribed books in Orange Co., lately done from the old books. I noticed this on my last visit to Orange Court House.

CONTENTS

* Browning's Abstracts
Omitted from volume II.

Tithables Orange County 1734

John Christopher......... 9
William Dann............. 3
John Hawkins.............13
Alex Waugh............... 6
Samuel Goerge............ 6
Valentine Morgan......... 6
William Clark............ 3
Capt Spencer.............13
Benjamin Horn............ 1
John Smith............... 3
Nathan Turner............ 3
James Whitum............. 3
William Minor............ 2
John Branham............. 9
William Morton...........14
William Smith............ 4
John Farrell............. 2
George Offett............ 2
Solomon Ryan............. 1
William Christopher...... 2
Nicholas Christopher..... 2
Old Adam................. 1
Thos Wharton............. 3
Charles Watts............ 3
Willima Chronoker........ 4
James Thorton............ 1
John Wells............... 1
John Dozer............... 5
Thomas Wight............. 1
A.C.Willis, 4. quarters
William Davis............ 2
Jonathan Ferrell......... 5
Will Hawkins............. 1
John H. Orin............. 1
John Edwards............. 1
George Wharton........... 3
Benjamin.................
Will Bussom.............. 2
James Sturner............ 1
Georfe Anderson, Sr...... 4
John Underwood........... 3
George Anderson, Jr...... 1
George Anderson, Jr...... 1
Samuel Anderson.......... 2
John Manewell............ 5
Richard Simms............ 1
John Dolwood............. 1
Theo Edings.............. 2

Thos Roceford................
Henry Jonson.................
Thos Russell................ 1
H. John Curtis...............
Steven Racoon............... 1
Thos Fore................... 2
Edward Price.................
Allen Newman................ 4
Thos Michael................ 1
Briant Sisson............... 3
Will Sisson................. 3
Robt. Urvil.................11
Thomas Ssims................ 2
Thos Rolloy................. 4
John Ingram................. 4
John Marks.................. 4
Samuel Graves............... 4
Richard Pennum.............. 4
John Pottoy................. 3
Thos........................ 1
Andrew Moore................ 3
Fran Moore.................. 3
John Fisher................. 2
Robt Russell................ 2
Thos Shambles............... 2
Will Connor................. 2
Luke Thorton................ 2
John Ranfield............... 1
George Wells................ 2

(Spelling in many cases guess-work)

Tithables in Precinct of George Smith
1736-37

Mrs Brockman.....Two Quarters.
John Brockman....One Quarter.

Correction 1753

Andrew Mannen............... 1

* From the private records of J. W. Browning, County Clerk of Orange County, 1730-36.

CLERKS OF COURT

Henry Willis 1734
Jonathan Gibson ... September 1740
John Nicholas ..... March 1745
George Taylor ..... March 1749
James Taylor ...... November 1772

KINGS ATTORNEYS

John Mercer 1734
Zachary Lewis......November 1735
John Lewis.........July 1764
John Walker (States Attorney) 1780

SHERIFF'S

Benjamin Cave 1734
Charles Curtis................1737
Robert Green..................1739
Richard Winslow...............1741
William Russell...............1743
Thomas Chew...................1745
Edward Spencer................1747
Benjamin Cave.................1749
Tavener Beale.....December 25, 1751
Joseph Thomas.....November 1753
James Madison.....November 1755
Alex Waugh........November 1757
Francis Moore.....November 1759
Thomas Jameson....November 1761
William Bell......November 1763
Rowland Thomas...October 1765
Richard Thomas...November 1767
Reuben Daniel....October 1769
James Walker.....October 1771
Zachary Burnley..October 1773
Thomas Barbour...March 1776
William Bell.....November 1780
Rowland Thomas...October 1782
William Moore....December 1784
Thomas Barbour...October 1788
Johnny Scott.....November 1790
Thomas Bell......November 1792
William Moore....November 1796
Mary Bell, appointed Jaiolor, July, 1781

SURVEYORS

James Wood, commissioner for William and Mary College...................... 1734
Thomas Lewis, for Augusta County.. 1744
George Hume.. 1751
Zachary Taylor, for William and Mary College..................... December 1751
William Moore, for William and Mary College...................... March 1768

Order Book PAGE	NAME OF CO. SURVEYOR	DATE
68	Richard Crittenden Webb. (Com. for W. & M. Col)	
	CORONERS FOR COUNTY	
53	Thomas Chew	Feb. 1735
	William Gooch	Feb. 1735
283	Robert Slaughter	Nov. 1740
	James Patton (for Augusta)	Feb. 1743
	Peter School (for Augusta)	May 1740
180	Benj. Cave	June 1749
538	William Taliaferro	June 1760
5	James Madison	May 1763
	Francis Moore	May 1763
5	Francis Moore	Nov. 1776
	William Bell	Feb. 1777
	JUSTICES	
1	Alcock, John	1787 Oct. & 1796 Feb.
1	Barbour, James	1734
1	Bell, Samuel	1734
8	Bordan Benj.	1734
51	Buchannan, John	1741 Nov.
	Bell, Wm.	1754 Feb.
235	Beale, Richard	1756 May
463	Barbour, Richard	1759 May
533	Burnley, Zachary	1760 May
492	Barbour, Thomas	1768 May
514	Bell, Thomas	1768 July
	Beale, Wm.	1787 Oct.
	Burton, May Jr.	1796 Feb.
	Brumley, Benj.	1796 Feb.
1	Chew, Thomas	1734
1	Cave, Benj.	1734
89	Curtis, Charles	1736
181	Coleman, James	1737 June
26	Catlett, John	1739 July
344	Campbell, Andrew	1742 Feb.
419	Clayton, Phillip	1743 Apr.
461	Chester, Thos.	1743 May
461	Campbell, Andrew	1743 May
66	Conway, Catlett	1777 May
	Campbell, Wm.	1787 Oct.
	Cowherd, Francis	1787 Oct.
	Cave, Belfield	1796 Oct.
463	Daniel, Reuben	1759 May
	Davis, Isaac Jr.	1787 Oct.
	Daniel, Robt.	1787 Oct.
180	Downs, Henry	1749 June
9	Eastham, Robt.	1734
	Ellis, Thos.	1787
1.	Field, Abraham	1734

PAGE	JUSTICES	DATE
1.	Finlason, John	1734
181	Field, Henry	1737 June
1.	Green, Robt.	1734
	Givins, Samuel	1739 July
66	Grymes, Benj.	1777 May
	Gordon, James	1787 Oct.
1.	Hite, Joist	1734
8.	Hobson, John	1734
89	Hobson, Geo.	1736
	Johnson, Benj.	1787
	Jameson, Thomas	1754 Feb.
1	Lightfoot, John	1734
2	Lightfoot, Goodridge	1734
	Lewis, John	1739 July
8.	Morgan, Morgan	1734
89	Mauldin, Richard	1736 July
107	McDowell, John	1739 Feb.
180	Madison, James	1749 Jan.
180	Moore, Francis	1749 Jan.
	Morton, Jeremiah	1754 Feb.
463	Morton, Elijah	1756 May
481	Moore, William	1768 Apr.
66	Madison, James Jr.	1777 May
66.	Mallory, Uriel	1777 May
	Moore, John	1796 Feb.
	Morton, George (refused to qualify)	1796 Feb.
	Mallory, William	1796 Oct.
1.	Pollard, James	1734
347	Patton, James	1742 Feb.
461	Pendleton, James	1743 May
492	Pannill, William	1768 May
	Porter, Chas.	1787 Oct.
	Porter, Champ	1796 Feb.
	Parrott, Wm.	1796 Oct.
89	Russell, William	1736 July
	Rucker, John	1739 July
461	Robinson, George	1743 May
	Robb, James	1787 Oct.
	Row, Thomas	1796 Oct.
1.	Smith, Augustine	1734
1.	Slaughter, Robert	1734
8.	Smith, John	1734
	Spencer, Edward	1737 July
57	Slaughter, Robert	1741 Nov.
461	Schule, Peter	1743
481	Shepherd, Andrew	1768 Apr.
481	Scott, Johnny	1768 Apr.
	Spotswood, John	1787 Oct.
	Scott, John Jr.	1796 Feb.
	Spotswood, John	1796 Oct.

PAGE	JUSTICES	DATE
	Shepherd, Andrew	1796 Oct.
1.	Taliaferro, John	1734
181	Taylor, George	1737 June
181	Triplet, William	1737 June
461	Thomas, Joseph,	1743 May
461	Thomas, Richard	1743 May
235	Thomas, Rowland	1756 May
180	Taliaferro, William	1749 Jan.
180	Taylor, Erasmus	1749 Jan.
235	Thomas, Richard	1756 May
556	Thomas, Joseph Jr.	1760 May (See May 1743, P. 461)
514	Taliaferro, Lawrence	1768 July
	Taylor, Hubbard	1787 Oct.
89	Taylor, Zachary	1736 July
	Uiquehart, Charles	1796 Oct.
461	Vaunce, David	1743 May
181	Winslow, Richard	1737 June
148	Wood, James	1742 April
180	Willis, John	1749 June
180	Waugh, Alexander	1749 June
533	Walker, James	1760 May
66	White, Jeremiah	1777 May
	White, William	1787 Oct.

MAGISTRATES PERIOD 1800-1822

Thomas Barbour	Peyton Grymes	Robt. T. Moore
May Burton	Armstead C. Gordon	Dabney Minor
William T. Burruss	Thomas Grasty	John Morrison
Sanford Beazley	George Grasty	John McCall
Tandy Bowcock	Charles P. Howard	William Parrott
Benj. Burton	Benj. Hume	Thomas Row
James Barbour	Edmund Henshaw	Edmond Row
Francis Cowherd	John Henshaw	John Spotswood
Belfield Cave	Wm. W. Johnson	Wm. H. Stanard
Thomas Coleman	Valentine Johnson	Thomas Sorrille
Philips C. Cave	Berryman Jennings	John W. Sale
Lawrence T. Dade	Reuben Lindsay	Baldwin Taliaferro
Isaac Davis, Jr.	John Moore	Richard H. Taliaferro
Thomas Ellis	George Morris	John Taylor
Goodridge L. Grasty	John Mallory	David Whitelow

CHURCH WARDENS AND VESTRYMEN

PAGE	NAME	PARISH	DATE
	Burton, May	Scotts	
146	Beale, Tavenor	St. Thomas c.w.	June 1748
316	Beale, Richard	St. Thomas Ves.	March 1757
512	Bell, William	St. Thomas	Feb. 1759
5	Barbour, Richard	St. Thomas Ves.	May 1763
234	Bell, Thomas	St. Thomas Ves.	Nov. 1764
	Ball, Samuel (appt. in 1731)	St. Thomas Ves.	March 1774

PAGE	NAME	PARISH	DATE
308	Burnley, Zachaiah	St. Thomas VES.	March 1774
	Barbour, James	Ch. Warden - (See Church Wardens vs. Williams - May, 1753)	
204	Catlett, Jno.	St. Marks C.W.	June 1740
169	Cave, Benj.	St. Thomas C.W.	June 1742
	Chew, Thomas	St. Thomas	Nov. 1746 (Suit vs. James)
146	Cave, Benj.	(appt. 1731)	June 1748
363	Curtis, Charles	St. Thomas	Feb. 1752
334	Coleman, James	St. Thomas C.W.	May 1757
367	Chew, Thomas	St. Thomas C.W.	Feb. 1758
532	Cave, Benj.	St. Thomas VES.	April 1761
	Clayton Phillip	St. Thomas C.W.	March 1746
	Downs, Henry	St. Thomas C.W.	May 1741
	Finlason, John (appt. 1731 or 1736)	St. Thomas	
54	Field, Henry	St. Marks C.W.	Feb. 1743
	Kirtley, Francis (Parish Hist.)	St. Marks C.W.	March 1746
182	Green, Robert (appt. 1731)	St. Marks	July 1744
81	Grymes, Benj.	St. Thomas vs.	March 1777
	Lightfoot, Goodrich	St. Marks (Ch. Warden)	July 1747
	Moore, Francis	St. Thomas C.W. (Ch. Warden vs. Lane)	May 1762
352	Madison, James	St. Thomas VES.	Dec. 1751
428	Madison, James	St. Thomas C.W.	Apr. 1753
525	Madison, James	St. Thomas C.W.	
523	Madison, James	St. Thomas VES.	Apr. 1761
532	Moore, Francis	St. Thomas VES.	May 1760
532	Moore, Francis	St. Thomas VES.	Apr. 1761
234	Moore, William	St. Thomas	Nov. 1764
125	Peyton, William (appt. 1731)	St. Marks	May 1748
308	Pannill, William	St. Thomas VES.	Mar. 1774
182	Russell, Wm.	St. Marks	July 1744
125	Roberts, Benj.	St. Marks (Ch. Wardens vs. Ruth Hace)	May 1748
	Spencer, Edward	St. Thomas C.W.	May 1742
291	Slaughter, Francis	St. Marks C.W.	Nov. 1742
204	Stanton, Thomas	St. Marks	1740
430	Slaughter, Robert (appt. 1731)	St. Marks	May 1743
430	Slaughter, Francis	St. Marks C.W.	May 1743
363	Sisson, Bryan	St. Thomas C.W.	Feb. 1753
100	Shepperd Andrew	St. Thomas VES.	Nov. 1770
	Sisson, Bryan	St. Thomas C.W.	Feb. 1751
393	Taliaferro, William	St. Thomas VES.	Nov. 24, 1752
169	Thomas, Richard	St. Thomas C.W	June 1742
	Thomas, Joseph	St. Thomas C.W.	Nov. 1754 (1751)
56	Taylor, Erasmus	St. Thomas VES.	Nov. 1754
76	Taliaferro, Wm.	St. Thomas C.W.	Mar. 1755
428	Taylor, Zach	St. Thomas C.W.	Apr. 1753
525	Taylor, Zach	St. Thomas C.W.	(Ch. Wardens vs. Copling)
	Triplet, William	St. Thomas C.W.	Nov. 1742
334	Taylor, Eras.	St. Thomas C.W.	Apr. 1760
76	Taylor, George	St. Thomas C.W.	Mar. 1755
538	Thomas, Richard	St. Thomas VES.	Aug. 1760

PAGE	NAME	PARISH	DATE
552	Taylor, George	St. Thomas VES.	Apr. 1761
532	Thomas, Richard	St. Thomas VES.	Apr. 1761
558	Taylor, Zachary	St. Thomas VES.	May 1761
558	Taylor, Eras.	St. Thomas VES.	May 1761
630	Thomas, Rowland	St. Thomas VES.	Apr. 1762
538	Waugh, Alex.	St. Thomas VES.	May 1761
101	Walker, James	St. Thomas VES.	Feb. 1771
101	Walker, John	St. Thomas VES.	Feb. 1771

ATTORNEYS

NAME	DATE	
Battaley, Moseley	Feb. 1748	
Buchannon, Andrew	Apr. 1772	
Burnley, Harden	May 1784	
Brook, Robert	Jan. 1785	
Bell, John	Feb. 1787	
Bruce, Richard	Jan. 1784	
Broughton, Edward	June 1737	
Dixon, Roger	Feb. 1748	
Dunlap, Ephriam	May 1773	
Edwards, John	Nov. 1742	
Hamilton, John	1739	(Book 2 - Page 47)
Lewis, Zachary	Nov. 1742	
Lewis, Zachary	1734	(Book 1 - Page 2)
Lewis, John	May 1761	
Mossom, David	Feb. 1739	(page 106)
Mossom, David	Feb. 1739	
Morton, Joseph	Jan. 1742	
Moore, Bernard	Apr. 1772	
Meickee, John	Mar. 1781	
Mercer, John	Jan. 1734	
Newport, John	Jan. 1743	
Pendleton, Edmund	May 1741	
Portheus, James	June 1746	
Pendleton, Henry Jr.	May 1765	
Porter, Benjamin	Feb. 1775	
Peacock, Robertware	Aug. 1792	
Quinn, John Page 277	Nov. 1742	
Rogers, Thomas	May 1753	
Robinson, Thomas	Mar. 1763	
Robinson, Charles	June 1766	
Robinson, Henry	June 1768	
Rose, John	Aug. 1772	
Row, Benj.	Dec. 1790	
Sherman, John	Sept. 1743	(Book 4, Page 6)
Semple, John	Mar. 1754	
Turner, Robert	1734	
Towles, Oliver	Apr. 1762	
Taylor, Robert	Aug. 29, 1783	

Vass, Robert B.	Mar. 1791
Underwood, Wm.	June 1766
Waller, William	Nov. 1736
Wyth, George	May 1748
Wyth, George	May 1746
Walker, John	Oct. 1765

PETITION OF INHABITANTS OF OPICKON June 1738-1739

To the worshipful his Majesty's Justices of Orange County Shewith: That ye petitioners at present lay under great Inconvenience for want of a road from Jost Hytes Mill to Ashby's Ford on Shanando humbly pray that ye worships will order that a wagon road be cleared. And ye petitioners be.

David Vance
Abner Hollingsworth
Robert Allane
William Hogg
Robert Smith
Peter Woolf
Jno. Nation
William Reed
Luke Vickery
Thomas Branson, Jr.
Thos. Postgate
Robert Wanth
James Vance
Ellis Thomas

Philip Kenny
Muhla Devine
Isaac Parkins
John Branson
William Vance
Edward Garder
Benj. Borden
Richard Wood
John: Hockli?
Joseph Colyer
John Harrow
John Harrow
Nathaniel Thomas
Isaac Davenport

John Hite
John MacDowell
Joseph Davenport
Charles Barns
Robert Mackby
George Bowman
Joseph Robins
John Goskin
George Lister
Charles Genodarick
Gesheim Woodel
Geshium Woodel
Jacob Christman
Stockli

PRESBYTERIAN

To the worshipful bench of Orange County Greeting 1735-36
The Petition of the Inhabitants of Opeckon and Shenadore humbly shewith:

The Bearer hereof the Rev. M. William Wms. Minister of the Gospel Hath promised to supply us in the administration of his office we humbly beg that Meeting places might be erected and rended in your Court one at the land of the abovesaid. M. Wm. near his house and another at Mr. Morgan Bryan near his house and your petitioners shall pray.

Morgan Morgan
John Hood
Elisha Pukin's
Benj. Hardin
Rich. L. Lane
Jacob Everson
Henry Lanscisco
Wm. Shirell
Thos Flora

Tunas Newkink
Robt. Railton
Davene Nukerlk
Michael Myar
Corn. Newkirk
Joseph Hardin
William Teague
Thos. Caudery
Eumch Freeland

Henry Friggs
Eben Rice
Robt. Turner
Tunes Hood
Thomas Cole
Thos. Cherry
John Sheneo
James Matson
Wm. Sheppard

To the Worshipful his Majesties Justices of Orange County instantly sitting.

We the undersigned subscribers begs leave to acquaint your Worships that we labour under great hardship for ye want of a good road that is suitable and convenient for us to go to market. Therefore we humbly beg that your worships would take it to your consideration and Mr. Jonah Danton and Mr. Thos. Branson, jun. Surveyors to lay out a road beginng about a mile below George Harrisons in that Road and so through that woods to Thos. Bransons and so along to Sherando River opposite to Manases Run and from thence through the Gap of the Blue Ridge between Ashbys bent gap & Chisters Gap which we have obtained an order of Prince William Court for ad road through the sd. Gap which is supposed to be the furst gap that ever was found in the Blue Ridge.

And your petitioners as in duty bound will ever pray. July 24, 1738.

Benj. Borden
James Boune
Thos. Branson
Benj. Borden
James Crawford
Sam. Cornegon
Robert Calvert
Ed. Coder
Jonah Denton
Jonathan Denton
Walter Drenin
John Denton
William Demose
Charles Daton

Henry Falkenborough
Andrew Falkenborough
Jacob Falkenborough
Henry Falkenborough
John Harrow
Jacob Hite
Jost Hite
Thomas Hawkins
Geo. Hoge
Peter Hopkins
Thomas Hawkins
John Janton
Thomas Locleto
James Mour
James Mc:ish

Robt. MacKevy
Thos Malcurn
James Macchews
Lewis Neil
Thos. Postgate
John Rose
Edward Rosson
James Mour
Will. Rentfro
Edw. Rogers
John Stephenson
John Shelden
Geo. Thuston
James Wgmory
David Vance

N. B. Chestnut Mts. now Clarks Mt., in my opinion)
Found in Judgments Sept. 1742 (A & L.)

To the worshipful court of Orange County:

The humble petition of Francis Moore be the other inhabitants of Chestnut mountains

Humbly preyeth that your worships may be pleased to grant to your Pet. an order to open the old road to be cleared along the Ridge of the Ad. mountains into the road that goes along by Mr. John Taliaferros Quarter to Fredericksburg, part of it being lately stopped by Mr. Taliaferros Overseer, it being the only way at present for rolling your plt Tobacco & also in a short time when the church is finished will be the best & only way thither, which your Pet. humbly hope your worship will be pleased consider.
And your petitioners will ever pray.

Tavenor Beale
John Bourn
Jno. Aranham
Andrew Bourn
Batllis Baker
Henry Bourn
Wm. Christopher
Tully Choyce
Wm. Cash
Wm. Christopher

Charles Foushee
John Foushee
Benj. Hawkins
Charles Lee
Harbin Moore
Harbin Moore
Wm. Minner
Wm. Morton
Fran. Moore
John Pennon
Thomas Pettey Jr.

Prices (Quarter)
John Roberts
John Smith, Jr.
Luke Thornton
James Thornton
Mark Thornton
John Thornton
Thomas Thornton
Geo. Wells
John Wells

1739.

To the Worshipful Court of Orange County
We the subscribers inhabitants on Beverly Mannor on behalf of ourselves and the other inhabitants of that part call'd the County of Augusta.
Humbly Shewith:

That we live beyong the Blue Ridge we cannot carry on any trade of consequence to the falls of Rapidan River unless a wagon road is cleared over the said ridge..... from John Trembles or thereabouts., by or through George Robinson to the top of the Blue Ridge and appoint David Davis, George Hutchison & Robert page to lay off and make the same and we as in duty bound shall ever pray

James Caldwell
Patt Campbell
James Davis
Thosm Henderson
John Lewis
Andrew McClure
Robert Turk
George Hutchison
James Cathey
Samuel Givins
Robert King
Daniel Monehon
George Robinson

To the worshipful Majestys Justices of Orange County. The petition of sundry inhabitants of Opickon. Shewith That ye petitioners at present lay under great ill convenience for want of a road from Jost Hyte to Ashby's bent Ford on Shenando humbly pray that ye worship. Will order that wagon road be cleared.
And ye petitioners

Robert allane
Thomas Branson Jr.
John Branson Jr.
Benj. Borden
Charl Barns
George Bowman
Edward Carder
Jacob Christian
Hukl Devine
Joseph Davenport
Isaac Davenport
John Gaskin
Abner Hollinsworth
William Hog
Johnnie Hocklè (Stockil)
John Harrow
George Harrison
John Hite
Jerry Lister
John MacDowel
Robert Mackoy
Isaac Perkins
Jno. Nation
Thos. Postgate
Joseph Robins
William Reed
Robert Smith
James Thomas
Ellis Thomas
Nathaniel Thomas
Luke Vickery
William Vance
David Vance
Peter Woolf
Robert Wauth
Richard Wood
Geshein Woodel

EARLY MINISTERS OF ORANGE COUNTY

Epharim Abell	1790	Baptist	
John Bicket	Nov. 1739	Episcopal	Presented for not celebrating Lord's Supper.
Aaron Bledsoe	Apr. 1778	(Oath Fidelity) Apr. 26, 1781, licensed to marry.	
Bartlett Bennett	Oct. 1778	(Oath Fidelity) Preaching in 1799	
John Barnett	1778	Episcopal (Bishop Meade)	
George Bingham	1791	Methodist	
Ambrose Brockman	1808		
John A. Billingsley	1815		
John Craig	Feb. 1740	Presbyterrain (Oath Fidelity) P. 311	
Elijah Craig	Mar. 22,1781	licensed to marry, Sept. 1777 Baptist (Oath Fidelity) was jailed in Orange & Culpeper.	
Richard Cave	May 1780	(Oath Fidelity)	
Joseph Craig	Apr. 1781	(Sargents Baptist license) to marry Apr. 26, 81	

Jeremiah Chandler 1800
Wm. Calhoun 1802
William Douglas 1803 Methodist
Robert Elkins Mar. 1779 (Oath Fidelity) dissenting minister
George Eve 1783 Baptist in Culpeper 1748, to Ky. in 1790, Charge of F. T. ch and Blue Run Orange Co. Va.
Henry Fry 1812 Methodist
John Goss 1813
William Gilberne 1760 (Biship Meade's old Churches)
James Garnett 1793 in Culpeper 1743 son of Anthony Garnett was pastor of Crooked Run Ch. for more than 55 years d. Apr. 16, 1830 M.Twice, 14 ch.
Hamilton Goss 1792 Baptist
John Garnett 1810
P. 69 Richard Heatwell of St. Marks, 1741 Nov. (exonerated for being drunk)
Robert Jones 1800
Page 48 George Samuel Klug Aug. 1739 German Protestant
Frederick Kabler 1800 (performed some marriage ceremonies)
John Leland 1788 Baptist
Wm. Mason 1815
Mungo Marshall July 1759 (also Bishop Meade 1753)
James Maury Jr. July 1759 (also Bishop Meade 1761)
Thomas Martin 1769 (Bishop Meade's Old Churches)
George Morgon 1794
Philip Pendleton 1813
John Price Aug. 28, 1777 (Baptist) (Desenting Minister oath allegiance license to marry Sept. 27, 1781.)
Page 400 Robert Rose Oct. 1738 (owned 900 acres on banches of James River.; known as "Buffalo Meadows".)
Page 461 John Casper Stover, May 17, German Protestant (Oath Fidelity)
Nathaniel Sanders Oct. 1777 Mar. 22, 1781 licensed to marry. Oath of Fidelity
Robert Sharman, Episcopal 1748 (Clerk of Upper Church of St. Thomas Parish petition about horse way)
Page 347 John Thomson Feb. 1742 German Protestant.
Isham Tatum 1800
Page 213 Wm. Williams, Sept. 1737, Presbytyrian (Oath of Fidelity)
William Williamson Nov. 1793 (Presbyterian.)
John Wingate 1774 (Bishop Meade's Old Ch's)
James Waddell 1788 (Presbyterian.)
Jacob Watts 1799

MILITARY CLAIMS CERTIFIED.

Claim of Cap. John Smith & his Co. certified to Rushy Assembly
Claim of Capt. John Christian & Co. Certifed to Assembly for allowance.
Claim of Capt. John Wilson Certified.
Claim of James Kerr Certified. (Not proved)
Claim of Capt. Sam. Grey Certified.
Claim of Capt. John Bohannon Certified.
Claim of Lim. Just. Stophonices Smith
Claim of William Russell
Claim of Lieu. John Douglas
Claim of John Branham

Claim of William Lucas
Claim of Joseph Cotton
Claim of John Newport, Gent.
Claim of John Walker
Claim of Aully Choice
Claim of Mich. Finney
Claim of John Smith

CHANCERY SUITS

July 1761 Anthony Strother vs. Alexander Waugh (Chy)
Sept. 1762 Francis Thorton vs. Smith (Chy)
Nov. 1763 George Livingston vs. John Noel
Apr. 1765 Robert Daniel vs. Daniel
Nov. 1767 Charles Beale vs. Beale et als.
Sept. 1769 Francis Wisdoms heirs vs. Benj. Cave.
Sept. 1772 Andrew Shepherd vs. William Hamm.
Sept. 1772 Same vs. Robert Martin
Sept. 1772 David Vawter vs. Wm. Kindell
Sept. 1772 Richard Vernon vs. William Taliaferro
Oct. 1772 Andrew Shepherd & Co. vs. Edmund Burrus
Nov. 1773 Francis Lowens vs. Urial Mallory
May 1773 Sarah Spicer etc. vs. Benj. Head
July 1773 Hugh Lenox & Co. vs. Isaac Bradburn
Nov. 1787 Wm. Thomas vs. Woolfolks exor.
Shepherd & Co. vs Ogg
May 1788 Jas. Walker vs. Roebuck & Brockman
Nov. 1788 Burnley vs. Robinson's adm.
Aug. 1788 John Thompson vs. Alex Newman
May 1789 Benonk Hansford vs. Nicholas Porter
L. to T. 1790 John Willis vs. Alex Waugh Sr. & Thomas. (Buckner vs. Bayne rum & wine for funeral.
Mar. 1791 Wm. C. Webb vs. James Madison
Aug. 1790 John Hawkins Ex. Wm. Willis Ex.
Mch. 1793 Francis Bruce et als vs. Charles Bruce et als (A to J)
Aug. 1796 A. To H. John Farguson vs. Wm. Watts
Aug. 1796 James Muckett vs. Nathaniel Gordon
Nov. 1796 John Glassill vs. Ludwell Grymes et als
Nov. 1796 Ambrose Madison & Johnny Scott vs. Robert Martin
Nov. 1796 William Powell vs. Powell Lewis G.
May 1796 Francis Powell vs. Wm. Riddell
May 1796 Geo. Richards vs. Wm. Richards Ex.
July Reuben Taylor vs. Hay Taliaferro
Polly Porter vs. Camp Porter et als
Mch. 1797 M. To W. Wm. Alcock vs. John Ryburn
Mch. 1797 Wm. Fowke & Co. vs. Wm. Alcocke
Mch. 1797 Waugh vs. Wm. Lyon
Sept. 1783 Beverly Winslow vs. Benj. Winslow etc.
May 1783 Wm. Bell vs. John Stockdell
May 1783 Zachriah Burnley vs. Joseph Jeffries
Nov. & Dec. 1785 John Oakes vs. Mary Burruss
June & July 1784 Reuben Roach vs. Wm. Monoe Ex.

CHANCERY SUITS DISMISSED

Ludwick Stover vs. Jacob Stover July 1737
David Williams vs. Thos. Hill May 1738
Robert Adams vs. Erasman & Geo. Taylor Feb. 1738
John Smith Adm of John Mch. 1738
Jacob Stober vs Strickler, Stone etc. Mch. 1738
Wm. Frazier vs Jacob Stover June 1739
Thomas Downer vs Elisha Perkins (appeal) June 1739
Mary Worthington vs. Robt Worthington Ex. June 1739
Robt. Worthington vs Jacob Worthington June 1739
Thomas Dillard vs Jacob Dillard Ex. June 1739
Nicholas Christopher vs John Christopher Taliaferro July 1739
Robt. Worthington Ex. vs Rees Smith Feb. 1739
John Grayhan vs. Charles McDowell May 1740
Thos. Wright Bellfield vs. Samuel Pound Sept. 1740
Hans. Jacob Kolp vs. Robt Row May 1741
John Littler vs Ambrose Nelson Nov. 1741
John Thorton vs Luke Thorton & Mildred Thornton Mch. 1742
John Seawright vs Joseph Stover
George Moffitt vs Benj. Borden July 1743
Robert Worthington vs Jacob Worthington et als Sept. 1743
Wm. Hunt vs. Wm. Deatherage
James Trimble Vs Benj. Borden Mch. 1743
Thomas Wright Belfield VS John Britain Mch. 1743
John Hanse VS Benj. Borden Mch. 1743
Wm. Gray VS James Rutledge etc. June 1744
Wm. Nutt VS Wm. Beverley & Jennings July 1744
Robt. Worthington vs Jacob Worthington Aug. 1744
Thomas Postgate vs Harry Downs (appeal) Mch. 1744
Isaac Smith vs Richard Halcomb July 1745

OFFICERS

Sept.	1740	Robert Slaughter	Military	2-268
Nov.	1740	John Inn	Atty.	2-277
Nov.	1740	Robert Slaughter	Coroner	2-283
Feb.	1740	Zachary Taylor	Ch. warden	2-308
Feb.	1740	John Craig	(Presbytarian minister oath alleginace)	2-311
May	1741	Edward Pendleton	Att.	2-354
June	1741	Rich Winslow	Sheriff	2-398
Nov.	1741	Wm. Bucly	Lieut. of Orange & Augusta	3-54
May	1742	James Wood	J.P.	3-148
May	1742	John Thomas	Military Com. Ensign	3-167
July	1742	Richard Thomas & Benj. Cave	(Ch. Warden)	3-169
Nov.	1742	Francis Slaughter	(ch. Warden St. Marks)	3-291
Jan.	1742	Naturilization of Andrew Gann Jr.		3-313
Jan.	1742	Samuel Ham. vs Wm. Ham		3-325
Feb.	1742	Courtney Boyle vs Nat. paper		3-346
June	1743	Wm. Russell	Sheriff	3-467
July	1743	James Portius	Atty.	3-502
Sept.	1743	John Sherman	Atty.	4-6
Nov.	1743	George Home Co.	Lawyers	4-25
Feb.	1743	James Patton	Coroners	4-49

Feb. 1743	John Lewis	J.P.	4-49
Feb. 1743	John Dobbin	Lient. of Horse	4-50
Feb. 1743	John Watts	Ensign	4-56
Jan, 1744	John Louis	Lawyer for Augusta	

July 24, 1783 Cert. by Chs. Yarbough 3rd regt. L. D. Sept. 10, 1782
Aug. 29, 1783 Rich. Young D. Q. Hr. Nov. 20, 1780
Sept. 25, 1783 Belfield Cave, impressed gun Lieu. for Orange Militia Jan. 11-1781
Sept. 25, 1783 signed by Jos. Hawkins A. C. T. year 1780
Sept. 25, 1783 Thos. Barbour, commandg. officer of Orange Co.
Sept. 26, 1783 Cert. by John Hawkins for Geo. Rice A. D. Q. M. Feb. 11, 1781
Sept. 26, 1783 Recpt. of Chas. Smith R. G. P. Albemarle Barrocks Nov. 24, 1780
Sept. 26, 1783 For premium rec'd at Albemarle Barracks by John Smith R. C. Sept. 14, 80.
Sept. 26, 1783 For premium rec'd at Albemarle Barrocks by John Thomas DCP Sept. 28, 80
Spet. 26, 1783 Cert. at Albemarle Barracks by Geo. Rice W.D.Q.M. ge Aug. 22, 1780
Mch. 25, 1784 Jno. Scott COC.
Apr. 23, 1784 Cert. by Thos. Stanley D. W. M. Ge. (1780)
May 28, 1784 Signed by Robt Tate R. C. for Fran. Tate A. D. C.
May 28, 1784 G. B. for use of Albemarle Barracks
May 28, 1784 Cert. by Benj. Johnson Capt. Orange Militia Mch. 22, 1784.
May 28, 1784 Signed by Maxey Ewell for use of Alb. Barracks.
May 28, 1784 Signed by Capt. John Sharp for use of Col. Armands Superior Apr. 12, 82
May 28, 1784 Signed by David Bullock F.M. Sept. 11, 1780.
May 28, 1784 Signed by Edm. Thomas R. C. Mch. 26, 1780.
Apr. 28, 1785 Certified by Jno. Thomas for use of Albemarle Barracks
Apr. 28, 1785 Certified by Maxey Ewell for Jos. Hawkins for Alb. Barracks
Apr. 28, 1785 Gun. impressed by Robt. Stubblefield for use of Orange Militia Sept. 19, 19, 1781
May 26, 1785 Cert. by Fran Taylor late Col. Regt. Guards
July 28, 1785 Cert. by P. Muklenberg B. T. June 11, 1782
Aug. 27, 1785 Cert. by And. Johnson WM May 7, 1781
June 22, 1786 By order of Lafeyette M.G.
July 25, 1782 Cert. by Jno Robertson D. C. for John Brown Com V. S.

Cert. by Chs Portlock Q. M. for use of detachment of infantry under command of Col. Call, June 9, 1781

Cert. by Joshua Lindaay W. M. for the use of the arm under the command of Marquis de la Fayette, June 20, 1781

Cert. by Wm. Cary cornet L.D. for use of Capt. Davenports Troops of Horse, June 11, 1781

Cert. by Wm. Gray Le & I.M. 1st reg. L.D. for pasturing 60 horses belonging to the 1st Reg. of L.D. & Maj. Nelsons Corps of Horse commanded by Maj. McPhearson June 6, 1781.

Cert. by Gorham Sargt. for May McPhersons Co., June 7, 1781.

Cert. by James Madison County Lieut. To Archibald Campbell dec'd for attending the sick Highland Prisoners at Orange Courthouse, July 8, 1776.

Cert. by Harry Allan Sarg. of Maj. J. Nelson's Corps V. Calway, June 10, 1781.

Cert. by Arch. McDonald F. M. for the use of the Brigade of Light Infantry under the command of Maj. Gen. Marquis de la Fayette, June 6, 1781.

Cert. by Joseph Wheaton Lt. L.D. W. H., June 7, 1781.

Cert. Senf. Col. Engmers, June 4, 1781.

Gun impressed by Capt. Robt Thomas for the use of the Orange Militia guardg. Convention Prisoners to Albemarle Barracks in the year 1779.

To Elijah Craig assigned of John Bledsoe, for his services as Wagon Conductor in the Southern Army, cert by Samuel Edmiston W.M. G. S. Army directed to Col. Elliott D.I.M.G. at Petersburg Jan. 24, 1781

Apr. 27, 1782 Gen. impressed by Capt. Robert Daniel for the use of the Orange Militia 1781

(April 18, 1919)

Apr. 27, 1782 Cert. by Jno. Hunnally I.M. June 3, 1781, for use of detachment of Infantry & Cavaliary from Ambia under Maj. Thos. Watkins.

Cert. by James Waggones Lt. for team going to Culpeper for arms by order of Col. Alcock July 27, 1781

Gen. impressed for Orange Militia by Capt. Robt. Daniel, Apr. 21, 1781.

Cert. by Jacob Holeman Com. P. Law Shenandoah Co., Dec. 23, 1780.

Cert. by D. Hammond Lieu. 1st Pen. Reg., June 22, 1781.

Cert. by Benj. Tutt I.M. for use of Culpeper Militia Sept. 13, 1781.

Cert. by Belfield Cave St. for use Orange Militia Jan. 11, 1781.

Gun. impressed by Johnny Scott for Orange Militia in 1777.

Cert. by George Smith Com. for Orange Militia May 19, 1781.

Gun. impressed by Zack Herndon Capt. O. M. for S. I. Militia in May, 1781.

Cert. by Anthony Foster, Aug. 24, 1781.

Doctor Charles Taylor claims for militia furnished for 5th Virg. Regt. certified by Strother Settle Ens. July 16, 1781.

May 23, 1782 Cert. by Rich. Baynham Q.M. for use of Caroline Militia under the command of Lt. Col. Saml. Temple, Apr. 28, 1781.

June 27, 1782 Cert. by Wm. Jennings, Capt. to Shenandoah & Fred. volunteer, Jan. 15, 1781.

Cert. by Jacob Lincoln I.M. for Rockingham Militia Oct. 20, 1781.

Signed by Geo. Morton Com. for Orange Militia under the command of Belfield Cave Capt. Aug. 15, 1781.

Cert. by Michael Robinson W. M. & Richard Young A.D.Q.M.G. teams to remain public stores from Fred. to Matapony by order of Gen. Weeden Jan. 7, 1781.

Cert. by Jno. Robertson D. C. G. for John Brown C. G. V. S.

Cert. by Geo. North Q. M. Brigade June 11, 1781.

Cert. by Jos. Wharton L. & D. W. M. June 8, 1781.

July 25, 1782 Cert. by James Davies Court for the use of Capt. Crawera Comp. of Militia on their March to Hillsboro in North Carolina, Aug. 14, 1780.

Apr. 16, 1782 Cert. by John Burnham Sargt. of Capt. Wm. Davenports.

Cert. by H. Young I.M. Gen S. V. for Entertainment of Wm. Clark (Express Rider)

Cert. by John B. Key for volunteers from Maryland July 29, 1781.

Cert. by Ben. Garnett County. for a party belonging to 3 Reg. L. Dragoons

Apr. 26, 1782 Cert. by Timothy Conner (who was appointed by Marquis Lafeyette to impress provisions for the army) June 30, 1781.

For the entertainment & his horse of John Barns a sick soldier of Col. Lighthorse.

Cert. by Jas. Head D. C. Sept. 3, 1781.

Cert. by Jno. Smith C. for use of Rockingham Militia on March to Richmond.

Furnished to Wm. Young I.M. for Rockingham Militia Sept. 26, 1781.

Cert. by Thos. Alderson I.M. for Rockingham Military Oct. 30, 1781.

Furnished to James Fitzpatrick Sarg. on his return from carrying piers to Stanton June 14, 1781.

Cert. by Thos. Shanklin wage master, May 3, 1781.

Receipt from Benj. Garven Feb. 10, 1781.

Cert. by Wm. McGill I. M. for Rockingham Militia under command of Col. Nall Apr. 18, 1781.

Cert. by Jno. Brock Dec. 16, 1780.

Cert. by Wm. Beckham Lt. Guard of ye pioneers to Winchester Mch. 13, 1781.

Cert. by Wm. Young for the use of the Rockingham Militia under the command of Gowen Hambleton Mag.
Cert. by Geo. Huston Capt. com. for the Rockingham Militia Aug. 13, 1781.
Cert. by Francis Taylor Capt. 2 Va. Regt. Apr. 1, 1778.
Apr. 27 Cert. by Robert Clark Jr. A. D. W. M. coal for public artificers June 13, 1781.
Cert. by Jos. Wood, Jr., Capt. for Culpeper Militia June 10, 1781.
Cert. by Lewis Webb, D. G. M. Gen. Clark, June 10, 1781.
Cert. by James French, June 20, 1781.
Apr. 16, 1782 Cert. by Wm. Triplet I. M. for team carrying baggage of Militia to Culpeper Co., July 28, 1781.
Cert. by W. MacPherson Maj. Con. for use of his legion June 8, 1781.
For gun, impressed by Capt. Robt. Daniel for Orange Militia Apr. 23, 1781.
Wagon & Team impressed for Orange Militia by John Taylor St. Col., Aug. 22, 1781.
Cert. by Wm. Thomas Lieu. July 5, 1781.
Cert. by Isaac Lane for the Volunteers from Frederick Co. Muchin to Fredericksburg Jan. 15, 1781.
Cert. by Robt. Morrow, Capt. 3rd Regt. S. D., Aug. 24, 1781.
Cert. by Wm. Young L.M. & Snow. Perkey St. for the Rochington Militia, Sept. 24, 1781.
For gun impressed for Orange Militia by Capt. Johnson in 1778.
For wagon & team impressed into the service in Richmond by Stephen Southall A. D. I. M. Gen.
For bacon for public use received by Abner Porter A.D.C. July 3, 1781.
Cert. by Thos. C. Bannon L. M. for a detachment of Militia returning to Fauquier Jan. 29, 1781.
Cert. by Baker Hassard for use of Gen. Morgan Baggage Feb. 24, 1781.
Rec'd. by Jno. W. Price for Jno. of Boswell D. F. Com., June 8, 1781
Rec'd by John Smith for the Rockington Militia Nov. 6, 1780.
For wagon & team impressed by Capt. Wood for the Culp. Militia and discharged by John Browne, Com. State of Virginia Aug. 6, 1781, cert. by Wm. Critten Crittenden W. M. Feb. 27, 1781.
Cert. by Els Edmonds Nov. 2, 1781.
Cert. by David Sloat W. M. June, 1778.
Cert. by Henry Bidinger Capt. in 3rd Regt. May 20, 1781.
Cert. by John Miller L.D., June 4, 1781.
Cert. by Thadey Kelly C. M. S., June 4, 1781.
Aug. 15, 1782 Cert. by James Walker A. D. C., Jan 27, 1781.
Cert. by Andw. Sharklin Q. M., June 20, 1781, for Pasturage for Rockingham Militia.
Cert. by Jno. of Boswell D. F. Com. to the army in Va., June 11, 1781.
Cert. by just Livington Surgeon, pasturage for horses belonging to Flying Hospital
Cert. by Wm. Young Q.M.R.M. & Gaw. Hamilton.
Maj. Com. for pastorage for Rockingham Militia, Sept. 20, 1781.
Thomas Aldonson, same for Rockingham Militia, Oct. 29, 1781.
Robt. Clark Gun.A.D.W.M. to the army, pasturage.
Cert. by John Walker W. M. for hay for use of a brigade going from Southern Army to Philadelphia, Mch. 4, 1781.
Gun impressed of Sam. Smith, Lt., for Orange Militia in 1781.
Cert. by C. Jones AA.D.Q.M.G. for use of Charles Porteers horse for Iratis for the Mayors D.L. three days June, 1781.
(Apr. 16, 1782 Cert. by Jeremiah McKay 2 k., July 4, 1781.
Cert. Geo. Morton C. O. M. benf. for Orange Militia Aug. 16, 1781.
Cert. by Thos. Barbour, Col. O C., June 23, 1781, & received for by John Higgins Maj. Com.

Recepted by Caleb Lindsay Capt. & Certified by Thos. Barbour Col. for Orange Militia Aug. 18, 1781.

Cert. by Edw. Power, A. S. F. M. for Genl. Military Brigade, June 10, 1781.

Cert. by Wm. Edmonson J. M. for Gen. Military Brigade, June 1, 1781.

Cert. by John Doswell, For & M. for Col. Calls Legion L. D., June 9, 1781.

Cert. by Chas. Lewis, B. F. M. for Gen. Nelsons Brigade, June 10, 1781.

Cert. by Enoch Ashby I. Master for grand at Brocks Bridge under command of Maj. Higgins June 22, 1781.

Apr. 3, 1782 Mich. Roberson W. M. & Rich. Young A. D. W. H. G. wagon and to move public stores to Mattapony (Jan. 19, 1781.)

May 3, Page 190, Apr. 15, 1782.

Apr. 15, 1782 O. Towles Lt. Col. 5th Reg. June 4, 1781 (P. 192).

Apr. 15, 1782 Received from Matt Kenney for party of troops under command of Col. Lamp Matthews, Jan. 20, 1781.

Cert. by Ben. Garnett Count. 3 R.L. Dragoons, Oct. 8, 1781.

Cert. by P. Squire I. M. Assistant for use of Light Infantry commanded by the Marquis de la Fayette, June 11, 1781.

Cert. by W. Thomas St. for Guard at Brock Bridge July 11, 1781.

Party of the 3rd. Regt. L. Dragoons commanded by Ben Garnett Comt. Syt, 1781.

Cert. by Nich Long W. Master, for wagons moving Military stores to Westham, Sept. 3, 1781.

Cert. by Matthew Fair for the use of the Rockingham Military commanded by Col. Hall, June, 1781.

Cert. by George North I. M. Brigade for pasturage for horses furnished for Gen. Wayne & family, June 10, 1781.

Cert. by Terce Connell F. M. B., June 9, 1781.

Cert. by Robert Morrow Capt. 3rd Reg. L. D., July 14, 1781.

Cert. by D. Hammond Lt. 1st Pen. Regt. Pasturage 11 horses with Gun., wagons, baggage.

Cert. by L. Thornton Col. for fodder for use of Culpeper minute men, May 23, 1781.

Cert. by John Crookshards, Capt. for volunteer from Shenandoah, July 2, 1781.

Cert. by Wm. Gray, Lieu. & Q.M. 1st. Reg. L. D., June 6, 1781, commanded by Maj. McPherson.

Cert. by Jeremiah McKay Q.M. for use of party of horsemen of Shenandoah Military commanded by Maj. John Denton ?

IMPRESSED

Apr. 1782 Capt. Richard Craves, impressed gun Conv. marched through Country (Mch. 30, 1782).

Apr. 1782 Capt. Gideon Spencer, dinner for self & men on march from Barracks to Charlotte Co., Nov. 11, 1781.

Provisions to Alex Kilpatrich of Col. Sampson Matthews Company, Feb., 1781.

John Mercer Com. of party of horses. June, 1781.

Apr. 2, 1780 Capt. Robt. Morrow Capt. 3rd Geg. L.D., July 14, 1781.

Lieu. Wm. Thomas, prisoner, Aug. 6, 1781.

Capt. Flemming Bates, for Halifax Militia returning from escorting the prisoners taken at York to Nolands Ferry, Nov. 11, 1781.

Capt. Chas. Williams of Pittsylvania Militia, on above trip.

Capt. Robt. Daniel, gun impressed for Orange Militia, May 17, 1781.

Benj. Garnett, cornet 30 R.L. Dragoons Sept. 2, 1781, horse

Tim. Conner, impressed by Marquis Lafeyette to impress provisions for the army. Aug. 18, 1781.

J. Robertson, D. C. for John Brown, Com. State.

Capt. Belfield Cave, Orange Military on way to camp, Prisoner Oct. 16, 1781.
James Pierce Ast. C. D. Com. for Army, June 10, 1781.
Chas. Lewis B.F.M. for use Brig. Gen. Nelson's brigade, June 1, 1781.
(Joseph Pollard Q.M. Orange Militia, Sept. 15, 1781.)
Wm. Edmonson F. M. for use of Gen. Muhlenbergs Brigade, May 31, 1781.
Peter Cline Sargt. 2 Reg. Pens., June 14, 1781.
J. Squire Q.M. Sarg., June 11, 1781.
Maj. Higgins, horse impressed 1781.
Capt. Rich. C. Webb., Capt. Orange Militia, May 16, 1781.
Wm. Thomas, Gun. Impressed for Orange Militia, May 17, 1781.
Gen. Stevens for use of Va. Military Marching to join Southern Army, Oct. 30, 1780.
Harrison Suillivan Corpl. for use of Capt. Reads L. Dragoons, Sept. 14, 1781.
John Hunnaly, Q.M. & Thos. Walters, Maj., June 3, 1781.
Rich. Call, Maj. L. D. Aug. 11, 1781.
Andw. Shanklin, Q.M. for Rockingham Militia, June 19, 1781.
Apr. 3, 1782-----Capt. John Rush for Rockingham Militia, Dec. 4, 1780.
Capt. Geo. Huston for Rockingham Militia, Aug. 13, 1781.
Wm. MaGill, Q.M., & Wm. Nalle, Lt. Col. Comdt. Sd. Militia, Apr. 17, 1781.
Thady Kelly, C. M. S., June 11, 1781.
Wm. Buckner, Capt. Orange Militia, May 17, 1781.
Col. R. O. Taylor, June 15, 1781.
Jas. Montiette, W.C.B., July 8, 1781.
Teree Connell, F. M. 1. P. B. for use Gen. Wagner Brigade, June 9, 1781.
Wm. Edmondson F. Master for Gen. Muhlenberg Brigade, June 8, 1781.
D. Hammond Lieu. Ist. Pena. Reg. on way to camp with Gen. Wagner baggage, June 22, 1781.
Capt. John Crookshawks, company of Volunteers on way to headquarters, July 3, 1781.
Rich. Cary Lieu. L. D. for Capt. Davenports Lt. Dragoons, June 9, 1781.
Ben. Garnett, Commt. of 3rd R. L. Dragoon, Oct. 3, 1781.
Ben. Robinson, Sargt. the guard for provisions & Militia machinery from Fredericksburg to Charlottesville Staunton, June 30, 1781.
Nick McNeely, Com. & Q. Martin for a detachment under comd. of Col John Posie, June 6, 1781.
Robt. Clark Jur. D.W.M. for Flying Hospital, June 11, 1781.
Wm. Young I. M. R. M. for Rockingham Militia, Sept. 17, 1781.
Benj. Garnett, 3rd R. L. Dragoons, Sept. 2, 1781.
Captain Zach. Herndon of Orange Militia.
Capt. Mich. Stump for use of Hampshire Militia, June 27, 1781.
Thos. Shanklyn Way. Master for use of continual teams from Rockingham to Headquarters, Oct. 4, 1781.
Rich. Call, Maj. 3rd Reg. L. D. for a Detachment of 3rd Regiment Light Dragoons.
Strother Settle Ens., 5th Va. Reg. & O. Towles Lt. Col. 5th Va. Reg., July 11, 1781.
Wm. Cary Cornet for Capt. Davenport troop horse, June 13, 1781.
Robt. Spicer, Sargt. for Capt. N. Reido Company Regulars, June 11, 1777.
Oct., 1739, James Strother added to Wm. Strother tethables, 2-83.
Nov., 1739, John Bicket Clerk presented for not giving Lord's Supper, 2-83.
Nov., 1741, Rev. Richard Hartswell presented by Grand Jury for being drunk, 3-69.
Nov., 1741, Rev. Robert Rose or Thomas Callaway 3-73
Mch., 1743, Rev. John Thompson 3-401
May, 1744, Owen Thomas, ex. of James Stevens 4-105.
Aug., 1744, Capt. John Christian & his Company, claim certified 4-201
Aug., 1744, Capt. John Smith & his company claim certified 4-201
Aug., 1744, Capt. John Wilson & his company claim certified 4-201
Aug., 1744, Capt. Sam Gray & his company claim certified 4-201
Aug., 1744, Capt. John Bohannon & his company claim certified 4-201

Feb., 1744, Timothy Crothwaite, Adm. of Wm. C. (in suit) 4-277
Apr. 1, 1782, John White the elder for provision furnished army.
May 28, 1798, Richard Farguson, Methodist Minister to preach.
Feb. 25, 1779, David Michie, Atty. at Law.
Dec. 23, 1799, Frederick Harris, Jr., Atty. at Law.
Oct. 26, 1790, John Groom in militia from Orange at seige of York lost alleg.
Nov. 22, 1790, Johnny Scott, Sheriff
Mch. 28, 1791, Robt. B. Vass., Atty.
Mch. 28, 1791, Judity Miller widow of John Miller, a pensioner, still living.
Mch. 27, 1792, John Bolling heir at law & brother to Wm. Bowling who enlisted a soldier in the 20th S. Reg. in Feb., 1777 in the Comp. commanded by Capt. Dudley sd. Wm. died in July 11
Aug., 1778, While in the service which was proved by Peachy Bledsoe who was a sargeant in So. Regiment.
Aug. 27, 1792, Robert Ware Peacock, Atty.
Mch. 25, 1793, Rich. Henry Yancey, Atty.
Mch 26, 1793, George Taylor, Atty.
Jan. 27, 1794, Richard Bruce, Atty.
Nov., 1794, Zach. Burnley, Sheriff.
Feb. 24, 1795, Thomas Ellis, coroner in room of Catlett Conway, resigned.
June 22, 1795 James Smith, Atty.
Aug. 24, 1795, James Blackerly, legal inspector of Thomas Blackerly, a soldier in the late construcal service who died in same.
Nov. 23, 1795, Francis Cowherd, Coroner.
Feb. 22, 1796, The court nominates the following magistrates May Burton, Jr., Champ Porter, Benj. Burnley, John Moore, John Scott, Jr., John Daniel, Wm. Alcock & Geo. Martin.
The acting magistrates are: James Madison, Zach Burnley, Wm. Moore, Thos. Barbour, Johnny Scott, Cat. Conway, Benj. Johnson, Wm. Campbell, Isaac Davis, Jr., Wm. White, Wm. White, Francis Cowherd, Thos. Ellis.
Sept. 26, 1796, Robert Coleman, Atty.
Nov., 1796, Wm. Moore, Sheriff.

Nov. 1742
All the inhabitants of Bordens land & _ ________ all in Brady Manor within 4 miles of the South River from the head branch downward as far as Joseph Lees.

Benj. Bordon	John Dalke	John Hays
James Robison	David ?	Andrew Hays
William Bucherson	Patrick Combb	Thos. Willson
John M. Cockrill	Francis M. Cowen	Thos. Douglas
Rob. Looney	Robert Erwin	Wilson Givens
Thomas Loney	John Canne	Jacob Anderson
Joseph Walker	Hugh Cuningham	James Anderson
John Walker	James Young	John Anderson
Charles Camphe	James Moore	Edward Boyle
Andrew Martin	John Cyler	James Moore
Joseph Cotton	Will Hall	James Gamble
Robert Coton	William Joyers	William Gamble
Bob Sturrt	James Cunegham	

Church Wardens

Robt. Green & Wm. Russell	St. Marks	July, 1742.
Philip Clayton & Goodrich Lightfoot	St. Marks	July, 1747
Thos. Chew & Joseph Thomas	St. Thomas Parish	Mch., 1747
Wm. Taliaferro & George Taylor		Mch., 1755
Zachary Taylor and James Madison		Apr., 1760

PETITION OF LEADING CITIZENS OF ORANGE COUNTY OCTOBER 20, 1779, ASKING THAT SOLDIERS NOT IN ACTION BE ALLOWED TO GO HOME TO PLANT CROPS SINCE LACK OF FOOD WAS CAUSING EXTREME DISTRESS.

BALLARD FAMILY
of
ORANGE COUNTY, VIRGINIA

Contributed by Kathrine Cox Gottschalk,
650 East Capitol St., Washington, D.C.

The record books of Orange County, Virginia, show several branches of the Ballard family name, but the only one of these which continued to reside in that county until after 1800 was the family of Philip and Ann (Nancy)(Johnson) Ballard. They had a large family of sons and daughters. Our intensive study of the material gathered in an extensive search was carefully analysed for time and place in order to identify the several members of the Ballard family. In our work we had the added advantage of the family papers written long ago by descendants of the above Philip Ballard. It has been a deep satisfaction to be able to check these chronicles against the authentic Court records and to find that a true account has been preserved by these family historians.

As so many errors have crept into print or by legend on this fine old Virginia family, descendants of Thomas Ballard, the immigrant, it may be that this true orientation of the family of Philip Ballard of Orange County, Virginia, will clear up some of these confusions and either connect or eliminate others by this name.

Philip Ballard had brothers named Thomas, William, John, and Bland Ballard, of Spotsylvania County. Two brothers, Thomas and John died in Albemarle County, they had land in Orange and in Louisa, before going into Albemarle County.

Philip Ballard owned land in Spotsylvania, part of which he purchased, part which he probably inherited as we find no grant or transfer to him on the records.

Philip Ballard sold a small piece before he removed to Orange County then after he removed to Orange County, he and his wife Nancy (Ann) sold the remaining property that he held in Spotsylvania.

References: See Crozier's Abstracts of Spotsylvania Co., Va. records.
See Orange Co., Deeds and other records: Many of which are in Mr. W. E. Brockman's Vol. 2, Orange Co., records.

Dates which have been approximated from records are denoted as ca (Circa). The absolute dates are dependable upon records and family data. Marriages are the dates the license or bond was signed or from a Minister's Return to the Court for performing the rite. The children of Philip and Nancy (Johnson) Ballard of Orange County may not be arranged in the right order of their birth, but as far as possible from the first record of their maturity or marriage.

Issue of Philip and Nancy (called also Ann)(Johnson) Ballard:

1. William Ballard married Elizabeth Step. She died 1830, in Monroe Co., (now) West Virginia. His descendant, Mr. Oliver Ballard, remained in Monroe Co., W. Va., and gave an account of his relatives who removed to Monroe Co., W. Va., from Orange Co., Va. Also see: Morton's Hist. of Monroe Co., p et seq. In this history Mr. Morton speaks about the characteristic "longevity" of the BALLARD FAMILY. This is also mentioned by other of the family historians and their dates bear this out.

Issue of William and Elizabeth (Step) Ballard were: 1. Johnson Ballard, went to Ky. 2. Jeremiah Ballard (1777-1867). 3. Lucy Ballard. 4. Millie Ballard, M. 1804, Jacob Mann. 5. Wm. Ballard (1784-1880). 6. Nancy Ballard. 7. Mollie Ballard. 8. Willis Ballard (1791-1880), Father of Oliver Ballard of Greenville, West Va., who wrote about his kinfolks in Monroe Co., W. Va. 9. James Ballard, m. 1804, Jennie Keaton (cousin).

2. Ankey Ballard m. James Keaton ca 1767. He was b. 1745,,had issu, among others, Rev. JOHNSON KEATON, who d. 1851. They went to W. Va., with (Ballard) Keaton's brothers.

3. Thomas Ballard m. in Orange Co., Va., 3-8-1778, (bond) Elizabeth Smith. He was Road Overseer in Orange Co., 1778. Is said to have served in Rev. War with his brothers Philip and Elijah. (Pen. of Philip Ballard, his brother who died in Logan Co., Ky. We have no list of children of Thos. Ballard.

4. Ann Ballard m. 1-16-1774, (bond) Orange Co., Va., William Vawter. They removed to Monroe Co., W. Va., and were known to the families of the sons of Philip Ballard who went to that county.

5. Morman (Mooreman) Ballard m. 1769, Minerva Bullock. There are many records of this son of Philip Ballard on the records of Orange County. He acquired much property. He removed to Madison Co., V., and had a large family. We have noted only a few of his children. He used as given names for them Johnson, Philip and Medley.

6. Philip Ballard, Jr., born in Orange Co., Va., served in the Rev. War, died in Logan Co., Ky. Received a pension. He died April 13, 1833, leaving a wife and no issue. He gave his age as 71 years in 1831. In his pension papers is an affidavit of his nephew, Joseph Keaton (Cotton), who stated that he had heard his uncles Elijah Ballard and Thomas Ballard spead of the services of their brother, the said Philip Ballard. In the family chronicles his nephews, son and grandsons of Larkin Ballard, they state that Philip , the brother of Larkin, died in Ky., and left a wife but no children.

7. Curtis Ballard b. ca 1758-59, died 1824 in Harrison Co., Ky. He married 4-23-1781 in Culpeper Co., Va., to Esther Gaines, the daughter of Humphrey and Sarah (Watts) Gaines. She was born 4-11-1761. Curtis Ballard and wife and family moved with his brothers and sisters to Monroe Co., West Va. From there he went to Ky. Spent a few years in Ohio then returned to Kentucky where he died 1824, and was buried in the Old Raven Creek (Baptist) Church yard. (A grand nephew, gr. son of Larkin Ballard) visited this grave of his gt. Uncle). Esther, the wife of Curtis Ballard, survived him. Issue: 1. Sarah Ballard who married in Monroe Co., W. Va., with her father's consent to Isaac Hutchinson. They went to Mo. 2. John Ballard of Ky. 3. Philip Ballard of Ky. 4. 4. a daughter m. John Michael in Ky. 5. a dau. m. Mr. Beck of Ky. 6. James Ballard b. 2-14-1791, Culpeper Co., Va., (Tombstone) died 5-10-1872, aged 81 years, Libertyville, St. Francois Co., Va. He m. Rachel Hitt in Cape Girardeau Co., Mo., 1831. Left issue two sons.

8. Larkin Ballard b. in Orange Co., Va., married Elizabeth Gaines, daughter of Humphrey & Sarah (Watts) Gaines (Bond) dated Jan. 13, 1786, Orange Co., Va. (her mother Sarah Gaines, widow, signed her consent.) Larkin Ballard and his family together with his brothers and sisters and their families removed to Monroe Co., W. Va., 1796-1800. Then the two brothers, Larkin and Curtis Ballard, and their sister, Millie, who m. 2. John Bolling went to Madison Co., Ky. Larkin Ballard died in Fayette Co., Ky., aged 84 years. Issue: 1. Hiram Ballard, 2. Howard Ballard, 3. Humphrey Ballard died under 21 years of age. 4. Henry Ballard, and several daughters.
9. Lucy Ballard b. 1761, Orange Co., Va., died 10-4-1851, Barren Co., Ky., m. 4-12-1778 Joseph Harvey, Orange Co., Va.
10. Johnson Ballard born in Orange Co., Va., died in Ky., married Betty Eastham, 12-22-1791 by George Eves, Baptist Minister. Culpeper Co., Va.
11. Milly Ballard born Orange Co., Va., m.1. Jesse Watson, marriage bond in Orange Co., Va., dated 8-10-1789, with consent of her father Philip Ballard, (she was under age in 1785). She m. 2., John Boling and went to Monroe Co., W. Va., with her brothers and to Kentucky with her brother Larkin Ballard's family.
12. Delphia Ballard m. Mr. Cummins and lived in West Va.
13. Elijah Ballard one of the older sons of Philip Ballard. He is found in Orange Co., Va., taxes, and also in Monroe Co., W. Va. He married Milly, the daughter of Thomas Dohaney of Orange Co., Va. (will of Thos. Dohaney) Elijah is named in the family papers as having a wife name Milly, and in the pension papers of Philip Ballard, Jr., his brother, in an affidavit given by their nephew. He may have remained in either Greenbrier or Monroe Co., W. Va., or removed elsewhere.

The extensive research undertaken for the ancestry and descendants of Philip and Nancy (Johnson) Ballard and the critical analysis of these data were carried on in over ten counties in Va., in Greenbrier and Monroe Counties in W. Va., in the several counties in Kentucky to which Philip Ballards sons and daughters migrated, in Madison & Monroe Counties, Ohio, a few counties in Illinois, and in Cape Gorardeau, and St. Francois Counties in Mo. Thus we could either connect or eliminate those branches of the descendants of Thomas Ballard, the immigrant sufficiently to either follow or drop them from further investigation. The greatest help was the clear delineation from the family papers of the two grand sons of Larkin Ballard and the Gt. Gr. son of Wm. & Elizabeth (Step) Ballard of Monroe Co., Va., and also from a descendant of Bland Ballard, who was personally known by the descendants of Larkin Ballard (son of Philip) Library material, Taxes, Census, Wills, Deeds, Court Orders, etc. from the Archives in Richmond, Va., State Library, and from the County Court Houses. The foregoing history of the family of Philip and Nancy (Johnson) Ballard has full documentation. (K.C.G.)

CATTERTON

By Pauline Brandt

(From an article in The Daily Progress, Charlottesville, Va., by Vera V. Via on the Catterton-Elliott home at Nortonsville, Va.)

The land on which this house is built, and in fact all of Nortonsville, was once part of one large grant, but which particular man acquired it first, we do not know.

Thomas Carr had grants in the general area, as did other large owners who speculated in land. In 1780, it was owned by a William Ball, who sold to Thomas Burruss and his wife, Ann, 800 acres on Lynch's River and along the County line. A clump of red and white oak figured in the boundary in several of the earlier deeds.

Judging from the deeds, the tract was an established plantation even in 1780. Thomas Burruss evidently bought it as an investment, for he held it only five years. On 1785, he sold to Michael Catterton, of Calvert County, Md., an estimated 715 acres. This deed spoke of houses and orchards, and there were evidently mills on Lynch's River, but we have no means of proving the house known as Capt. George Elliott's place was standing at that time.

Julian Catterton, of Free Union, who is a descendant of Michael Catterton, says that according to family tradition two brothers, Michael and William Catterton, and a woman, possibly a sister, came from Maryland and settled at what is now Nortonsville. It is entirely possible this old house is the homestead."

TWO DEEDS

It took two deeds to clear Michael Catterton's title, as Ann Burruss was too feeble to sign the deed, so a special deed had to be made later in the year to release her dower rights. This gave the size 750 acres, but it was the same tract of land, it seems.

My Great Grandmother, Elizebeth Catterton Brockman, was born and reared at Nortonsville, Va. I believe this is either her old home or the home of her uncle. William Catterton, Sr., married Agatha Sims. Amanda A. Catterton married Parrott Elliott. One Elizabeth Catterton married George Parrott.

Norfolk, Va.
March 12, 1957

Dear Cousin

I just received your letter. In the copy of the will that I sent you of Michael Catterton of Calvert County, Md., 1782, I think you will find that Gattwood Catterton is a daughter and not a son of this Michael Catterton. The will reads as follows: "Item - I give and bequeath to my daughter Gattwood Catterton, one negro girl, Deli, and one negro boy named Tom. To her and her heirs forever."------ This Gattwood Catterton married Samuel Austin December 2, 1791, no doubt, after she came from Maryland and settled in Alb. Co. A Wm. Wood, son of John Wood, of Alb. Co., married Mildred Austin December 22, 1822. Possibly she was a descendant of this Gattwood Catterton and Samuel Austin. This Wm. Wood was a brother to Levi Wood (a grandson and a great granddaughter of Levi Wood's married Brockman descendants.) Benj. Wood was also a brother of this Wm. and Levi Wood. Benj. Wood married Nancy Catterton, a sister of Great Grandmother Elizabeth Catterton Brockman. John Wood, father of the above Wm., Levi, and Benj. Wood was from Maryland originally. He came to Albemarle County and settled near Earlysville at an early date.

Pauline H. Brandt

Will of Michael Catterton 1782

In the name of God Amen----

I Michael Catterton of Calvert County in the State of Maryland, being weak and infirm in body but of perfect mind and memory, do make and ordain this may last will and testament in the following manner and form. That is to say.

Imprimis my will and desire is that my beloved wife shall have the use of all my land and three Negroes, Vozsue, London and Harry, during her widowhood.

ITEM--I give and bequeath unto my Daughter Elizabeth Owens, one negro man named Tom. To her, and her heirs forever.---

ITEM---I give and bequeath unto my daughter Mary Catterton, one Negro girl named Rachael. To her and her heirs forever.---

ITEM---I give and bequeathto my daughter Gattewood Catterton, one Negor girl named Deli, and one Negro boy named Tom. To her and her heirs forever.---

ITEM---I give and bequeath to my son, Michael Catterton, one Negro woman named Jenny. To him and his heirs forever,--and also one Negro boy named Jean.

ITEM---I give and bequeath to my son William Catterton one Negro man named Jerry and one Negro boy named Jack. To him and his heirs forever.---

ITEM---I give and bequeath unto my son Francis Catterton one Negro boy named Nacy, and one Negro girl named Flers. To him and his heirs forever.---

ITEM---I give and bequeath unto my daughter, Sarah Hansell and her heirs forever, one Negro man named Joe and one Negro firl, Gamar, and no more.---

ITEM---my will and desires is that after the death of my beloved wife, all my land be divided equally between my two sons Michael and William, my son Michael to have that part whereon my dwelling house stands thereon and his heirs forever.

LASTLY--- I constitute, make and ordain my beloved wife and my son Michael jointly Exeecutrix and Exectuter of this my last will and Testament, and I do hereby utterly Disallow, Revoke and Disannul all former will and Testaments by me heretofore made---Ratifying and confirming this and no other,.to be last will and Testament. In witness Whereof I have here unto set my hand and seal.

This second day of June in the year of our Lord God one thousand seven hundred and eighty two--------

Signed sealed and acknowledged)
by the within named Michael)
Catterton to be his last will)
and testament.)

MICHAELL CATTERTON

In the presence of us
HENRY DOWELL
his
SAMUEL x AUSTIN
mark
DANIEL FIBBENS

Children of William Catterton and Agatha (Agnes) Simms Catterton

1. Frances Catterton born Oct. 27, 1795. Married Nancy Clarkson Oct. 12, 1815. Frances Catterton died 1834.
2. Ann or (Annester) Catterton born July 16, 1796-Died Aug. 19, 1849-Spinster.
3. Nancy Catterton born Sept. 1, 1798-Died 1852.
4. Michael Catterton born Dec. 6, 1799. Married Lucy Wyatt Mills May 2, 1826. Lucy Wyatt Mills was born Jan. 9, 1812-Died Sept. 21, 1875. Michael Catterton died April 26, 1854. (This Michael Catterton was the grandfather of the Mr. Julian Catterton that sent me the notes)
5. Elizabeth Catterton born July 29, 1803. Married Bluford Brockman 1822 (My great grandparents P.H.B.)
6. Sarah Catterton (Mr. Catterton wrote that their names were mixed up in the
7. Mary Catterton (Bible and not plain enough for him to read.
   This Sarah Catterton married Pleasant Maupin Aug. 21st, 1837.
   I believe this Mary Catterton married ? Wood as she was mentioned in her father's will as Maney (Could have been Mary) Wood.

Michael Catterton (son of William and Agatha Simms Catterton) married Lucy Wyatt Mills. Their children were:

1. Pamelia Catterton born 1829-Died Oct. 21, 1885. Never Married.
2. Mary Jane Catterton born 1832. Married Samuel Ward July 2, 1851. She died July 5, 1898.
3. Nancy Catterton born 1834. Married George Hedrick Oct. 5, 1858.
4. George Newton Catterton born Feb. 1, 1838. Married Malindo Woodson May 16, 1861. Died Jan. 6, 1895 - Fought in War between States.
5. Angeline Catterton born July 23, 1841. Died June 4, 1922. Never married.
6. Albert M. Catterton born July 26, 1843. Died Aug. 23, 1909. Never married. In War 1861-1865.
7. Elizabeth Catterton born May 13, 1846. Married John Crow. Died Feb. 25, 1899.
8. Susan Catterton born Sept. 10,1848. Married John Fleming April 21, 1885. Died June 2, 1923.
9. William Z. Catterton born Oct. 14, 1851. Married Ida Bell Davis Dec. 21, 1890. Died Feb. 28, 1923. (Father of the Mr. Catterton that sent me the notes P.H.B.)

William Z. Catterton (son of Michael) and wife Ida Bell Davis had the following children.

1. Julian Catterton born July 5, 1899. Married Mae Hildebrand Aug. 20, 1939. One dau. Catherine Catterton born Nov. 12, 1940.
2. Stuart Catterton born Sept. 18, 1900. Died Oct. 11, 1927. Never married
3. Carroll Catterton born Jan. 26, 1902. Married Louisa Black July 16, 1938. They have two girls: 1. Carolyn Catterton b. June 7, 1943. 2. Sandra Louise Catterton b. April 10, 1947.
4. Wyatt Stella Catterton born March 16, 1904. Married Frank Garth Aug. 6, 1925, One son, Hugh Clingman Garth b. July 8, 1927.
5. Etta Mae Catterton born Aug. 26, 1906. Married William Chapman Nov. 20, 1933, one daughter, Joan Chapman b. Oct. 28, 1946
6. William Z. Catterton Jr., born Jan. 22, 1909. Married Janet Payton Brand. Two boys; 1. William Z. Catterton. 2. Bob Catterton.

"This is Michael Catterton, brother to William and Gattwood Catterton, who came from Calvert Co., Md. about the year 1784-1785, and settled at Nortonsville Va., in Albemarle Co.

Michael was born Feb. 8, 1761, and was married May 3, 1793, to Frances Williams who was born April 17, 1776.

Michael Catterton and his wife, Frances Williams had the following children:

1. Nancy Catterton born April 1, 1794. Married Isaac Sims 1809.
2. Elizabeth Catterton born April 8, 1795. Married ? Parrott (A Elizabeth Catterton married George Parrott in 1813 - Min. Geo. Bingham)
3. Benjamin W. Catterton born Jan. 6, 1797. Married _ Austin (He went to Missouri in 1837 in a covered wagon from Nortonsville. We have letters he wrote back).
4. Mary Catterton born May 6, 1799. Married ? Williams.
5. Frances Catterton born Oct. 24, 1800.
6. Sarah Catterton born Sept. 24, 1802. Married a Durrett.
7. William Catterton born Feb. 11, 1804. Married Matilda Durrett Oct. 13, 1827.
8. Eliza Catterton born April 28, 1806. Married a Sherman. (There is a record of a Eliza Catterton married George W. Shurmond - 1835 - in Albemarle County.
9. Permilia Catterton born July 16, 1808.
10. Collins Catterton born March 5, 1812.
11. Nimrod W. Catterton born Nov. 9, 1815.
12. Michael Catterton born Nov., 1816.

I wrote Mr. Catterton regarding information of the late Nim Catterton of Charlottesville. The following is a reply to my letter.

"You ask about Nimmie Catterton. His name was Nimrod Parrott Catterton and he was born August 6, 1880. Died Nov. 30, 1951. He married (?)Lelia Elizabeth Powell, Sept. 24, 1902, and has one son, Powell Catterton, born Oct. 31, 1904, who lives in Charlottesville. Nimrod's father was named William Wallace Catterton and was born Feb. 11, 1845. Died Oct. 26, 1924. He married Sarah Ann Elliott Oct. 25, 1868. William Wallace Catterton's father, named Nimrod W. Catterton, born Nov. 9, 1815, and died May 11, 1898- and married Elizabeth K. Key Jan. 15, 1840. Nimrod W. Catterton's father was named Michael Catterton and was born Feb. 8, 1761 in Calvert Co., Maryland, and was married to Frances Williams on May 13, 1793, and his wife (Francis Williams Catterton) was born April 17, 1776."

From Julian Catterton.

My Grandfather, Michael Catterton, married Lucy Wyatt Mills May 2, 1826. She was the daughter of Zachary Mills and Zachary Mills was the son of Capt. David Mills. Capt. David Mills came over from England, and first settled in one of the counties near Jamestown, for about two years. Then he came to what is now Albemarle Co., and took out grants of land from the King of England in the year 1745, amounting to 11,600 acres. The land we live on now, is a small part of that grant. It has come straight down to us from my Great-great Grandfather, David Mills. At the time Michael Catterton married, the Mills owned lots of land, so he came to live with the Mills on the Mills land. My father, Willie, was born in the house that I live in.

The old Mills home where Lucy Wyatt Mills was raised, is about a half mile from our house. It was built in 1752, and it was the first frame house built in this section. Before that the houses were built of logs. All the framing in the house was hued out with an ax, and all the plank was sawed out by hand, and the house was put together with wooden pegs. The few nails that were used were shop made nails. (The old house still stands).

I know the house where William Catterton lived, part of it still stands. I know where Michael Catterton lived when he came from Maryland. It is a large house there now. I think part of it is the same house that he lived in. It is about a mile and a half from William Catterton's home.

I know where William Sim's old home stood. I think it fell down about 1915. It was about 2½ miles from Michael (Catterton's) home and 3½ miles from William (Catterton's) home.

I found an old muster roll of a Company of Militia Commanded by William Michie, 2 Bat. 88 Regt. Va. (Dated 1837) and one (Dated 1842). One of the names on the muster roll was Eli Howard. I wondered if this would be any of your people. (Eli Howard married his cousin, Ann Marshall. Eli Howard witnessed the will of my great-great grandfather, William Catterton. (P.H.B.)

I have written down the names I found in William Catterton's old shopbook. One 1810 and 1818. I thought you might want to see the names of some of the people that lived around here at that time:

Waller Brockman	James Dunn	Chali Goins
William Brockman	Capt. Reuben Davis	William Dowel
William Havard	John Elliott	Richard Durrett
Isaac Sims	John Morris	Thomas Foster
James Sims	James White	Benjamin Catterton
Samuel Gibson	John Davis	John Slater
Thomas Marshall	Johnathan Goodall	William Goins
David Austin	John Gentry	Isaac Morriss
Josha Dunn	Jacob Martin	John Fraizer
Isaac Shiflett	Allen Hall	John Furgerson
John Dunn	James Gentry	Boney Shiflett
George Bingham	Handens Shiflett	Susanah Patterson
Overton Shiflet	Nat Goins	John Higdon
John Dickerson	John S. Shiflett	Johnathany(?) Tyre
Jacob Shiflett	Jack Gibson	John Shob
Thomas Davis	James Marshall	Henry Shiflett
Tomson Mason	Mace Pickett	Joseph Huckstep
Corn Blam Shiflett	Nathan Mason	George Douglass
Granshaw White	Benjamin Goins	John Dollins
Sherred Goins	Buck Estes	Richard Howard
James Shiflett	Edward Hamsell	Darby Sullivan
Tom Brock	James Harris	John Wood
Michael Catterton	London Bruce	Winston Shiflett
John Mallory	Macazial Wood	Enoch Slamons
Richard Bruce	James Keton	Foster Morriss
Peter Gibson	James Hansell	John Turner
John Peel Shiflett	Butckeh Knight	Richard Harvey
Mecozer Shiflett	John Hall	Morgan Garver
John Snow	Lewis Davis	Joseph Bingham
William Cave	Willey Morris	

One receipt I found 1804. William Catterton paid James Sims 2 pounds, 10 shillings and 7 pence for teaching his children that year. I found other receipts that he had paid James Sims through 1812 to teach his children. The last receipt was for

$8.50 for the year 1811 and 1812. After that a man by the name of Stringfellow taught his children.

In the year 1790 he had statements of merchandise he bought from Thilimon (?) Key, and in 1812 for a few years he bought from Richard Michie.

From 1790 through 1840 you can tell the names of the men who kept store, by the statements and bills he kept of the merchandise he bought.

We might have papers that date back further than 1789. I have never looked through all of them (the old papers that we have). I found books printed in 1803-1823-1835-1837-1840 and 1860 and up.

CHAPMAN FAMILY OF ORANGE COUNTY, VIRGINIA

by

Kathrine Cox Gottschalk, Washington, D. C.

Mr. Reynolds Chapman and Mr. Richard M. Chapman of Orange County, were brothers and were the sons of Mr. Richard Chapman, and Elizabeth Reynolds, his wife. This Mrs. Chapman (the mother) married secondly, a Mr. Green. She resided at one time in Hanover County, Virginia. This is learned from the following obituary of Mrs. Elizabeth Green who died at the home of her son, Richard M. Chapman, in Orange Co., Virginia.

Obituary from the National Intelligencer (District of Columbia) May 11, 1825, and published in National Genealogical Society Magazine Vol. XXXIII, Dec. 1950. This was in a series of Vital Records copied from the above old newspaper by Mr. George A. Martin, who made a collection of Vital Records from this paper.

"..Mrs. Elizabeth Green died in Orange Court House, Va., at the home of her son Richard M. Chapman. She was aged 73 years, and had formerly lived in Hanover County, Va., but for the last twenty years has been a resident of Orange Co. and a member of the Protestant Episcopal Church."

From the above we learn that Elizabeth (Reynolds)(Chapman) Green was corn ca 1752, and died in 1825. That she survived her two husbands. We do not have a full list of the children of Richard and Elizabeth (Reynolds) Chapman. (not definitely)

Known issue:

1. Judge Reynolds Chapman of Orange Co., Va., m. Rebecca Madison. She survived him. He died ca 1844, intestate. A division of part of his estate names his heirs, and the will of widow Rebecca (Madison) Chapman is of record in Orange County Court House: dated March 20, 1860, probated Feb. Court 1863. She was sojourning in Madison Co., Va., in 1852.

   Issue: Jane Chapman m. 1828, Thos. Slaughter
   John M. Chapman m. 1841 Susan Cole, they were living in Washington D.C., 1852.
   Alfred Chapman m. Mary E.......
   Richard Chapman m. ... living in Augusta Co., Va., 1852.
   Mary Ellen Chapman (may have been widow of Wm. M. Chapman)
   Wm. M. Chapman d. 1846 - no issues.

Issue of Judge Reynolds Chapman and Jane Conway Madison, Cont. Elizabeth Chapman.

See the appended notes from the Court Records of Orange Co., Va., for the authentic data on this family.

The second son of Richard and Elizabeth (Reynolds) Chapman was Mr. Richard Meriwether Chapman of Orange County, Virginia. He married in Orange Co., by license dated Feb. 7., 1813, Maria, the daughter of Paul Vedier, the daughter of Paul Paul Vedier. Her father sent a note giving his consent to this marriage of his daughter. This was necessary as she was under the legal age of consent. The will of Richard M. Chapman was recorded in Book 12, page 325, Orange Court House Va. Will dated July 13, 1853, and probated Sept. 4, 1858. In this will he names his five children, as follows:

1. Johnson Chapman probably the eldest child and had been given land before the will was made as he shares, only in a part of the estate of his father. Or possibly a son by a first wife.
2. James Chapman b. in Orange Co., about 1820. He was a lawyer.
3. Susan M. Chapman m.1. in 1839 Wm. Quarles Taliaferro. no issue by this marriage.
   m.2..............Reed. She is named as Susan Reed in her father's will, but on her marriage bond with William Q. Taliaferro she is given as the daughter of Richard M. Chapman (1839) who gave his consent to the marriage. She was born after 1819.
4. William Henry Chapman m. Mary E. Stanard March 3, 1751.
5. Maria Chapman m. Dorsey J. Reed (bond) 7-31-1851 Orange Co., Va.

Court Records of Orange Co., Va. for the foregoing Chapman Family.

Bk. 43, p. 00, dated Oct. 28, 1853, Richard M. Chapman to Wm. H. Chapman for $2,000.00 lots in the twon of Orange...

Bk. 43, p.243, dated Sept 27, 1855, Wm. H. Chapman party of the first part, to James Chapman party of the 2nd part and Richard M. Chapman party of the 3rd party. This was a mortgage to Wm. H. Moore, in which it is recited "and also all his interest and title in the reversion of an estate in which a Mrs. Ellen B. Stanard held a life interest and in which the said Wm. H. Chapman has a right (if any) through his wife." This obligation was paid after the death of Wm. H. Chapman by his widow, Ma E. Chapman and heirs.

Will Bk. 12, p.325 The will of Richard M. Chapman (with a codicil) will dated July 13, 1855, codicil dated Sept. 4, 1858: Will probated Sept. 27, 1858. Frees his slaves and makes provision for their care. "All of my property except that in the village of Orange to be divided into four equal parts and given to: my son James Chapman ¼. my daughter Susan Reed ¼, my son Wm. H. Chapman ¼, my daughter Maria Reed ¼.

The property in the village of Orange to be sold and the proceeds divided equally among my five children, my son Johnson Chapman to be included among the five. Executors named were sons James & Wm. H. Chapman.

Note: Johnson Chapman is found on records in HANOVER CO., VA. (K.C.G.)

MARRIAGE BONDS in ORANGE CO., VA.

Richard M. Chapman m. Maria Vedier, 2-6-1813, consent given by her father Paul Vedier.
Wm. Henry Chapman m. Mary E. Standard 3-31-1852.
Susan M. Chapman m. W. Q. Taliaferro, 7-16-1839. Consent of her father Richard M. Chapman.
Mary Louise Chapman m. Dorsey J. Reed, 7-31-1851. Consent of her father Richard M. Chapman.
Mary Ellen Chapman m. Moses Myers 3-2-1847.

For other marriages see W. E. Brockman's Vol. 2, Orange Co., Va., Records.

The namessof other Chapman families appear on the Orange County, Va., records, which from our research on this name are NOT related to the two brothers, Reynolds and Richard M. Chapman, with the exception of JOSHUA Chapman, he is said by the Richard M. Chapman descendants to have been his brother. This seems highly probable. K.C.G.

William and Mary Magazine, Vol. 19. (1) p. 137
Richard Chapman, son of Richard Chapman and his wife Jane Johnson was born at Chericoke", King William Co., Va., Sept. 1741.
Elizabeth Reynolds was born at "The Island in New Kent, Febry, 18, 1757. Elizabeth Reynolds and Richard Chapman were married by Rev. Mr. Ford, Sunday 16th, 1775.
Jane Chapman, their dau. was born at "Prior Park" Thursday, Feb. 29th, 1776.
Reynolds Chapman, her brother, was born at Prior Park We., July 22, 1778.
Johnson Chapman, their brother was born at Prior Hall Tues., Dec. 26th, 1780, died age four years.

Madison Co. Records.
Book 1 - Reynolds Chapman m. Rebecca Conway Madison Feb. 18, 1802. Parent - Wm. Madison.

Orange Co. Records.
Wm. T. Wood married America Mitchell Oct. 3, 1832 - Wit. W. M. Chapman.
David Spicer married Nancy Sims Sept. 22, 1829. Wit. Reynolds Chapman - Bondsman, Wm. Williams
Catherine Brockman, daughter of William Brockman Jr. of Alb. Co., married 1. Dabney Spicer. 2. John Lewis

Madison Co. Record
Book 1 - Benj. L. Mitchell married Isabella Chapman Sept. 26, 1829 - Father Thomas Chapman (Elizabeth Early, daughter of James M. Thomas Chapman) Wood's History of Alb. Co.

Orange Co. Records.
Isabella M. (Chapman) Mitchell married (2nd) Holland Ozborne Jr. April 2, 1835, Wit. Reynolds Chapman.

Madison Co. Records
Book 1 - Thomas Chapman married Ann Rouzee Nov. 9, 1808. Parent Jno. Rouzee. Married by Wm. C. Carpenter Nov. 10, 1808.

Book 1 - Wm. Chapman M. Hattie Gains April 29, 1799.
Book 1 - Sims Chapman m. Ann Bohannon Nov. 9, 1808.

(From a newspaper article on the Myers family of Norfolk - Virginian - Pilot and Norfolk-Landmark Jan 18, 1931.

"Barton Myers Home Gem of Georgian Architecture and Treasuer Home of Priceless Antiques. Chairs that belonged to Marie Antoinette. President James Madison, who brought back from France the furnishings of Marie's Palace, gave these two chairs to his great-niece, Mary Ella Chapman. She married the second Moses Myers, grandson of the builder of the home. And she lived there for one year, and died."

COLLINS OF VIRGINIA

So far as I am able to tell this is the line of descent of Joseph Collins who left Will at Spottsylvania, 1757.

First Generation

William Collins came to Virginia in 1635 at age 23 landing on May 15 from the Plain Joan, Richard Backam, Master. "Having brought attestations of their conformation to the orders and discipline of the Church of England." He took up 561 acres in the Isle of Wight and in 1691, and 620 acres with Tim Corners in King and Queen Oct. 10, 1791, where he was listed as a merchant. His wife was Ann Wilds, widow of Thomas. The record there shows that one Ann Collins, widow married (3rd marriage) Alex Murre or Merry. William had a son John, who married, but whether his wife was Eleanor Oliver daughter of John, or whether she was a daughter of Amy Wyatt (Will 1666) is not known.

Second Generation

John Collins, son of William had at least four children:

1. Jospeh Collins, who was living in Essex in 1718 and 1720, where his brother William was living in 1751. Joseph married Catherine Robinson or Robertson, indicated by land transfers from Robinson to Joseph, sons: Joseph, Thomas and William. He died 1748. Fleet's abstracts of King and Queen County pages 39 and 176 have this official record: "ordered that summons be issued for William of Essex, and George Collins of King and Queen to cause them to appear at the next court held for this county to declare whether or not they will execute the last Will and Testament of Joseph Collins, deceased, May 3, 1748". In 1741, John Robertson transferred 400 acres to Joseph Collins; in 1744, 300 acres to Thomas Collins; in 1744, 254 acres to Joseph Collins (presumable son of Joseph), and 1744, 200 acres to William collins. These transfers are all to son-in-law Collins and his children. William Collins transferred his 200 acres to James Haley whose wife was then Beliah and presumably daughter of William Collins. James Haley is shown as having wife Susanna (believe to be Brockman) in 1749 when he and wife transferred 126 acres in Orange to Samuel Brockman. This Joseph Collins and wife Catherine Robinson then had at least four sons and he was dead by 1748.
2. John Collins, had son Edmund. See Will of brother Thomas.
3. Thomas, of King and Queen, Will January 3, 1748, mentions father John and brothers John and Joseph and nephew Edmund, son of brother John.
4. George Collins.

There were probably other children.

Third Generation

Children of Joseph Collins and wife Catherine Robertson:

1. Joseph, married Susannah Lewis, believed to have been daughter of Zachary Lewis.
2. William of Essex, wife Elizabeth.
3. Thomas, Will June 3, 1751, proved Sept. 12, 1752, Spottsylvania, wife Elizabeth, Sons: Joyce, under 21, Thomas, Jr., Richard. Witnesses: brother Joseph, Benjamin Glaze, William and John Collins, Thomas Collins, Jr.

Fourth Generation

Children of Captain Joseph Collins and wife Susannah Lewis:

1. John, married Ann Cook.
2. James married Elizabeth Wylie.
3. William married Elizabeth Bashaw.
4. Thomas married Susannah Wyatt Davis Bartlett.
5. Lewis, married Elizabeth, and left Will at Granville, N.C., 1783, naming wife Elizabeth and Children (See Volume 11 Orange County Families) and his wife Elizabeth left a Will at Kershaw, S.C., 1796, naming most of the children mentioned in her husband's Will.
6. Ann married John Wisdom.
7. Mary married John Brockman.
8. Tabitha married Henry Gatewood; 2nd. John Holliday.
9. Caty married Benjamin Glaze.
10. Susannah married William Gholson.
11. Granddaughter Amy Collins, presumably daughter of a deceased son.

DOWELL - SALMON - BROCKMAN

The earliest Dowell we have is John who sold land to Thomas Graves about 1725, and he had land holdings in old Louisa, now Albermarle County north of the Rivanna, and which he sold to Richard Durrett in 1730, and this land was then sold to Robert Duncanson, who sold it to William Brockman 1761, and is the property referred to in an article in the Charlottesville Progress newspaper by Vera V. Via. John Dowell, left a Will at Louisa 1760 disposing of land that became a part of Albermarle, about 1758. While John lived in Caroline at one time the family may have come from Maryland, where Henry Dowell was witness to the Will of Michael Catterton in 1700, and the latter family were old residents of Albermarle. We are presenting some Salmon data, because of early association with Thomas Salmon of Maryland, and the intermarriages between the Salmons and Dowells. The following item from the Daily Progress has been corrected in some parts as to spelling and some parts deleted because of duplication of data in other parts of this book.

"In this series on old Albemarle homes, we have given the stories of two places called "Bleak House", and shown that the two places were connected by marriage. The one at Free Union, which was the old William Ferguson homestead, is the oldest house by that name. The old Rogers house at Earlysville was built at a later date, and the mother of the builder was a Ferguson.

We are informed by Mrs. M. A. Brandt II of Norfolk who is a descendent of the Brockman family, that her ancestral home at Burnleys was called "Bleak Hill." From family notes we find a connection with both the Ferguson and Rogers families so "Bleak Hill" can be considered another of the "Bleaks."

According to notes from the "Brockman Scrapbook" by W. E. Brockman, this family came to America very early. Henry Brockman was brought to St. Marie County, Md., before 1674 by a Capt. John Jourdaine. For services to the captain, he was given 50 acres of land, which he sold to Thomas Salmon. Henry was thought to be a son of Thomas Brockman of the Barbadoes, and he married Rebecca Salmon. He had one son, Samuel, of King and Queen, Spotsylvania and Orange Counties, who died in 1766. His will is in the Orange County records.

Samuel's son, William, whose wife's name was Betty Mason, lived on Proddy's Creek in Albemarle County where he had large holdings not far from the present site of Bleak Hill. He also had one of the first mills erected in that section. He and his brother, Samuel of Orange County, were willed 300 acres in Albemarle, which they sold. A codicil of this will of the first Samuel Brockman was witnessed by James Madison.

Willed Church

William Brockman died in 1809, and in his will he left a church on his land, which was the predecessor of the present Priddy's Creek Church, to the congregation. One of William's sisters, Rachael, married John Rogers, and she was a widow by 1762. This John Rogers may have been a brother of Giles, who was father of the line which built the Bleak House.

Samuel Brockman, son of William who lived on Priddy's Creek, married Ann Sims, and they had ten children. The oldest of these, Richard Sims Brockman, was a witness to President James Madison's will. But it was the third son, Bluford Brockman, whose line we will follow. He married his first cousin Elizabeth Catterton, on Dec. 22, 1822.

According to family notes, Bluford and Elizabeth Brockman lived in the house called "Bleak Hill." No one knows when it was built, but it is known to have been standing in 1822, and it is possible it dates all the way back to William Brockman. William willed the children of his son, Samuel, 150 acres of land on which he then lived in 1809.

Several other members of the family married in northern Albemarle. Tazewell Brockman married Sarah Salmon in 1847. Julia Ann Brockman married Anderson B. Carr.

Family Connection

Bluford Brockman is the first for whom we have definite record of living at Bleak Hill, but the oldest son of Bluford was Walter D. Brockman, born in 1823, who married Ann Ferguson in 1848. So the name could have come through the earlier Rogers connection, or through the Ferguson connection. No one seems to know why it was given the name 'Bleak Hill,' but not it would seem, because of its bleakness. It is much more likely it was named after the old original Bleak House. There were other connections between the Ferguson and Brockman families, as Fergusons were witnesses to some of the early Brockman deeds.

We believe the land on which Bleak Hill stood was originally part of the William Brockman holdings, acquired by him probably before the Revolution. His son, Samuel, died before his father, and Samuel's widow and her children sold their place, "Green Plains" near Barboursville, and moved to the place at Burnleys. Her father-in-law then willed his home to his son's children. Bluford died in 1878, and by will gave the property to his daughter, Lucetta Elizabeth Brockman Mitchell. She was the youngest child, having been born in 1843, and she married Andrew Jackson Mitchell in 1860. She outlived her father by only three years, dying in 1881, and the property went to her six children, with her husband more or less having charge of it.

This land was not partitioned until around 1916, and then sections of it were sold off. Some of it went to relatives of the Brockman lines. Bleak Hill is still owned by the Mitchell family.

Two Centuries

William married Betty Mason by 1748, so he must have come to Albemarle soon after.

Bluford Brockman seems to have done his full share in furnishing supplies during the Civil War. In 1864, a receipt was given him for five bushels of corn as forage. On Dec. 19,1864, he supplied 42 bushels and a half of corn and six hundred pounds of fodder, his tithe for the year 1864.

Elizabeth Catterton Brockman was given on her marriage a slave called Mammy Cindy, who stayed with the family even after the Civil War. She was greatly loved by the family. She married Willson, who was bought by Bluford Brockman from Sims Brockman. Both slaves remained faithful to the family.

In 1840, Bluford Brockman paid Everett Gay $4.48 for 112 days of schooling of his children, at the rate of four cents a day. In 1855 he paid Eliza P. Douglas $4.50 for the tuition of his daughter for the year 1854.

"Bleak Hill" is still in the hands of Brockman descendents, but on one is living in it at present. The huge chimney on the Bluford Brockman home once had a large fireplace, but that has been closed up. His grave is marked by a tombstone B.B. in the Brockman-Mitchell Cemetary there."

WILLIAM BROCKMAN LAND

Patented by John Dowell 1738; sold to Henry Haines 1749, Sold to Richard Durrett 1754; Purchased by William Brockman 1761.

DEED

Dated: July 23, 1754

Richard H. Durrett and wife, Sarah
To
Robert Duncanson, Merch. of Fredericksburg
Consideration: 80 lbs. current money.
Conveys 400 acres in County of Louisa, Parish of Fredericksville, as contained in Patent dated February 1, 1738, granted unto John Dowell & from him by several means

and conveyances and described in said Patent as follows: BEGINNING at William Cradock's red oak white oak and pine running thence N. 50 deg. E. 86 poles to two pine saplins thence N. 220 poles to Several Oak bushes, thence W. 96 poles to a maple in a small branch, thence S. 50 deg. W. 204 poles to pine saplin in a valley, thence S. 15 deg. E. 252 poles to two pines in Cradock's line, thence along same N. 50 deg. E. 150 poles to beginning.

Signed: Richard Durrett (Seal)
Sarah Durrett (Seal)
Witnesses: ------------
Recorded: July 23, 1754.
Teste: Jas. Littlepage, Clk. Crt.

Recorded: Deed Book "B", page 13.

An Abstract:-
Teste: Kate B. Pattie Deputy Clerk
for L. A. Keller, Jr., Clerk,
Louisa County Circuit Court,
Virginia.

WILL of JOHN DOWELL (wife Christian) of Louisa County

Dated: December 16, 1759.

To my Son Thomas Dowell tract of land I purchased of Thomas Collens joining Mr. James Coleman, Samuel Munday & Daniel Fargason. Also 2 negroes Jack & Aggy.

To my Son John Dowell 250 acres of land I purchased of Jasper Haynes, Joining Richard --Durrett & John Quarles also 2 negroes - - -& Phillis, also all my household goods, stocks, etc.

To my son Will---Dowell, my Mountain Tract of Land joining Mr. James Coleman and one negro girl Hannah and first living child born from loins of Aggy.

To my son Ambrose Dowell, 300 acres Joining Mr. Dixon William Dier & John Quarles, 1 negro girl, Peg, & first living child born of loins of Phillis.

To my son, Richard Dowell, 1/2 of tract land whereon I now Dwell he to have first choice also 2 negroes, James & Lett.

Remainder of tract to son Ambrose Dowell.

To Samuel Munday and Robert Grinnen Tract of land joining William Dyer, John Davis and my own plantation only reserving 50 acres Joining my own line from my son Thomas Dowell to my son John Dowell.

To my son, John Dowell 200 acres joining Joseph Martin James Coleman and William Granger.

To my daughter, Sarah Grinnen, 5 lbs. sterling debarring her of all other rights and properties belonging to my estate.

To my daughter, Mary Lankford, 5 lbs. sterling debarring her of all other rights and properties belonging to my estate.

To my daughter, Milley Dowell, 5 lbs. sterling debarring her of all other rights and properties belonging to my estate.

To my daughter, Sukey, 5 lbs. sterling debarring her of all other rights and properties belonging to my estate.

Appoints son John Dowell and friend Daniel Fargason, Exors.

Signed: John his I mark Dowell (Seal)

Witnesses: George Martin John Maccauley his X mark

Joseph Davenport

"The wife of John Dowell was Christian Monroe".

Recorded: March 25, 1760

Teste: James Littlepage, Clk. Crt.

Will Book "1", pages 50-51-52.

An abstract:-
Teste:-________________________Deputy Clerk
for L. A. Keller, Jr., Clerk,
Louisa County Circuit Court,
Virginia.

Norfolk, Va.
Jan. 18, 1958

Dear Cousin:

Thank you very much for the copy of the will of John Dowell (will 1759) I believe Sarah Dowell Grinner-Greening-Grinnils was the same person. Perhaps just a different way of spelling the name in the court records. Rebecca Grinnils-Greening(?) who married Wm. Mitchell and James Greening who married Sarah Crosthwaite were children of Sarah Dowell Grinner-Greening-Grinnils. The above children along with their mother, Sarah sold land to Achillis Douglass. In 1803, James Greening and Sally, his wife, and Thomas Dowell and Sally, his wife, sold Achillis Douglass 150 acres of land. (Sally Salmon who married Tazewell Brockman was a granddaughter of one Thomas Dowell and wife Avery). Thomas Dowell could have been married twice, or there could have a Thomas Dowell Sr. and Jr. The land Ambrose Dowell sold Wm. Brockman Sr. in 1782, bordered the Dixon, Charles Dickens and Peter Ferguson land. Wm. Brockman, Sr., in his will refers to parts of his land as the "Dixon tract" and some as the Dickerson tract". Getting back to the John Dowell will, I notice that Joseph Davenport was a witness to the will of John Dowell. Joseph Davenport was a son of Richard Davenport. Richard Davenport's will mentions a daughter, Mary, wife of Thomas Jones. This Richard Davenport's will was witnessed by a Samuel Dyer. John Dowell's land joined that of Wm. Dyer.(the tract that he willed Samuel Mundy and Robert Grinner). One Thomas Jones had a son Thomas Jr. Perhaps he married Mary Davenport and the other Thomas Jones married Patty ?. One thing sure, the Dowells, Brockmans, Crosthwaits, Dyers, Jones, Douglass and Dickersons lived in the same neighborhood. I believe there was a close family tie between them, but it is like trying to put a cross word puzzle together to identify them. From the deeds etc., Mrs. Marshall sends me in connection with the research that we are doing on our Mitchell-Greening families- I am convinced that these families have some connection with our Brockman family. The same names are always on the deeds etc., Crosthwaite, Douglass, Jones and Dickerson. I am interested in the John Dickerson, wife Mary, who died in Albemarle Co., 1788. Wood's History gives the names of his sons, but not those of his daughters. I have asked Mrs. Marshall to send you any Dowell-Groening data that she finds. Between us, by piecing bits of data together, we learned the name of Nelly Wood Mitchell's parents, brothers and sisters. We only had the name Nelly Wood Mitchell to go on. I believe we can do the same on our Brockman line if we try hard enough.

Mrs. Mrshall Douglass, a Dowell descendant, says that her John Dowell came from England married Patience Franklin, niece of Benj. Franklin, and died in Alb. Co., near Advance Mill. See your map of Alb. Co. Follow route 641 from Burnleys Station to a junction of route 743 and you will find the location of Advance Mill. Mrs. Douglass gave this Dowell information to Mrs. Marshall's mother.

I found the following in "Va. Genealogies and County Records" by Burns" (Alb. CO.) Vol. 1, page 2.

8-15-1751-Benjamin Franklin. Wife Patience Franklin. Children: Anne, Elizabeth, Mary, Dorcas. Executors: Patience Franklin, Ambrose Profus and Reuben Franklin. Witnesses: Phillip Davis, and Thomas Tillie. Probated 11-12-1751.

I wrote an elderly cousin pertaining to the Jones family whose land was shown as joining our land at Burnleys in the survey made in 1869. She wrote me that an old Jones home place joined our land. From what she wrote, it was between our land and the Roy Brockman place. She said in latter years a Johns family resided there. The Johns family are also related to us.

Sincerely, Pauline H. Brandt

Albemarle Co., Records

Book 3	Thomas Salmon	division	
page 224	wife Ann Salmon		
1786	Children:		
1794	Thomas Salmon Jr.		
	Betsy Salmon	Wit:	Chiles Terrell
	Peggy Salmon		Peter Clarkson
	John D. Salmon		Gravit Edwards
	Mary Salmon		Madison Breedlone

Book 3	Ann Salmon	division	
page 253	Thomas Salmon		
1795	Peggy Salmon	Wit:	Peter Clarkson
	Elizabeth Salmon		Madison Breedlone
	Mollie Pritchett		Samuel Brockman

Some Salmon marriages-Alb. Co., Va.

1. John D. Salmon M. Mary Dowell Feb. 5. 1798
   Bond- John D. Salmon and Jeremiah Nicholas

2. Jeremiah Nicholas M. Ann Salmon 1789
   Bond- Jermiah Nicholas and Edward Banker
3. James Prichett M. Mary Salmon Dec. 5 1793
   Bond- James Prichett and Jeremiah Nicholas
4. Thomas Salmon M. Elizabeth M. Carr Dec. 17, 1808

1815 Will Book 6, page 40 --- JOHN D. SALMON
Nancy Salmon, daug. of Thomas Dowell, wife of John D. Salmon
Fendal F. Salmon, son of John D. Salmon
Thomas Salmon, son of John D. Salmon
John Salmon, son of John D. Salmon
Nancy Salmon, daug. of John D. Salmon, wife of Wm. Pritchett
Sally or Sarah Salmon, daughter of John D. Salmon
Julia Salmon, daug. of John D. Salmon, wife of Walter Pritchett
Elizabeth Salmon, daughter of John D. Salmon, wife of Charles Mundy

Information: Dowell vs. Dowell, Alb. Co. Court and Salmon vs. Salmon, Alb. Co. Court.

1813 Book 6, page 83 --THOMAS DOWELL (wife Avery Dowell)
Major Dowell son of Thomas Dowell share
John Dowell, son of Thomas Dowell share
Wm. Dowell, son of Thomas Dowell share
Elijah Dowell, son of Thomas Dowell share
Reuben Dowell, son of Thomas Dowell share
Nancy Salmon, daughter of Thomas Dowell, wife of John D. Salmon
Betsy or Elizabeth Taylor, daughter of Thomas Dowell, wife of George Taylor.

(From Dowell vs. Dowell Alb. Co. Court)

1794 Deed Book 12, page 346, JOHN DOWELL
ANNE DOWELL, wife of J. John Dowell
Mary Dowell, daug. of J. John Dowell, wife of Major Dowell
John Dowell, son of J. John Dowell
Patience Gunter, daug. of J. John Dowell, wife of John Gunter
Darkus Dowell, son of J. John Dowell
James Dowell, son of J. John Dowell
Benjamin Dowell, son of J. John Dowell
Mildred Dowell, daughter of J. John Dowell
Nancy Dowell, daughter of J. John Dowell
Major Dowell, son of J. John Dowell

(From Dowell vs. Dowell Alb. Co. Court)

1812 Will Book 5, page 204 --- JOHN DOWELL, wife Molly or Mary Dowell
See Deed Book 41 page 235

Wm. Dowell, son of John Dowell
Harrison Dowell, son of John Dowell
Nancy Coleman, daughter of John Dowell, wife of Wm. Coleman
Jane Pickett, daughter of John Dowell, wife of Charles Pickett
Richard Dowell, son of John Dowell
Sally Garrison, daughter of John Dowell, wife of Volley Garrison
Major Dowell, son of John Dowell,
Betsy Keaton, daughter of John Dowell, wife of James Keaton
John Dowell, son of John Dowell, went west
Polly or Mary Dowell, daughter of John Dowell, died unmarried

(Dowell vs. Dowell, Alb. Co. Court)

The above information form Mr. W. P. Maupins records.

Deed Book 18, page 528
Jan. 1, 1814
26 acres
$1.00

John Dowell and Major Dowell, adm. for Thomas Dowell decd., to John D. Salmon

"being the claim which Salmon has to the landed estate of Thomas Dowell decd."

John Dowell (Seal)
Major Dowell (Seal)

SALMON-MUNDY BIBLE RECORD

Sally Salmon was born August the 23rd, AD 1807
Tazewell Brockman was born April the 24th, A.D. 1806
Tazewell and Sarah Salmon Brockman were married the 16th of November in the year 1847
Tazewell S. Edwards and Julia Em Mundy was married March the 10th, 1852.
William H. Salmon and Sarah Jane Mundy were married Octeber the 13th, 1859
John D. Salmon was born March the 22nd, A.D. 1773.

DEATHS: (different handwriting)

Sarah Mundy Salmon died Dec. 3, 1914
William Salmon died Dec. 4, 1923
Walker L. Mundy died Feb. 11, 1928
Rosalie S. Mundy died May 29, 1931
Clarie Mundy died Dec. 3, 1924

BIRTHS:
Elizabeth Salmon was born May the 13th, A.D. 1799
Thomas Salmon was born November the 16th, A.D. 1800
John Salmon was born June the 28th, A.D. 1803
Nancy Salmon was born June the 17th, A.D. 1805
Sally Salmon was born August the 23rd, A.D. 1807
Julia Ann Salmon was born Aug. 19, A.D. 1809

BIRTHS:
Lovellian Mundy was born June 1st, 1826
John D. Mundy was born Nov. 18th, 1827
Julia Emma Mundy was born September 3, 1829
Lucyann Mundy was born March 9, 1831
Sarah Jane Mundy was born May 24th, 1833
Jonathan R. Mundy was born Nov. 4th, 1835
Thomas W. Mundy was born June 29th, 1838
Margarett J. Mundy was born Jan. 16, 1842
Charles T. Edwards was born Dec. 14, 1852
Julia E. T. Edwards was born Aug. 27, 1855

DEATHS:
Lovellian Mundy departed this life Oct. 1st, 1844
John D. Mundy departed this life Oct. 12th, 1844
Lucyann Mundy departed this life Oct. 19th, 1852
Julia Emma Edwards departed this life Aug. 27th, 1855
Charles Mundy departed this life June 27, 1859
Elizabeth Mundy died Nov. 28, 1894 (different handwriting)

Lizzie W. Salmon was born Dec. 21, 1864

The above records are from a family Bible owned by Mr. L. W. Mundy, Rio Dr., Charlottesville, Va. Date in front of Bible, 1834.

EDWARDS BIBLE RECORDS

The dates of births of the children of Thomas Tandy Edwards and his wife Agnes C. Brockman Edwards (Agatha Cowherd Brockman Edwards)

1. Still birth
2. Horace Booker Edwards, born Dec. 6, 1819
3. Bluford Bibb Edwards, born Dec. 3, 1821
4. Brice Jones Edwards, born June 24, 1823
5. Tazewell Sims Edwards, born May 5, 1826
6. S muel William Edwards, born July 18, 1828
7. Thomas Tandy Edwards (Jr.) born Oct. 20, 1830
8. Julie Anne Edwards born April 1, 1833
9. Martha Jane Edwards born May 19, 1835
10. Elizabeth Helen Edwards, born May 17, 1837
11. Nancy Susan Edwards, born Dec. 20, 1840
12. Henry Clay Edwards, born June 30, 1842
13. John Carr Edwards, born Jan. 20, 1845
14. Elizabeth Agnes Edwards, born Feb. 5, 1847
15. Valentine Gravitt Edwards, born May 13, 1849

Nancy Edwards was the daughter of Agatha Brockman Edwards.
Tazewell Brockman, brother to Agatha B. Edwards
M.O.Douglas, Father of Henry B. Douglas.
Henry B. Douglas's first wife was Mildred "Milly" E. Edwards. She was the daughter of Mary Mitchell and Samuel W. Edwards. Mary Mitchell was the 1st wife of Samuel W. Edwards. His 2nd wife was a Shotwell.
Edwin T. Douglas, son of Nancy Edwards Douglas, and husband of Elizabeth D. Gilliman.

D.B. 19, page 400, 1815 -- 184½ acres (Levi Wood from Sam Brockman and Patsy Brockman of Orange Co.)

Alb. Co. Va. Land Book - 1861 - Levi Wood, 184 acres on Priddy's Creek.

Levi Wood witnessed the division of land of Samuel Brockman, husband of Ann Sims Brockman. Evidently Sims Brockman and Patsy Brockman were living in Orange when they sold land to Levi Wood. This land was on Priddy's Creek - 184½ acres.

Information to Mrs. Mildred Marshall from Mrs. Ells Wood Smith (age 99).

Jeremiah Shotwell married a Taylor. Their Children:

1. Jeremiah Shotwell married Columbia Brockman.
2. Minar Shotwell married a Harrison
3. Mary Shotwell married Jefferson Wood
4. Sally Shotwell married Ira Wood (Mrs. Ella Wood Smith's parents)
5. Louise Shotwell married John Smith
6. Caswell "Dock" Shotwell married 1st.- ? Wood. He married 2nd.- Rebecca "Becky" Mahones.

This Jeremiah Shotwellmust have been Sr. I have not been able to find this marriage record. It may be in Orange. Possibly the Taylor girl he married was related to the James Taylor family, that married Frances Brockman.

Jeremiah Shotwell Jr. married my great aunt, Columbia Brockman.

Mrs. Smith did not list Caswell Shotwell as a son, but I know that he was a brother to great aunt, Columbia Brockman Shotwell's husband. Caswell Shotwell's first wife was a Wood, daughter of Johnnie Wood, and she was a sister of the Mary Wood who married Horace Edwards.

ELLIS

The Ellis Family has lived in Orange since it became a county. In fact they may have acquired land there when Essex and Spottsylvania extended their borders merging toward the West. The name is found at Jamestown in the second contingent of English settlers and the family moved up to Henrico, Goochland and Albermarle. The Orange family were in Gloucester, Essex, Spottsylvania and Hanover. My research on this family resulted from finding an old deed at Orange wherein John Brockman in settling the estate of his father Samuel, in 1792, went to the county clerk and took possession of a deed executed April 22, 1779, between Thomas Graves and his wife Isabel (Bartlett) of Louisa to John Ellis (One John Ellis was in Essex, 1718) of the Parish of St. Paul's, Hanover, 195 acres on the North Anna river next to William Neale and Samuel Brockman, and this land I believe to be the present farm or part of it now owned by Caroline

Brockman Ellis, widow of Russell Ellis, son of John. Also I was intrigued by locating the descendants of Lindsay Ellis Brockman, at Moberly, Missouri, son of William and Mary Lindsay Brockman, and this is the first time that I had found that Ellis was the middle name of son Lindsay. His grandmother was Rebecca and not knowing her surname, this suggested that it may have been Ellis but no proof of this has been found. Altho the records at Henrico are filled with Ellis Wills, the direct connection with the Orange family of Thomas Ellis of Pine Park has not been established. Discovery of the diary of Capt. Robert S. Ellis, of Pine Park, son of Thomas throws some light on the descendants. This diary in the hands of Mrs. Henry Ellis or Orange I read and it is dated April 13, 1830, when Robert S. Ellis began a journey to the West. Some of the Spottsylvania branch found their way to Orange also. Sallie Ellis, daughter of Hezikiah, whose Will at Spottsylvania dated February 13, 1772, and proved April 16, 1772, was son of William Ellis, Will May 19, 1766, proved August 4. His wife was Elizabeth, and William had a brother Robert. March 19, 1779, John Ellis was named guardian of William, Thomas, Elizabeth, Mildred, Hezikiah, Sarah (Sallie) Ellis. Sallie Ellis married Aaron Quisenberry whose first wife was Rachael Shelton. Daughter Lucy Ellis married Asa Brockman 1819, and daughter Nancy married Curtis Lindsay Brockman, cousin of Asa.

The Graves family has been associated with the early developments and settlements in most of the Eastern Counties. Mrs. Martha Hiden, in William and Mary Quarterly, October, 1936, gives a well documented history of Capt Thomas Graves who arrived in Virginia 1608. He may or may not have been father of perhaps brother of William Graves who baptized a daughter Rebecca in Abingdon Parish, Gloucestor in 1702. Thomas who joined with Hickman in taking up large grants in Albemarle, and Fredericksville Parish, Louis County, was likely son of William. He was in Essex in 1718. He bought 170 acres from Lawrence Franklin in Spottsylvania (Orange) on February 3, 1725, and 400 acres from John Dowell March 2, 1730, the latter having large holdings in Fredericksville Parish, Louisa County. Thomas Graves, believe to be his son was born in Louisa 1730, and died in Fayette County, Ky. 1801. His wife was Isabella Bartlett, daughter of William Bartlett, who left a will in Spottsylvania, naming among others a daughter Isabel Graves. Will of Thomas Graves, Book H, page 5, Fayette Co., mentions wife Isabella, children, William, Bartlett, John, Rosannah, Randolph, Isabel Hall, Ann Hancock, Sally Graves, Mary Beeler, and Liddy Graves. Will proved Oct. 24, 1801, and witnesses were James Martin, William Dickey (John Graves of Spottsylvania, Will 1747, named daughter Rebecca and his wife was Susannah Dicken) Jeremiah Buckley; Executors son Bartleet and Bartlett Collins. This seems to tie up this Thomas Graves with the John Graves of Spottsylvania and Capt. Thomas, to Va. 1608. Thomas Graves was signer on many documents connected with Samuel Brockman, 1, and Samuell, II, seemed to have an interest in the property which Thomas Graves and wife Isabel, sold to John Ellis, in 1779. Rebecca seems to have been a constant name in the Graves family and it is likely that Rebecca, wife of Samuel Brockman II, was a sister of Thomas Graves of Louisa County and daughter of Thomas who took up early land in Albermarle, Spottsylvania and Louisa. In Lancaster Co., 1662, Thos. Graves, Sr., of Gloucester bought 700 acres from Francis Morrison. On March 6, 1704, John Graves of King and Queen bought 100 acres in King William.

THIS DATA FROM MRS. JOSEPHINE HENDERSON NEAL OF LOUISA, VIRGINIA

From a letter written 1935 from Mrs. Elizabeth C. Haggatt, address unknown, to Mrs. Susan Henderson Wright.

ELLIS

The name Ellis appears at an early date in connection with the Colony of Virginia. David Ellis came out in its second supply of emigrants from England and was one of the men sent by Capt. John Smith to build a house for King Powhatan at his favorite seat Warowocomico on York River. John Ellis was one of the grantees in the second Charter of the Virginia Company of Welsh extraction.

John Ellis settled on Peter's Creek, Henrico County, he was born 1661, his wife was named Susannah. His Children:

John Ellis, William Ellis, Thomas Ellis, Henry Ellis, James Ellis, Joseph Ellis, Mary Ellis and Charles Ellis. (Note: From other data I have, he, Charles Ellis, was born 1719, m. 1739, d. 1759, that John(2) married Elizabeth Ware, That his daughter Susannah m. 1758 Thomas Lewis).

William Ellis, the second,son, lived to be 83 years old and left 4 sons and 4 daughters. (not named) A grandson William Burton Ellis married Elizabeth West.

Thomas Ellis, the third son, married Elizabeth Patterson and had two sons, three daughters. (not named) (From Douglas Parish Register I found Sally a daughter b. June 27, 1777; Sukie b. Dec. 27, 1786; Nancy b. Aug. 1, 1775).

Henry Ellis the fourth son never married and died 1768.

James Ellis married died without issue.

Joseph Ellis married Elizabeth Perkins (he had a grandson Daniel Ellis b. May 2, 1774) his will dated June 11, 1785 proven Jan. 7, 1793, his wife died 1798. (does not say where)(From other source children: D. Elizabeth b. 175-; Son Charles b. Oct. 13, 1764; Son Samuel b. Mar. 3, 1786. Then Joseph E. Ellis and Christian Farrar (Ferrar) m. 1769, a son Robert b. Jan. 14, 1770 (this copied as written I presume Joseph E. m. 1769 son above Joseph and that Robert is his son.)

Mary Ellis the only daughter of John Ellis I married John Smith.

Charles Ellis the seventh son born in Hanover County Va. 1719, m. Susannah Harding daughter of Thomas Harding and Mary his wife (nee: Giles) in 1739, and had 2 sons and 8 daughters. He removed with his family to Amherst, then Albemarle in 1754 and settled at the seat of Ellises called "Red Hill" on Pedlar River. He died May 4th, 1759. His widow is buried by his side at "Red Hill", she lived to be 95 years old. Children: (1) Hannah m. W. Haynes (2) Edith M. Devereux Gilliam (3) Susannah m. Isaac Wright (4) Josiah m. Jane Shelton (5) Mary Ann m. Peter Carter (6) Charles (Jr.) m. first Elizabeth Waters, second Sarah Tucker (?) (7) Sarah m. John Harrison (8) Bertha m. Thomas Leftwich (9) Elizabeth m. William Gilliam (10) Rosanna m. Charles Davis.

NOTE: For children of Josiah above see Bishop Meade's "Old Churches and Families Vol. II p. 461-3. There was Rev. Josiah Ellis from this line an Episcopal Minister on Va.

What is quoted from Douglas Parish Register I found out and added to this. (Mrs. Neal)

At Henrico I found a number of Ellis Will, all in Will Book No 1. Page 31, John Ellis, son of John, September 8, 1779, names children John, Hezikiah, puryear, Susannah Lewis, Elizabeth Clarke, grandson Robert, son of Joseph. Proved April 2, 1782. Page 78 September 27, 1779, Jesse Ellis, wife Sarah, son John under 21, Susannah, father-in-law Joseph Woodson, lands occupied by Elizabeth Stodgill in Goochland. Ex. John Ellis, son of Joh, Stephen Ellis, son of Joseph, and Jos. Woodson. Proved May 5, 1783. Page 68. Thomas Ellis, son of Jesse, Susannah Crunch, Mary Maddox, son John, daughter Sally, wife Anne. Proved July 7, 1783.

October 20, 1788. John Ellis, son of Thomas, names son Josiah, wife Martham, daughters and sons not named, brother Thomas (Book 2, page 119).

William Ellis, October 18, 1775, children John, Susannah Clark, William, Jacob, David, Lucy Johnson, Elizabeth, Mary. There are other records in Henrico but none that connected with the Orange family. Thomas Ellis of Pine Park, Orange County, is reproted to have married 1st, Rebecca Moorman and 2nd, Elizabeth Hurt. Thomas left a Will at Orange Book 5, page 160, dated May 27, 1816, in which he names children Thomas, Robert, Richard, Clara, Mary Ann, Maria (Thompson), Frances, Agnes (under age) John, James, Becky Thompson (Rebecca) Sally Thompson and relative Elizabeth Gray. August 11, 1828, Elizabeth Ellis, widow of Thomas entered into a marriage agreement with Thomas Woolfolk, Jr., known as Judge Woolfolk, Deed Book 32, page 332.

ELLIS FAMILY OF PINE PARK, ORANGE COUNTY, VIRGINIA

From a letter addressed to C. W. Woolfolk, mailed in St. Louis, Mo., May 1st, 1901. On stationery "Hotel Howard", Holladay & Son, Fayette, Mo.

First and Second Generation

Thomas Ellis born November 9th, 1758
Elizabeth Hurt born June 11th, 1759

Children of Thomas Ellis and Elizabeth Hurt
Rebecca Ellis m. Wm. Thomson
John Ellis born April 26th, 1791
Jas. Hunt Ellis born Feb. 5th, 1793
William Ellis born August 11th, 1794
Elizabeth H. Ellis born March 26, 1796
Sallie Ellis born October 6, 1797
Clara Ellis born July 5th,1799
Thomas Ellis born Feb. 26, 1801
Mary Ann Ellis born Sept. 13, 1802
Maria L. Ellis born June 26, 1805
Robert S. Ellis born April 25, 1807
Richard P. Ellis born Nov. 6, 1809
Fannie A. Ellis born August 21, 1811

Mrs. Henry Ellis says that Thomas Ellis married 1st Rebecca Moorman; no proof, however later Jas. Ellis named a daughter Moorman, and my mother was her teacher.
W.E. Brockman

Rebecca Ellis married William Thompson, Jr., November 18, 1805
John Ellis married Mildred Furgerson
Sallie Ellis married John Thompson, Nov. 19, 1812
James Ellis married Mary Woolfolk, March 26, 1816
Clara Ellis married William Woolfolk, Nov. 28, 1816
William Ellis married Louisa Duke, Sept. 17, 1817
Maria Ellis married David Thompson, May 24, 1820
Mary Anna Ellis married Collin Johnson, Dec. 22, 1824
Thomas J. Ellis married Cynthia A. Fergerson, Jan. 14, 1829
Richard P. Ellis married Margaret Fergerson, Nov. 25, 1830
Fannie Ellis married Chas. Y. Crawford, Oct. 26, 1831
Robert S. Ellis married Emily A. Sneed, Nov. 5, 1833

Third Generation

Children of William Thompson and Rebecca Ellis
Frances Thompson married Thomas Woolfolk
Mary Thompson married Spotswood Smith
William Thompson married Catherine Saunders
James Thompson married Judy Ann Buckner
Alfred Thompson married Sallie Sneed
Ellen Thompson married Wm. Graves
Mildred Thompson married Alfred Baker
Sallie Thompson married Horace Furgerson
Lucy A. Thompson married Nicholas Lewis

Children of John Ellis and Mildred Furgerson
Marshall Ellis married a Miss Davidson
Sarah Jane Ellis married a David Hunter
Mildred Ellis married --------------------
Frances S. Ellis married Marshall Furgerson

Children of William Woolfolk and Clara Ellis
Thomas Woolfolk died unmarried at the age of 21
William Woolfolk married Elizabeth Thompson
John Woolfolk married --------------------
Elizabeth H. Woolfolk married Littleton W. Sneed
Susan Cole Woolfolk married Mat Goodwin
Robert Woolfolk - unmarried
Lee Woolfolk killed at the age of 18
Clara Woolfolk married Samuel P. Hackett
James H. Woolfolk married Louisa Thompson

Children of William Ellis and Francis Louisa Duke
Thomas Joe Ellis married Martha Fore
William H. Ellis married Ann Mana Johnson
Elizabeth Hurt Ellis married David Patteson
Mary Louisa Ellis married Peter Smith and 2nd, G. P. Smith
Martha Gray Ellis (child by second wife) married Dr. J. B. Thomas

---

Children of Mary A. Ellis and Collin Johnson
Agnes Johnson married Samuel M. Teel
Ann Maria Johnson married Dr. W. H. Ellis
Louisa Duke Johnson married John W. Murphy
Ellen James Johnson married James H. Ellis
Texanna Johnson married Dr. John R. Lewis
Octavia Johnson married Charles Quarles
Victoria Johnson married Charles Quarles
Emslie Johnson married Bettie Miller

Children of Thomas J. Ellis and Cynthia A. Fergerson
Thomas Vivian Ellis married Clemantine Smith
James H. Ellis married Ellen Johnson
Wm. F. Ellis married Sallie Poindexter
John Marshall Ellis married ---------------
Lucy J. Ellis married Taylor Goodwin
Eugene Ellis died unmarried
Bettie Ellis died unmarried

Children of Richard P. Ellis and Margaret Fergerson
Wm. Vivian Ellis unmarried
Richard Thomas Ellis unmarried
Mary Ellis married Edward Harris
Frances Ellis married McDowell
Thornton Ellis married Annie McCutchen
Ann M. Ellis married Dr. Blevins
H. M. Ellis married Sallie Blevins
Walter Ellis died at age of 18
Melville Ellis --------------------------

Children of Fannie Ellis and Chas. Y. Crawford
Jennie Crawford married Lewis Johnson
Blanche Crawford married -----------------
Lizzie Crawford married -----------------

Children of Robert S. Ellis and Emily A. Sneed
Sarah Elizabeth Ellis married Joseph Miles Henderson
William T. Ellis married Lizzie Teel
James H. Ellis married Mary Ellis Teel
John E. Ellis married Lizzie H. Burruss
Mary E. Ellis married George L. Grasty

Fourth Generation

Children of Francis Thompson and Thomas Woolfolk
William Woolfolk died unmarried
William Thomas Woolfolk married Sallie M. Goodwin
John W. Woolfolk married Nannie Bowie
James T. Woolfolk married Sally M. Terrill
Joseph E. Woolfolk married Sallie Gilmer
Alfred Woolfolk married ------------------

Children of Mary Thompson and Spotswood Smith
Clementina Smith married Thomas Ellis
Charles Quarles Smith married -------------
Woodson Smith married Mamie Houston and Mamie Ellis
Geo. C. Smith married--------------------
Annie Smith married Rev. Rowland Pitman

Children of James Thompson and Judy Ann Buckner
William Thompson died unmarried
Mary Thompson married Robert Ehle
Fannie Thompson married Louisa McCutchen
Edward Thompson unmarried
Maria Thompson married Joshua Jones
Henry Thompson married Clara Bell
Kelly Thompson married Sallie Lee
Jennie Thompson married W. Speed Stevens
James Thompson married Laura Humphrey

Child of Sarah Elizabeth Ellis and Joseph Hiles Henderson
Robert Ellis Henderson married Linda M. Fox, parents of Mrs. Josephine Henderson Neal, of Louisa

---

Children of James H. Ellis and wife Mary Teel (not given according to ages)
Moorman Ellis, died unmarried
Robert S. Ellis married Bessie Watts
Agnes Ellis, married 1st, William Eliason, daughter Willie married Crump Pannel; married 2nd, J. R. Johnson
Emmett Ellis
Henry Ellis married Hattie L. Watts
Tell Ellis married Ola Lacy
John Ellis, a brother to James, married Lizzie H. Burruss, and they had two boys, Russell, who married Caroline Brockman, daughter of Allie, and Evan, who married Mary Massie

---

GRAVES BIBLE RECORDS

The old Garnett homestead sold in St. Mary's Ill., Dec. 15, 1933 after having been in the possession of the Garnetts for nearly a century. These records were in the personal effects of Aunt Vira Garnett and I record them in order that we may compare the facts, names, etc., with the Graves Family information recorded in my family records. Copied by Ermie Williams Garnett (Mrs. Chas. Garnett)

Note by W. E. Brockman: In the August 28, and Sept. 4, editions of the Virginia Gazette, Williamsburg, Charles Hughes Hamlin, 4604 Forest Hill, Richmond, Va., in a copyright article gives the ancestry of the Graves Family. He states that John Graves, Will 1747, was born 1706, son of John and wife Rebecka, son of Thomas and wife Mary, son of Thomas, son of John and son of Capt. Thomas and wife Katherine. He notes that Rebecka, daughter of John and Susanna Dicken is unaccounted for and she may have married Samuel Brockman, as per speculation in my previous books.

BIRTHS

John Graves, son of John and Susans Dicken Graves, b. Dec. 19, 1737
Ann Rice, daughter of William and Sarah Helms Rice, b. Nov. 21, 1741.
Sarah Graves, daughter of John and Ann Graves, b. Sept. 6, 1761
William Graves, son of John and Ann Graves, b. June 10, 1762
Susanna Graves, daughter of John and Ann Graves, b. Dec. 30, 1764
John Graves, son of John and Ann Graves, b. Jan. 19, 1767
Absolom Graves, son of John and Ann Graves, b. Nov. 28, 1768
Ann Graves, daughter of John and Ann Graves, b. Jan. 15, 1771
Joseph Graves, son of John and Ann Graves, b. June 20, 1773
James Graves, son of John and Ann Graves, b. Mar. 1, 1776
Edward Graves, son of John and Ann Graves, b. Oct. 10, 1778
Stephen Graves, son of John and Ann Graves, b. June 19, 1780 (1781)
Jeremiah Graves, son of John and Ann Graves, b. April 10, 1784
Reuben Graves, son of John and Ann Graves, b. May 18, 1786

Above is whole family of John and Ann Graves.

Reuben Graves being progenitor of the branch we follow into the Garnett family.
Elizabeth Willis, daughter William and Elizabeth Willis, b. Aug. 13, 1788
William Willis Graves, son Reuben and Elizabeth Willis Graves, b. May 18, 1810
Benjamin Garnett Graves, son Reuben and Elizabeth Graves, b. May 27, 1812
Joseph Addison Graves, son Reuben and Elizabeth Graves, b. Feb. 23, 1815
Ann Eliza Graves, daughter of Reuben and Elizabeth Graves, b. Oct. 16, 1817
John James Graves, son Reuben and Elizabeth Graves, b. Oct. 18, 1819
Elizabeth Ann, Daughter of Reuben and Elizabeth Graves, b. Dec. 18, 1822
Edward Dicken Graves, son of Reuben and Elizabeth Graves, b. Feb. 12, 1825
Mary Graves, daughter Reuben and Elizabeth Graves, April 16, 1827
Isaac Newton Graves, son Reuben and Elizabeth Graves, b. Aug. 8, 1830

DEATHS

William Graves, son John and Ann Graves, departed this life August 17, 1808, age 45 years
Stephen Graves, son of John and Ann Graves departed this life September 11, 1818, age 37 years
John Graves, son John and Ann Graves, departed this life August 13, 1824, age 37 years
Sarah Garnett, wife of Edmund, and daughter of John and Ann Graves, departed this life September 15, 1824, age 63 years
John Graves, son John and Susanna Graves, departed this life December 8, 1825, age 88 years
Absolum Graves, son John and Ann Graves, departed this life August 17, 1826, age 57 years
Ann Graves, daughter William and Sarah Rice, departed this life November 12, 1826, age 86 years.
William Willis, son John and Elizabeth Willis, departed this life May 21, 1833, age 90 years
Elizabeth Willis, wife of William Willis and daughter of Anthony and Elizabeth Garnett, departed this life January 4, 1835, age 90 years
Elizabeth Ann Graves, daughter of Reuben and Elizabeth Graves, departed this life July 23, 1824

Elizabeth Willis Graves, daughter of William and Elizabeth Willis, departed this life August 29, 1840

Reuben Graves, son of John and Ann Graves, departed this life July 24, 1872

Benjamin Garnett Graves, son of Reuben and Elizabeth Graves, departed this life September 1, 1846

Mary Elizabeth Graves, daughter of William and Ann Graves, departed this life January 4, 1847

Ann Garnett Graves, daughter of William and Mary Garnett, departed this life September 26, 1847

Martha Ann Graves, daughter William W. and Ann G. Graves, departed this life December 13, 1847

William Sydnor Graves departed this life March 17, 1862

Joseph Addison Graves son Reuben and Elizabeth Graves, departed this life June 18, 1869

Cornelia A. Graves, daughter of Absolum and Elizabeth Graves, departed this* (*no further entry as to date)

Reuben Graves, son John and Ann Graves, departed this life Oct. 20, 1873

Edward D. Graves, son Reuben and Elizabeth Graves departed this life November 11, 1879

HUME

The history of the Hume Family will be found in "Early American History, Volume 1, by W. E. Brockman. The following supplement is by W. N. Bate, of Corpus Christi, Texas.

GEORGE HUME - THE EMIGRANT FROM SCOTLAND.

George Hume, the emigrant, was born at Wedderburn Castle, Scotland on May 30, 1698. Together with his father, Sir George, and his uncle Francis, he participated in the Jacobite rebellion of 1715. Defeated at the Battle of Preston, they were imprisoned in the Marchelsea. After two years in prison George was released and placed on a Glasgow slave ship, much against his will. At the request of Captain Dandridge, ancestor of Martha Washington, George was exchanged to his vessel and put ashore at Norfolk, Virginia. With a letter from Capt. Dandridge he went into the country to Williamsburg, the seat of the newly founded College of William and Mary, where he found his cousin, Gov. Spottswood, and presented the letter of Capt. Dandridge to him. He was later employed as assistant to the chief surveyor of William and Mary College and sent to the field to work. In 1726, he was engaged by King George II as official surveyor of the County of Orange. In 1727-28 he laid out the present city of Fredericksburg. He was a surveyor all his life. He died in 1760 in Culpeper County. On Feb. 16, 1727, he married Elizabeth Proctor. Their children were:

1. George Hume, married Jane Stanton.
2. Francis Hume, married Elizabeth Duncan.
3. John Hume, married Helinor Manson of Boston.
4. William Hume, married 1st, Susan Elzephan, 2nd, Miss Granville, 3rd, Mrs Sarah Benson Baker.
5. James Hume, married Frances Patterson.
6. Charles Hume, married Hannah James.

(Two genealogists of the direct Hume line have stated in their works that this emigrant, George Hume, was the surveyor that taught surveying to George Washington. However, documentary proof has not been found, although circumstantial evidence is present.)

GEORGE HUME, JR., ELDEST SON OF EMIGRANT GEORGE HUME.

George Hume (1), born in Culpeper, Virginia, in 1729. Married Jane Stanton. Was a surveyor and assisted his father in that trade. He was a sargeant in the company commanded by William Payne, Jr., in the First Virginia Regiment, under the command of Colonel George Gibson, during the Revolutionary War, serving from September 14, 1777, to March 1778. Was at Valley Forge. Their children were:

1. George Hume, married Susannah Crigler.
2. Reuben Hume, married Anna Finks.
3. Charles Hume, married 1st, Lizzie Banks; 2nd, Elizabeth Kirtley.
4. John Hume, married Anna Crigler.
5. William Hume, married -------
6. Elizabeth Hume, married ------
7. Frances Hume, married Joe Delaney.
8. Sarah Hume, married John Crigler on December 25, 1789.

SARAH ANN HUME, YOUNGEST DAUGHTER OF GEORGE HUME (1) AND JANE STANTON, married John Crigler on December 25, 1789, at Culpeper, Virginia. They moved to Madison County, Kentucky about 1800. Their children were:

1. Jennie Crigler, married 1st, James Gillaspy; 2nd, Alexander Bradley.
2. Elizabeth Crigler, married Adam Wood.
3. Katherine Crigler, married John Wilhoit.
4. Frances Crigler, married William McWilliams.
5. Polly Crigler, married Madison Colvin.
6. George Crigler, married Mary Utz.
7. Christopher Crigler, died unmarried.
8. John Crigler, married Gabrella Tavis.

JENNIE CRIGLER, eldest child of Sarah Hume and John Crigler.

Jennie Crigler, married 1st, James Gillespie; 2nd, Alexander Bradley on December 26, 1830, in Howard County, Missouri. Children from the second marriage were:

1. James Bradley, married Elnora Blanton, Howard County, Missouri.
2. Christopher Crigler Bradley, b. 1833, in Howard County, Mo., married 3-11-1858 Jane E. Ballew, b. 3-24-1836, Burke Co., N. C., in Livingston Co., Missouri.

CHRISTOPHER CRIGLER BRADLEY, youngest son of Alexander Bradley and Jennie Gillespie Bradley.

Christopher Crigler Bradley, born 4-17-1833, in Howard County, Mo., moved with father, Alexander Bradley, to Livingston County, Mo., in about 1848. In about 1850 Christopher went to California in the gold rush. Returned in a few years and married Jane E. Ballew in Livingston County, Missouri, on 3-11-1858. They went at once to California via the Panama Canal route. Their home was at Lafayette, California. Christopher died in 1863. Their children were:

1. Alice V. Bradley, b. 1-2-1859, Contra Costa County, California.
2. Frank Bradley, b. 12-25-1860, Contra Costa County, California, unmarried.
3. Dora Bradley, b. 2-10-1863, Contra Costa, County, California, married Joseph Cox.

ALICE VIOLA BRADLEY, born January 2, 1859, in Contra Costa County, California, was brought to Missouri in 1869 over the Union Pacific Railroad which had been completed only about two weeks. On December 5, 1880, she married George W. Bate in Livingston

County, Missouri. She died on June 15, 1947, in Livingston County, Missouri. Their children were:

1. Maude E., b. 9-13-1881, married 1st, Jay Bodle in 1907; 2nd, Chas. Mitchell, in 1936. She died 2-18-56 in Nampa, Idaho.
2. Newton M., b. 1-5-1884, married 1st Emily; 2nd, Anna ---. Living at Isabel, South Dakota.
3. Frances F., b. 7-18-1886, married Golba Groves, died about 1938, Colorado.
4. Raymond G., b. 7-10-1890, married Jennie Thompson. Living at Chillicothe, Mo.
5. Walter N., b. 6-29-1893, unmarried. Living at Corpus Christi, Texas.
6. Harris C., b. 1-13-1897, married --------. Living at Wadsworth, Kansas.
7. Herman W., b. 7-27-1900, married --------. Living at Willamina, Oregon.

JACOB CRIGLER, EMIGRANT FROM GERMAN BOHEMIA, 1717. Was married to Suzanna -------- Children:

Nicholas
Christopher, born about 1721
Michael

CHRISTOPHER CRIGLER, married Catherine Finks in 1750. He was born in Spotsylvania, Va. His wife was the daughter of Mark Finks. (Eleven Children.

JOHN C. CRIGLER, son of Christopher and Catherine (Finks) Crigler, born June 10, 1767. He was an Ensign in the Culpeper Militia - 1763. He is listed as a patriot and the National Daughters of the Am. Revolution.

He was married to Sarah Ann Hume Dec. 25, 1789. She was the daughter of George Hume II of Spotsylvania County, Va. They moved to Madison Co. Ky. They had 8 children

---

JOHN CRIGLER, JR., son of John and Sarah (Hume) Crigler, born July 26, 1812. 9 children.

GEORGE CHRISTOPHER CRIGLER, son of John Crigler, Jr., born April 13, 1847. 5 children.

WILLARD T. CRIGLER, son of George C. Crigler, born. July 21, 1882. Has 3 children.

BETTIE MAY CRIGLER GEIGER, daughter of Willard T. Crigler, has 4 children:

1. Sarah Lionel

Lloyd Elliott
Willard Noble
Betty Caroline.

- Bettie May Crigler -

MACON

The genealogy of this family is related in a book by Jane Macon, "Gideon Macon of Virginia and Some of His Descendants." My interest in this family comes through marriages between it and the Madisons. At the request of David Conway Macon, Jr., 407 N. Charles Street, Baltimore, Md., I went to see some of the old homes and copied data from the Tombstones in the family burying ground of the Madisons at Montpelier. The original Macon property in Orange, so I am told by local residents, was a part of

an immense property known as the "Octagon' and referred to in county records. The problems that arose over the ownership of these properties is recorded in the real estate transactions in the County Clerk's Office at Orange. The data on the descendants of Thomas Macon and wife Sarah Catlett Madison was furnished by Mr. David Conway Macon. Thomas Macon, was son of William and Lucy Scott Macon, son of William and Mary Hartwell Macon, son of Gideon Macon, b. New Kent, 1650, m. 2nd, Martha, daughter of Wm. Woodward and his widow, mar. Capt. Nathaniel West. Martha Macon, a daughter of Gideon married Orlando Jones, ancestors of Martha Custus Dandridge Washington. Gideon Macon, Hugenot Secretary and Indian Interpreter under Sir William Berkley, is buried at the foot of the chancel of Bruton Church, Williamsburg, Va., of which he was a vestryman and one of the original subscribers for its first building. Thomas Macon was born June 11, 1765, and died February 20, 1838. On February 4, 1790, he married Sarah Catlett Madison, sister of President James Madison. Sarah was born August 17, 1764, and died October 17, 1843. They lived near Somerset on a plantation of 1821 acres purchased from Zachariah Burnley in 1799, where they built a house in 1803.
Children:

1. James Madison Macon, b. July 3, 1791, d. Feb. 3, 1877, married Lucetta Todd Newman Oct. 10, 1815. Lucetta was born Jan. 9, 1799 and died Jan. 8, 1878.
2. Conway Catlett Macon, b. 1792, d. 1860. Married Agnes Mayo
3. Lucy Hartwell Macon, b. Feb. 21, 1794, died Mar. 13, 1871. Married Reuben Conway July 24, 1811. Reuben was born Mar. 11, 1788 and died Jan. 3, 1838. "Greenwood" their home. No children.
4. William Ambrose Macon, b. 1797, died in 1856 at "Greenwood". Unmarried.
5. Edgar Macon, b. 1802, died 1829. Unmarried. Col. Edgar Macon died in Key West, Florida.
6. Reuben Conway Macon, b. 1808, d. 1853 at "Greenwood". Unmarried.
7. Henry Macon --- Unmarried.

Children of James Madison Macon and Lucetta Todd Newman. (Marriage dates on following are register dates.)

1. Lucy Conwayella Macon, married Dr. John Knox of Richmon on July 2, 1846. Dr. Knox died 1890.
2. Sarah Frances Macon, married John W. Goss September 15, 1853. Later she married Thomas Hill, brother of Gen'l. A. P. Hill of Culpeper.
3. Edgar Barbour Macon, b. April 5, 1830, d. March 11, 1923. Married on Sept. 4, 1851 to Virginia A. Cason of Princess Anne who was born Jan. 18, 1833 and died June 20, 1905. Lived in Princess Anne from 1851 until death.
4. James Madison Macon, married Jennie McLean Bridges of New Orleans. Moved to Richmond.
5. Reuben Conway Madison Macon, b. May 14, 1839, died March 21, 1927. Married in 1865 to Emma Cassandra Riely of Winchester who was born Oct. 1, 1847 and died Jan. 13, 1942. Lived in Orange.
6. Thomas Newman Macon unmarried.

(probably 3 daughters, 1 son)

Unable to trace children of Conway Catlett Macon and Agnes Mayo. Slaughter says an only son was killed at Manassas. A daughter, Sarah Elizabeth Macon died July, 1831. She died at 15 when they lived at Mt. Erin. An Edgar Macon, probably their only son, was licensed to practice law in Orange in 1833. A grandson, Edgar Macon, was a lawyer in Richmond in the 1880's, according to Slaughter. C. C. Macon lived at Walnut Hills for a while. In 1848, he sold Mt. Erin and moved to Richmond where he died in 1860. He was a tobacco inspector there. In 1843, he was Com. Sheriff of Orange, and in April, 1844, Com. Justice of Peace.

Had brief contact with Mrs. Conway Macon Knox in Richmond and heard of Mrs. Malcolm Bridges there. They gave the Sarah Madison Macon Bible to the Va. Historical Society a few years back.

James Madison Macon, III, gave me some typed Macon-Madison sheets. I was unable to get further information as to his own line.

I don't have anything on the Sarah F. Macon-Goss-Hill descendants.

Edgar Barbour Macon established the Princess Anne Norfolk line.

Children of Reuben Conway Madison Macon and Emma Cassandra Riely:

1. Emily (Emma) B. Macon b. Oct. 20, 1866. Married March 12, 1890 to Jacob Stair. His sister, Virginia Stair, of York, Pa., is active in family lore.
2. Clifton Macon married Janet Bruce
3. Kate Conway Macon, b. (register)Nov. 30, 1871 (tombstone gives 1872), d. July 10, 1947. Married Frank G. Paulson of Pittsburgh April 12, 1892. Married secondly to George Edward Hoffmeister, b. Dec. 13, 1864, d. Apr. 19, 1944.
4. Latimer S. Macon, b. Oct. 12, 1878. Married Millie Stagle. She lived with Emma Riely Macon until the latter died in 1942.
5. James Conway Macon married June 22, 1910 to Armistead Taliaferro. She was from "Mt. Sharon" in Orange County.
6. Riely Macon married Helen Khrissler. Until recently at least, he was in the insurance business in Florida. Helen divorced from Riely, but she alone remained in 1958 as a Macon in Orange. The Macons by birth had all scattered.
7. Evelyn M. Macon married secondly Harry Talcot of N. Y. First marriage was to Henry Atwood April 23, 1902.

MADISON-MACON-BARBOUR HOMES

"Barboursville"	- James Barbour. A sister, Lucy Barbour, m. Thomas Newman. Their daughter Lucetta Todd Newman, m. James Madison Macon.
"Frascatt"	- Philip Pendleton Barbour - brother of James Barbour and Lucy Barbour.
"Burlington"	- James Barbour Newman, brother of Lucetta Todd Newman, m. Sarah Battaille Fitzhugh. (One source has Frances B-F.
"Somerset"	- Thomas Macon and Sarah Catlett Madison built in 1803. Originally 1,821 acres (1,050 acres in 1840). Sold to Ebenezer Goss in 1840-1841. Sale-1840, settled-1841. Public Auction. Brought $14,000.
"Arlington"	- Thomas Newman m. Lucy Barbour
"Montpelier"	- Ambrose Madison M. Frances Taylor James Madison, Sr. m. Eleanor Rose Conway James Madison m. Dorothea Payne Todd
"Greenwood"	- Wedding present by Thomas Macon to daughter Lucy H. Macon and her husband, Reuben Conway. Was the real haven of the Macons in Orange.
"Chestnut Hill"	- Reuben Conway Madison Macon and Emma Cassandra Riely, his wife.
"Meadowfarm"	- Zachary Taylor (Grandfather of Pres. Zachary Taylor) and brother of Frances Taylor (wife of ambrose Madison) m. Elizabeth Lee of the "Ditchley" Lees. Daughter of Hancock Lee.
"Walnut Hills"	- Daughter of Conway Catlett Macon married a Cave. He lived with them a short time.

"Mt. Erin" - Home of Conway Catlett Macon sold in 1848 when he moved to Richmond. Isn't clear, but it seems that his wife, Agnes Mayo didn't go to Richmond with him.

"Woodberry Forest" - William Madison, brother of James Madison, Sr. and Sarah Catlett Madison Macon

"Mt. Athos" & "Montchere" - Residences of James H. Macon and wife.

TAYLOR

James Taylor, II, m. Martha Thompson

A Daughter,	A Son
Frances Taylor m. Ambrose Madison	Zachary Taylor m. Elizabeth Lee
James Madison, Sr. m. Nelly Conway	Richard Taylor m. Sarah (Pannill) Dabney Strother
James Madison, Jr. (president) m. Dorothea Payne Todd his sister, Sarah Catlett Madison, m. Thomas Macon	Zachary Taylor (President) m. Margaret Machall Smith
	Sarah Knox Taylor (died age 20) was first wife of Jefferson Davis ("Knox" came from Ft. Knox, Ind., where her father was stationed when she was born. She died of Malaria in La. or Mass., after 6 mos. of marriage. J. Davis nearly died of it then too.

Elizabeth Lee married Zachary Taylor - Grandparents of Pres. Zachary Taylor. She was daughter of Hancock Lee of the Stratford line of Lee's. "Lighthorse Harry" Lee married his cousin, Matilda Lee, thus joining Leesylvania Lee's with Stratford Lee's. Second marriage to Ann Hill Carter, daughter of King Carter. Robert E. Lee born to them in 1807.

Mary Conway (b. 1686) aunt of Nelly Conway (m. James Madison, Sr.) married Major James Ball in 1707. Their daughter, Mary Ball, married Augustine Washington. Parents of Pres. George Washington. (Lancaster Co.)

CONWAY

Edwin Conway m. Martha Eltonhead
Edwin Conway, II, m. Elizabeth Thompson
Francis Conway, I, m. Rebecca Catlett
A daughter Nelly Conway m. James Madison, Sr.

A son Francis Conway, II, m. Susannah Fitzhugh
Catlett Conway (1751-1827) m. ?
Reuben Conway (1788-1838) m. Lucy Hartwell Macon (1794-1871) no children

---

FITZHUGH

OF STAFFORD COUNTY

Henry Fitzhugh (1723-1783) m. Sarah Battaille
Henry Fitzhugh II, (1750-1777) m. Elizabeth Stith
An only child, Henry Fitzhugh (1773-1830) m., in 1791, Elizabeth Conway, sister of Reuben Conway (1788-1838). There were 13 children:
Henry Stith Fitzhugh (1796-1844)
Catlett Conway Fitzhugh
Francis Conway Fitzhugh
Drury Stith Fitzhugh
James Madison Fitzhugh
Drury Bulling Fitzhugh
Elizabeth Catlett Fitzhugh
Elizabeth Fitzhugh
Louisa Conway Fitzhugh
Susanna Fitzhugh
Susanna Conway Fitzhugh
*Sarah Battaillg Fitzhugh (b. 1811)
Anne Wray Fitzhugh

*Sarah Battaillg Fitzhugh b. 1811, m. in 1830, James Barbour Newman, brother-in-law of James Madison Macon to whom he deeded "Montchere" in 1844.

The family of George Mason was related to the Statford Fitzhughs. If the Brockman-Fitzhugh relationship can be established, then the Brockman-Madison-Taylor-Mason connections are proven.

ORANGE COUNTY PASSING ITS ZENITH:

1836 - James Madison died at "Montpelier".
1838 - Thomas Macon and Reuben Conway died at "Greenwood".
1840 - "Somerset" sold at forced auction after death of Thomas Macon.
1842 - James Barbour (Governor 1812-1814)(Secretary of War - U.S. Senator) died.
1843 - Sarah Madison Macon died at "Greenwood".
1843 - "Mt. Athos" sold for debts of James Madison Macon.
1843 - William Hartwell Macon, brother of Thomas Macon, died at family seat, "Mt. Prospect" in New Kent County, Also owned "Northbury" in New Kent and "Fairfield" (Birthplace of Thomas Macon) in Hanover County.
1844.- "Montchere" deeded to James M. Macon and Lucetta Todd Newman by her brother, James Barbour Newman.
1845 - Philip Pendleton Barbour died. (Speaker of House, Supreme Court Justice).
1845 - Last part of "Montpelier" sold by Dolly Madison, widow of President James Madison.
1848 - Conway Catlett Macon sold his "Mt. Erin" holdings and moved to Richmond where he died in 1860.
1849 - Dolly Madison died.
1850 - Zachary Taylor died.

By every method of measurement, Orange County "died" in the 1840 decade.

Thomas Macon was in trouble as far back as 1818. That coincides with the terrible circumstances of Thomas Jefferson in Albemarle from about that time until his death in 1826.

James Barbour built "Barboursville" in 1822, and seemingly knew little distress. James Madison had mostly bad years from 1825 until his death, but was solvent.

Just as I warned, I have only disjointed notes, with no original research involved. Miss Crafton did a lot of copying for me and Miss Jane Macon supplemented her book. Miles Cary Johnston, a Richmond relative, gave me the chain of title down to his 29-year-old son as to the original (1680) Gideon Macon stand in New Kent County. He sent me a plaque of "Mt. Prospect" on the Pamunkey River.

If there are questions, please ask them, but since you have been doing this for 40-odd years, I am sure I can add little to your storehouse of information.

There is much more of the family, but since Orange County was just an interval for the 10 generations (only four generations in Orange, and not full ones at that), I didn't include the rest.

Sincerely,

David Conway Macon, Jr.

---

407 N. Charles Street
Baltimore 1, Md.
July 12, 1959

Dear Mr. Brockman,

Just yesterday I came across the following which you may, or may not, have:
Source - K.C.M. Paulson - Sewickley, Pa., December, 1911

Descendants of Reuben Conway Macon (1839-1927) and Emma Cassandra Riely Macon (1847-1942)

CHILDREN		GRANDCHILDREN
The Reverend Clifton Macon Oakland, California (Janet Bruce)	(1)	Margaret Bruce Macon Emma Macon
Emma Brent (Macon Stair York, Pa. (Jacob Stair)	(2)	Jacob Stair, Jr. Virginia Gordon Stair
Kate Conway (Macon) Paulson Sewickley, Pa. (Frank Gormley Paulson)	(3)	Charles Henry Paulson Daniel McKee Paulson
James Conway Macon Sewickley, Pa. (Armistend Taliaferro)	(4)	

Latimer Small Macon Orange, Va. (Milly Slagle)	(5)	Latimer Small Macon, Jr. Jacob Slagle Macon
James Riely Macon Pittsburgh, Pa.	(6)	
Evelyn Madison (Macon-Atwood) Talcott New Rochelle, N. Y. (Henry Dickson Atwood, deceased) (Harry Pickard Talcott)	(7)	Henry Martyn Atwood

Appeared in Appendix to Reminiscences of the Civil War - written in 1896, published in 1911 - by Reuben Conway Macon and Emma Cassandra Riely Macon. Copyrighted K.C.M. Paulson.

Also from the book:

Reuben Conway Macon - adjutant, 13th Va. Infantry, Ewell's Division, "Stonewall" Jackson's Corps.

He left his home, "Mt. Chone" (Montchere? DCM) in Orange County on April 23, 1861 to join confederate army at Harper's Ferry.

Of not knowing manual of arms or facings, and of receiving private instruction for an hour or two by Lt. Wood.

"Of course, it was a matter of mortification with me to see so many men who were inferior to me in education, social position, and every other respect, going through these movements that I could not, so I determined to learn as quickly as possible".

Wounded in thigh, June 6, 1862, at Cross Key, six or eight miles east of Harrisonburg. Went home for a month. Unable to extract the ball. Healed over.

Returned in time for Battle of Slaughter's Mountain.

Had his negro servant, Cornelius, with him. Cornelius died on the March to Sharpsburg.

At that time his boots had worn out and he had just bought a pair of worn shoes for $20.00. When a friend back from leave, brought another pair of boots sent by his mother.

Was at Battle of Fredericksburg. Was amazed that his ragged fellows were more than a match for the well-equipped federal forces.

Was sent to Winchester, missing the Battle of Gettysburg. There met his wife of 2 years later.

Had leave in Feb. 1864. Spent it with his betrothed in Winchester.

May 6, 1864, wounded in shoulder. The wound discharged periodically until his death in 1927. Last of active service, Feb. 1865. On retired list, orders to report to Gen. Kemper for conscript duty, but war then ended.

Sincerely,
David Macon

MASONS OF GUNSTON HALL

During the year I have been reading a number of books on English history dealing with the era before and after Charles I and while one recent book says much in support of Oliver Cromwell and his contribution to government and this one will have to concede, I end up by respecting his statesmanship, with scorn for Charles II, and with tenderness for Maria Henrietta of France and her spouce Charles I. Taking all of the known facts it appears that the latter was a good father, a devoted and loyal husband but not the strongest King or ruler. Having descended from a long line of Virginia Baptists who overthrew the so-called yoke of the English Church, I look back at the influence of Maria Henrietta, who only did what she was expected to do traditionally, but her influence on Charles in supporting the Bishop in England was surrounded with nonê of the reported evils of the Catholic rule in France. A recent reading of the Duchess of Marlborough, which tells the story of Sarah Jennings, wife of John Churchill, the forefather of Sir Winston, much emphasis is given to the writings of Francis Osborne and his recording of the trend of English Government is impartial and factual. It was Francis Osborne who came to Virginia in 1637 bringing with him William Brock (Brockman) and it was a Richard Osborne who was host to Charles I in the Isle of Wight where he stayed at Carisbrook Castle, not imprisoned but in "custody" and the Osbornes lived in Osborne House nearby and Queen Victoria once stayed there after the property had been bought by the English Government and in recent years has been a convalescent home for officers of the Royal Naval College. Another man prominent in the recluse of Charles I, was a Gen. Hammond, and it was Gen. Mainwarring Hammon who got a Royal Crown grant of 4,000 acres near West Point, Virginia and built thereon a mansion which he called the White House. This property passed into the hands of the Bassetts and eventually the Custis family, and this is where George Washington courted Martha Dandridge Custis on his route from Mt. Vernon area to Richmond. In his life of a recluse, Charles I, was a disturbing factor in the English Government and it was with reluctance that Cromwell permitted him to die with the loss of his head. During his stay on the Isle of Wight many of the Virginia Colonists urged him to seek refuge in Virginia, but he still held out nearly three years till he was beheaded in 1649. During this troublesome time in England many English sought refuge in the new America, and the ruthless policy of the Government under Cromwell forced them to flee for their lives or else they were sent as prisoners to the West Indes. However much earlier other political refuges went to the New World and among them Thos. Brocke went as a prisoner from Taunton, Eng., where he lived and served his time in the Barbados. This section is about the Masons and they and the Brockmans were embroiled together in the defeat of Charles I and it is thought that Henry Brockman came to the Barbados about the time of Colonel George Mason, the latter in 1751, fleeing for his life and threatening hazards, the latter not only being a cabinet minister to Charles I, but an active revolutionist in behalf of Charles II. In my study of early Virginia families I learned that two Brockmans had married Masons, and that led me to look more into the latter family. Supposition that Henry Brockman came to Barbados about 1649 is based on his statement that "when the Protestants took over, I could no longer worship as I wanted to" and this would be after Cromwell took over from Charles I. This statement, if quoted correctly would indicate that Henry was not a refugee in that his life was in danger for supporting Charles I, but his security was threatened by edicts of Cromwell. Sir William Brockman of Beachborough, Kent County was defeated at Maidstone by General Fairfax, 1648, and belonging to the gentry he was fined by Cromwell as a penalty and punishment but Henry (son or nephew) sought relief in a new world. Now Colonel George Mason, born 1629, was a cabinet minister under Charles I, and apparently became an insurgeant during the Cromwell reign and organized an army to fight for Charles II, therefore his position was more of a dangerous character to Cromwell, and he was defeated at Worcester, 1651, and sensing his danger he took ship at once and landed at Norfolk, Virginia that same year. Since he was then 22, his two marriages to Mary French and Frances Norgrave probably took place in Virginia. His son also Colonel George married Mary Fowke, Elizabeth Waugh and then Sarah French, and they lived in Stafford. Col. George the third, 1690-1735, married Ann, daughter of Stevens Thomson of Loudoun County. He had much land in Orange County and in 1735, Ann Mason widow, was made guardian of son George and the other children.

Few genealogists, in fact not any that I have met, refer to the life of George Mason in Orange. Somehow that seems to have escaped their notice. Son George was George Mason of Gunston Hall, and author of the Virginia Bill of Rights. His sister Catherine, married John Mercer of Marlboro. She was a daughter by the second marriage to Elizabeth Waugh which took place in 1706, and her husband, John Mercer, left a Will at Duplin County, North Carolina, naming among others a granddaughter, Nancey Brockman. Identification of Elizabeth Mason who married William Brockman about 1749, cannot be identified by the Genealogical Chart, copyrighted by Stevens Thomas Mason of Baltimore in 1907 and for sale by the Gunston Hall management. Many of the Masons were in Fairfax and left Wills there and at Culpeper and in Augusta. The Culpeper Masons spread into Albemarle and their names on deeds in the Priddy's Creek area and next to the land of William Brockman and one acquired some of the land of his son Samuel, known as Green Plains, so that there is a tie that has not been unravelled. Mrs. Lamont DuPont Copeland of Greenville, Delaware, is a student of this line and she, I am told by Mr. Fred Griffiths, director of Gunston Hall, is striving to make up an authenticated family tree that is all-inclusive. William Mason, Baptist minister left a Will at Culpeper Sept. 17, 1821. His brother John married Mary Nelson Nov. 27, 1747, and these and other births and marriages are given in the Overwharton Register, Old Stafford County Virginia. William a son of John and Mary Nelson Mason had a daughter Ann who married James Sims of Culpeper and Madison and this brings this relationship of the Masons of England back to the Sims and Brockmans of Orange and Albemarle. Both the William Mason Will, Stafford between 1729 and 1748 and the Will of George Mason, the second, son of immigrant were recorded in Stafford but the original Wills disappeared, probably taken by some unscrupulous hunter of historical documents. The Gunston Hall chart does not show any of the children of the immigrant Col. George Mason, except, George II, and of course there was a son William and perhaps many other children from two marriages, and from either son William, or another son, the Beockmans and Sims get their connections.

On April 10, 1676, Joane, widow, petitioned for administration of the estate of her deceased husband, William Mason, and the property was divided between widow Joane and daughter Elizabeth. This William was likely son of immigrant George. Since, his brother William is recorded as having lived in Norfolk and had at least one son and several daughters. One Elizabeth Mason is recorded at York Courthouse as having some land in that area born St. Peters Parish, New Kent, 1729, and she could very well have been wife of William Brockman of Albemarle. The transfer of Orange land to John Brockman by Samuel and William Bronough and Margaret William's wife, grandchildren of George Mason II, suggests an earlier Mason connection, since John was grandson of Sanuel Brockman I, and administrator of the estate of his father Samuel II, and in the settlement there were chancery suits over titles, so that Samuel's wife may have been a Mason also. We know her only as Mary. Like others engaged in research, I bemoan the loss of Virginia records, and damn those responsible, but there are some unmistakeable signs and evidence left by those early settlers who left the English shores without a passport and often under assumed names. One is the fact that Colonel Thomas Patterson Brockman who married Mary Kilgore, named a daughter Henrietta Maria, reversing the name of the little French Princess who was wife of Charles I. With

Charles I, characterized as the good man but poor ruler going to the scaffold, Henry Brockman described his desertion of the homeland by saying "When the Parliament forces (the Protestants he called them) took over, my father went to the Barbados."

This is not a genealogical history of the Mason family as others are working on that. However scraps of information come to me and for fear that they may be lost, I am recording them. Virginia Wilson of 114 Woodland Avenue, Lexington, Ky., has sent me her connection with the family. She gives this data. Thomas Sims, Sr., presumed to be son of William who died Richmond County, 1716, whose wife was Rebecca. Some say Rebecca, granddaughter of Paul Harrelson of New Kent, and other Rebecca, daughter of John Petty, son of Thomas Petty. One researcher says that he married both of the Rebeccas, Rebecca Petty being the second wife. Thomas Sims left a Will at Culpeper, proved July 18, 1785, naming 10 children. His son, James, Sr., married Elizabeth Nalle, and left a Will at Culpeper, 1802, altho all not named in his Will, other data shows that he had twelve children. James Sims, Jr., son of James, married Ann Mason, daughter of Elder William Mason. Ann was born November 30, 1748, in Stafford and died April 26, 1823, at Culpeper. William Mason, was son of John and wife Mary Nelson Mason. James Sims, Jr., was born about 1761, and died 1851, in Jessamine, Ky. His son John Gilbert Sims was born October 11, 1811, in Virginia and died in Jessamine Ky., Sept. 27, 1875. A daughter Elizabeth Ann married Hawkins, and she was the grandmother of Virginia Wilson.

THE MONTAGUES

From the file of Miss Julia S. Stevens,
5211 Dartmouth Avenue, St. Petersburg, Florida

All of the published records on this family have contained one error of spelling. Even the very accurate Crozier in his County Record Series and that refers to the name of the wife of Peter Montague, the 4th, which was Ann Theriet, (The Theriot's were a prominent French Family in the time of Voltaire.) and not Authorit, as a Christian name. Dominick Theriet, sheriff of Northumberland, 1656, was son of William, wife, the widow of Henry Lee, and he had a daughter Hannah who married Henry Towles. There were probably others and Ann Theriet, wife of Peter Montague was of this family. Now from Mrs. Steven's files:

Peter Montague was the son of Peter and Eleanor Montague of Boveney, in the Parish of Burnham, Buskinghamshire, England, born 1603. At the age of 18 he emigrated to Virginia on the ship Charles, landing at Jamestown, Va., in 1621. He was in Nasemond County and afterwards in Lancaster. He represented Nasemond in the House of Burgesses November 25, and July 5, 1653. He died 1659. Wife, Cicely, children: Ann, born 1630; Ellen, born 1632; William, born 1638;;Margaret, born 1640; and Peter born 1634.

Peter (2) married Mary Minor and had a son Peter born about 1666.

Peter (3) had a son Thomas born 1694, in Middlesex, married Grace as his first wife.

Peter (4) born 1718, married in 1737, Ann Theriet (also Therriot) and they had a daughter Sara, born January 29, 1739.

Sara Montague married John Stevens about 1756. Their children were Nancy, born Sept. 22, 1757, who married Joseph Ducan; Elizabeth, born Nov. 10, 1758, married Thomas Burruss; James, born July 23, 1760, went to Kentucky and John, Jr., born May 26, 1765, married Polly Smith of Spottsylvania; Sally, born Jan. 23, 1767; William, born June 22, 1773.

William Stevens, son of John and Sara Montague Stevens, born in Orange County, married Margaret Mills, daughter of Nathaniel Mills of Louisa. Children: Eliza Tompkins, married Dr. John Minor Goodwin; Julia Thomas, born 1804, married Rev. James L. Powell, died, 1870; Frederick M. went South about 1850; Nathaniel; Margaret A. married Isaac Graves; William J. married Julia Lindsay, a cousin and granddaughter of Sara Montague Stevens. The Stevens home was at Thornhill and Goodwin home near Cuckoo.

Mary Therriot was wife of Thos. Salmon, Will Culpeper, 1748.

QUISENBERRY

Aaron Quisenberry, Senior, was father of Aaron Jr., who married first, Rachael Shelton, and second, Sallie Ellis, daughter of Hezikiah of Spottsylvania. This family has a published genealogy, so this data is given because candidates have had difficulty in establishing the Revolutionary Service of James Quisenberry, because one by that name died 1777, who had Revolutionary Service. Record of James enlistment in the State Militia has been covered in the Brockman Scrapbook, page 250. Enlisted at age 17, and his name is on the Revolutionary Service monument at Boonesboro, Ky.

DEED BOOK # 18-P. 455 - ORANGE, ORANGE, COUNTY, VIRGINIA

27th of July 1786 - DEED OF GIFT

To all persons to whom these presents shall come before that I, AARON QUISENBERRY SENR., of Orange Co., parish of St. Thomas, Planter, for and in consideration of the love, good will and affection which I do bearto my Son JAMES QUISENBERRY of the Co. of Fayette, Caintukey, have given and granted and by these Presents do truly give and grant unto the said JAMES QUISENBERRY, his heirs and Administrators one Negro Fellow by the name of Bob - about twenty-four years old. Now being in the Co., and perish aforesaid of which before the signing of these Presents I have delivered to the said JAMES QUISENBERRY and Inventory signed by my own hand and bearing even date, To have a and to hold the said Negro Fellow Bob in the said premises of the said JAS. QUISENBERRY his heirs, Exors and Admrs. from henceforth in their proper right, absolute without any manner or condition.

In Witness whereof I have hereto set my hand and Seal this 27th day of July 1786.

Witnesses:
Geo. Quisenberry
John Quisenberry

AARON his X mark QUISENBERRY

At a Court held for Orange Co., Va., on Thurs. 27th of July, 1786-this deed of Gift from AARON QUISENBERRY SENR. TO JAMES QUISENBERRY was proved by Oath of Geo. Quisenberry & John Quisenberry Witnesses thereto and ordered to be recorded.

JAS. TAYLOR C.O.C.

April 20, 1959

Dear Mr. Brockman:

In my wife's file, she has the following information on Rev. James Quisenberry: Founder of the Kentucky branch of the family. Born in Spottsylvania County in Virginia on July 5, 1759, and died in Clark County in Kentucky on August 5, 1830. (The above was taken from MacKenzies Colonial Families of the United States--Page 423, Vol. 1.) A note follows: Our ancestor, Rev. James Quisenberry in Revolutionary War in Capt. Timothy Dalton's and afterwards in Capt. Richard Glasscock's Company of Virginia Volunteers, also in Capt. Joseph Weddishes' Company of Col. Samuel H. Peyton's 45th Virginia Regiment. An insert further says he belonged to Orange County Virginia Militia. If your client has difficulty with James' record for admission to the DAR group, she can turn to old Aaron who furnished supplies to the Army. My wife joined on his record and she would be glad to help the lady in question without charge, of course.

Yours very cordially,

D. N. Davidson, Rhoadesville, Virginia

Order Book 8, page 162, Thurs. 23rd day of Jan., 1772

A deed of gift from AARON QUISENBERRY SENR. and JOICE, his wife to AARON QUISENBERRY, JR. (He was married twice).

In Deed Book 20, page 33, Sept. 26, 1791

Deed of Gift from AARON QUISENBERRY SENR. To My Son JAMES QUISENBERRY of the Co. of Fayette Caintucky-etc.
Also one from him to "My Son, JOHN QUISENBERRY of the Co. of Fayette, Caintucky.
AARON QUISENBERRY'S WILL is here in Will Book #4, page 152, Wife Sally.

Minute book #2, page 172-1782

To AARON QUISENBERRY for 500 pounds of beef - Certified by Ben Winslow.

Of course these would have to be certified - we cannot photostat from books in this office.

(Comment from Mrs. C. M. Crafton, 186 Peliso Avenue, Orange, Va., who copied the above.) (April 20th, 1959.)

RHODES

Daniel Horace Rhodes was born in Albemarle Co., Va., 1842, and died April 23, 1906. He was a son of Harace Rhodes and Sarah Jane Spicer Rhodes.

Mildred Catherine Poindexter was born August 28, 1844, in Madison Co., Va., and died Nov. 6, 1921. She was a daughter of Joseph Poindexter and Clarissa Mitchell Poindexter. Daniel Horace Rhodes m. Mildred Catherine Poindexter Dec. 23, 1868. He was 25 years old and she was 23 years old. (Albemarle Co., Va., Records). Children of Daniel H. Rhodes and Mildred C. Poindexter Rhodes:

1. William Daniel Rhodes (d. Oct. 14, 1942) m. Ella Katherine Pyles (b. Aug. 24, 1893) April 14, 1915, in Summers Co., W. Va. Her parents were James Wesley Pyles and Fannie Capenton Diddle. Children:
   a. William Dale Rhodes (b. Jan. 13, 1916) m. Isabel Elizabeth Dobson Nov. 20, 1948, in New York City. (Isabel Dobson was b. Oct. 29, 1918)
   b. Virginia Carol Rhodes (b. Nov. 26, 1919) m. Theodore Ripberger, Jr., Mar. 27, 1939, in Summers Co., W. Va. (Summers Co., W. Va., Records)
      (1) Carol Theodore Ripberger III, b. Oct. 14, 1939, in Kenbridge, Va.
      (2) Charles Ripberger, b. Dec. 9, 1941, d. Dec. 9, 1941 in Richmond, Va.
      (3) William Rhodes Ripberger, b. Feb. 12, 1943, in Richmond, Va.
      (4) Nancy Cushwa Ripberger, b. March 9, 1947, d. March 9, 1947.
      (5) Stephen Ashby Ripberger, b. Nov. 6, 1950 in Richmond, Va.
      (6) Philip Roger Ripberger, b. June 9, 1955, d. July 2, 1955.
   c. Ashby Marshall Rhodes, b. July 5, 1923, unmarried.
2. Florence Virginia Rhodes b. in Lawrence Co., Ill., July 10, ---?. Died Jan. 23, 1934. M. David Jacobs Jan. 26, 1916. (no children) (Alb. Co. Records)
3. Charles Ross Rhodes (b. in Saline Co., Mo., March 17, 1874, died Dec. 3, 1931 in Hamlet, N. C.) married Annie Edna Nowlan (b. Aug. 18, 1885) August 5, 1903 at Pence Springs, W. Va. Her parents were Joseph Nowlan b. April 3, 1839, d. Oct. 6, 1908, and Mary Bertha Keeney, b. Aug. 9, 1847, d. May 20, 1929. Children of Charles Ross Rhodes and Annie NowlandRhodes:
   a. Silas William Rhodes b. June 3, 1904, in Pence Springs, W. Va. Died July 15, 1911, Hamlet, N. C.
   b. Lawrence Joseph Daniel Rhodes b. April 23, 1906, Alderson, W. Va.
   c. Charles Reginald Rhodes b. July 22, 1908, married Amy Marie Suttle Aug. 18, 1940, at Marion N. C. Amy Marie Suttle was born April 28, 1909. Her parents were Ella Hamrick Bower, b. Feb. 24, 1880, and Nevills Claxton Suttle, b. Nov. 20, 1880.
   d. Annie Elaine Rhodes, b. Feb. 9, 1911, in Hamlet, N. C.
4. George Lossie Rhodes (b. Dec. 22, 1877) married Fannie Houston Nowlan (b. June 2, 1875, d. May 28, 1938) Jan. 14, 1914 in Talcott, W. Va.
   a. Mary Rhodes b. May 29, 1915
5. Mila Roger Rhodes (b. March 13, 1881) m. David Johnson Miller Jan. 17, 1917, at Barboursville, Va. (Alb. Co. Va.)
   a. Mildred Catherine Miller (b. April 17, 1918) m. Woodie Gordon Marshall (b. Feb. 1, 1915) Nov. 28, 1935. (Alb. Co. Va.)
      (1) Walter David Marshall, b. Jan. 7, 1937, in Charlottesville, Va.
      (2) Adele Louise Marshall, b. Sept. 21, 1950, in Charlottesville, Va.

LINEAGE OF JULIA RHODES DUNN, HAMLET, N. C.

Grandfather: George W. Rhodes; Born Nov. 4, 1847, Died April 23, 1880.
Buried in Gordonsville, Virginia, in community cemetery.
Place of birth believed nearby
Married Emily (or Emma) Hicks of New York, (who died in Staunton, Va.)
Their children were:

Erwin Nelson Rhodes
Alexander)
Charles) These four reared in Miller School
Eugene) near Charlottesville, Va.
Cornelia)

Father: Erwin Nelson Rhodes; Born in Orange County, Va., July 16, 1869
Married Nellie Perry at Alderson, W. Va., May 14, 1902
Died April 21, 1950, at Hamlet, N. C.
Buried in Mary Love Cemetery at Hamlet, N. C.
Their children are:

1. George Perry Rhodes; Born Nov. 8, 1903, Hamlet, N. C., Married Mary Hitt (2 daughters)
2. Raymond Judson Rhodes; Born Dec. 23, 1908, Hamlet
3. Robert Randolph Rhodes; Born August 18, 1911
4. Julia E. Rhodes Dunn; Born August 29, 1919. Married Tyler James Dunn, Aug. 29, 1937.

Children of Julia and Tyler Dunn:
Emily Nelson, born July 18, 1939
Patricia Rhodes, born June 13, 1945
Nancy Irene, born July 31, 1952

George W. Rhodes was the son of Thomas Rhodes and second wife Christine (Drumright) Rhodes.

SHOTWELL FAMILY BIBLE RECORD

Jeremiah Shotwell and Sarah, his wife was married 19th day of December, 1810.
Martha Shotwell was married the 16th of Aug., 1831.
Arrinas Shotwell was married the 16th of April, 1835.
Minor Shotwell was married the 29th of Sept. 1844.
Cazwell Shotwell was married the 4th of Sept. 1845.
Jeremiah Shotwell was married the 23rd of Dec. 1851.
Sarah Shotwell was married the 10th of Nov. 1853.
Mary A. Shotwell was married the 3rd of Dec. 1857.

BIRTHS:
Martha Shotwell was born the 7th day of August in the year of our Lord, 1814.
Arrena Shotwell was born the 30th day of Jan. in the year of our Lord, 1818.
Minor Shotwell was born the 25th day of May in the year of Our Lord, 1820.
Cazwell Shotwell was born 29th day of Jan. A. D., 1825.

different hand writing (Ora Frances Hall, 1905
Eleanor Elizabeth Estes, June 21, 1941

DEATHS:
Jermiah Shotwell, Sr., departed this life on Sunday, Aug. the 28th in the year of Our Lord, 1864.
Sarah Shotwell, Sr., departed this life on Wed. March 13th in the year of Our Lord, 1878.
Caswell Shotwell died Sat. Nov. 19th, 1898.

(different hand writing on following three:)
Elizabeth Rebecca Shotwell departed this life May 7th, 1923.
Louise Sims Bentherd to Donovan Coude Estes, Dec. 31, 1938, Spring Hill Church
George Powell was born the 12th of Nov. 1878.

BIRTHS:
Jermiah Shotwell was born on the 4 day of Jan. in the year of Our Lord, 1789.
Sarah-----------------------Jan. 1795.
Louise Shotwell was born the 6 day of Jan, 1828.
Jeremiah was born the 1st day of July, the year of our Lord 1830.
Sarah Shotwell was born the 4th day of March, 1833.
Mary A. Shotwell was born the 13th day of Nov., 1835.

DEATHS:
Claude M. Estes, March 8, 1940. (different hand writing)
Irene Shotwell Estes, March 9, 1940. (different hand writing)

Date in Bible 1816

Mrs. Mundy, Rio Road, Charlottesville, Va., has this Shotwell family Bible. Her grandfather was Cazwell Shotwell.

Thos. Mundy left Will at Essex, 1702.

Information from Mrs. Ella Wood Smith, age 99, granddaughter of Jeremiah Shotwell, Sr.

Jeremiah Shotwell m. Taylor Children were:
1. Minor Shotwell m. Miss Harrison from Amherst
2. Cazwell Shotwell m. 1st, Wood; 2nd, Becky Mahaner
3.3. Mary Shotwell m. Jefferson Wood
4. Sally Shotwell m. Ira Wood (Mrs. Smith parents)
5. Louise Shotwell m. John Smith
6. Jeremiah Shotwell m. Columbia Brockman

ORANGE CO. MARRIAGE RECORD

Martha Shotwell m. Benj. Powell, Aug. 12, 1831.
Parent - Jeremiah Shotwell
Eli Collier m. Arena Shotwell, April 17, 1834
Parent - Jeremiah Shotwell

SIMMS OF VIRGINIA

Two families by the names of Simms found their way into Orange County. One of these was Thomas, son of William Simms of Richmond County who left a Will there dated 1716, (dead by June 30, 1719) and the other was Richard Simms who was poisoned by a slave of Mrs. Harriet Potter while staying with the latter in Middlesex. He died, however, at his home in Orange County, and his wife Joanne was made administratrix in 1746. At one time, 1739, he showed seven in the family over 21 in the tax list. His home was on the Pamunkey River as shown by a transfer of 300 acres of land after his death by his son William Simms, who married first Anestar Step (Stap) and second, Agatha, thought to have been a daughter of a James Simms and Elizabeth his wife. The Culpeper family seems to be well documentated by the records in that county, but the names of the other children of Richard are obscure and I am not enough sure of them to give their names. A Sims genealogy by Henry Upson Sims deals with the family of

Robert Sims, who had a land patent in Nasemond County, 1694, and a book "Adam Symes and his Descendants", by Jane Morris, give the lineage of Thomas Symes of England, and his descendants through George of Antiqua and his son George of Surry County, Va. A son Richard of the original Thomas, died 1723 leaving his estate to his nephew Richard, so of his deceased brother William for life and then to his great nephew Richard, son of his nephew Thomas. Then we have James of the Isle of Wight, who had sons John, Robert and Richard. Just which one of these Richard's came to Orange, I have not been able to tell. The Culpeper crowd, in a study by one of that family, say that our Richard of Orange and Albemarle was son of William of Richmond, but the latter's will did not say so, but they feel that he may have been given property before the death of William or else he was son of Thomas, brother of William. In 1958, I did find the Bible of Captain William Simms and in it the marriage of Agatha, daughter of Jams and Elizabeth and what looked like Simms, to Captain William in 1761.

SYMES (SIMMS, SIMS)

English Lineage

Courtesy of Mrs. R. M. Anderson, Chatham, Virginia

These records show that Thomas Symes, son of John of Poundsford, was the ancestor of the Virginia Symses (mentioned in the book entitled Adam Symes and His Descendants by Jane Morris), and the father of George of Antiqua; that Geo. of Antiqua was the father of George of Surry Co., Va.

Wm. Symes of Charde, in Co. of Somerset, pedigree in 1623, Vol. II, Pub. of Harleian Society, p. 110; had arms granted in 1591; d. July 1597; m. Eliz., dau. of (2) Robert Hill of Yarde (Somerset), arms in same Vol. II, and his wife, Alice Clark.

ABSTRACT OF WILL OF WM. SYMES OF CHARDE:

"Wm. Symes of Poundsford, Somerset, Merchant. Will dated June 4, 1597; proved July 27, 1597, by Eliz. Symes the relict (66 Cobham). Poor Charde and Pitminster. The Rt. Hon. Sir Edw. Seymour, Knt. Lord Seymour of Pomeroy, Devon, by deed, Nov. 29, 31 Eliz.; hath granted me an annuity of 100 marks out of the demise of Bury Pomeroy for 99 years; if Eliz. my wife and Henry & James my sons shall live so long. To my son John Symes, 2000 Lbs. according to certain covenants between me and Sir John Popham, Kt. Chief Justice and Thomas Horner, Esq. To Henry my son 1000 marks. My dau. Margeret Payne 100 marks. Jasper Payne my son-in-law living in Charde. My manors of Barwick, Bowre, Stoford, Somerset, & Franklin, Dorset. Mill in West Coker & lands in Taunton. My manor house in Charde to Eliz. my wife during her life, Extrix. Supervisors, John Payne, Esq., Roger Hill, Gent., & my brother-in-law, Hugh Hill, Gent." From Somerset Wills - First Series (Brown) P. 52, Library of Congress Washington, D. C.

Henry Symes (son of Wm. & Eliz. (Hill) Symes, d. in 1599 without issue. From Brown's Somerset Wills - First Series, p. 52, "Henry Symes of Poundsford, Somerset, Gent. Will dated Mch. 19, 1941 (¢) Elizab., proved June 15, 1599, by his brother John Symes (54 Kidd) To be buried at Pitminster. To my sister Jane Howe, Alice Hodges & Margery Payne, 4 angels. My bro. John Symes. Roger Hill, a witness". Henry's sister Jane has been elsewhere given Lady Jane Pole. John Symes, eldest son and heir of Wm. and Eliz. (Hill) Symes, was b. in 1581; d. Oct. 21, 1661, aged 80; long epitaph in Frampton Cotteral Church, m. (Amy, dau. of Thomas Horner, Esq., of Mill Co., Somerset (Brown's Somerset Wills, p. 52).

Abst. of the Will of John Symes, of Poundsford:
Oct. 5, 1658; prov. Dec. 19, 1661 (206 May). To be buried at Frampton Cotteral Co., Glouc. To my nephew Arthur Symes 100 pounds at end of his apprenticeship. I am possessed for many years to come & undetermined of the Mansion of Poundsford my Exors shall convey it to Wm. Symes, eldest son of John Symes decd. He not to vex or prosecute any suit against Henry or Thomas Symes. To my two nieces Eliz. & Grace Symes 800 pounds to be paid out of Poundsford. My nephews John and Edw. Symes sons of my son Thomas Symes. Residue to my sons Henry & Thomas Symes Exors."

From Somerset Wills, First Series (Brown), p. 53
Library Congress, Washington

In the Church of Bishop Hull there is a monument to "Georgio Farewel...".. Another to the memory of John Symes of Poundsford records that he was "greatly renowned for wisdom, justice, integrity, and sobriety, which talents he did not hide in a napkin but religiously exercised in the whole conduct of his life, especially in the government of the county wherein he bore all the honourable affairs incident to a country gentlemen as knight of the shire, high sheriff, deputy lieutenant for many years, and justice of the peace for forty years and upwards."

From Quarter Session Records, for the Co. of Somerset
James I. (Somerset Records Society, Vol. 23, p. XXV).

John Symes of Poundsford and his wife Amy Horner had issue:

1. John, who d. before his father.
2. Henry m. Amy, dau. of Sir John Seymour
3. Thomas, of whom later

John Symes (eldest son of John of Poundsford and his wife Amy Horner) d. before 1658; m. Abigail, dau. of Arthur Arscott of Tolcott, Devonshire, and had issue Wm., to whom Poundsford was conveyed, Henry, and Abigail.

Wm. Symes of Poundsford, son of John of Poundsford and his wife Abigail Atscott, was b. in 1623; d. 1687; m. Rachel Bluett, dau. of Francis Bluett (killed at Lyme, 1664) and his wife Joan Moore (Brown's Somerset Wills - Second Series, p. 33).

Collison's "History of Somerset," Vol. 3, p. 54: "North Pextherton is a very large parish between the towns of Bridgewater and Taunton. Within it are North Newton and about 15 other hamlets. It was one of Wm. the Conqueror's towns, and came into possession of the Bluett family which is so closely allied with the Symes family."

Abstract of Wm. Symes Will
Wm. Symes of Poundsford in Pitminster, Somerset, Esq. Will dated Nov. 30, 1687; proved Feb. 16, 1687-8 (Archdeaconry of Taunton). All my goods to my wife, Extrix. If not money enough to pay my debts to sell my estate & return the overplus to my bro., Henry Symes of Bristol, Gent. My brother-in-law John Bluett of Holcombe, Rogus, Devon, Esq., & my bro. Francis Bluett to be my friends in trust, etc. Estate of Hancreech & West Monckton. Geo., John & Elinor, ch. of my bro. Henry Symes 100 lbs. each. To my cousin Rachel Davison, dau. of Joseph Davison of Freshford, Gent. 500 lbs. at age of 21. Poor of Poundsford 10 lbs. To my bro. John Bluett, my young Strawberry mare. To my bro. Mr. Francis Bluett, my silver hilt sword & all my arms. Sealed with a coat of arms."

(Brown's Somerset Will - Fourth Series pp. 70-71.)

Abst. of Will of Henry Symes, bro. of Wm. of Poundsford: "Henry Symes late of Bristol now of London, Gent. Will dated May 15, 1693. (100 Coker) To be burd., at Tyson (Ruyshton) Somerset. Estate given me by my late bro. Wm. Symes's Will. My wife Elinor, my youngest son Geo. Symes 200 lbs. My dau. Elinor. My son John shall have my estate. Edward and Robert Westcombe, sons of my late sister Abigail" (Brown's Somerset Wills - Fourth Series, p. 71). John d. without heirs: "John Symes of Poundsford, Somerset, decd. Admin. May 20, 1698, To my sister Elinor, wife of Francis Duncombe" (Same source as above). His bro. Geo. became heir-at-law of Poundsford. This Geo. Symes had children, Sarah, Henry, and Elinor, christened in London between years 1702 and 1710.

Henry Symes, second son of John of Poundsford and his wife Amy Hornew: "Henry Symes of Frampton Cottrell, Gloucre., Esq. (*) Will dated Jan. 28, 1678; proved Feb. 12, 1682" (*) Henry Symes was a son of John Symes of Poundsford, by Amy Horner. He md. A mye, dau. of Sir John Seymour, of Bitton, Glou.". (From Brown's Wills, p. 52 - Visitation of Glos. in 1682-3 p. 183. Edited by Fenwick & Metcakfe).

From Mr. W. H. Bason, Genealogist, "I copied a part of the will of Henry Symes because of the genealogical footnote. This Henry mentions no sons but 5 dau. Seymour is a Royal Line".

Thomas Symes, son of John of Poundsford and his wife Amy Horner, In Brown's Somerset Wills, p. 48, there can be found the tabulated descendants of Edw. Bridges, showing that he md. Phillippa, dau. of Sir Geo. Speke, and that his fifth child, Amy md. Thomas Symes in 1640.

Will of Elizabeth Symes, dau. of Thomas Symes & his wife, Amy Bridges: "Eliz. Symes of Doynton, Glouc., spinster. Will dated Nov. 22, 1675; pro. July 12, 1676 (Gloucester Will). My body to be buried at the disposing of my loving'Ants', Mrs. Eliz. Langton & Mrs. Katherine Bridges. To brothers Henry, Geo. & Richard Symes, 5 lbs. each. Rings to my bro. Edw. and John, my sisters Amy, Katherine, and Mary Symes, my cousin Eliz. Guise, my cousin Still, Mr. and Mrs. Wilkes, Mr. Ware & my cousin Ann Merideth. 5 lbs. to my 'Ant' Langton "Ant' Bridges, bro. Wm. Symes. Poor of Doynton. To my Uncle Geo. Bridges -- Robert Wilskes for sermon. To Mary Seymour. To my bro. Thomas Symes. To my uncle Mr. Guise. To my bro. Charles; bro. Edw. & John Symes. Residue to my sisters Amy & Katherine, Extrices.

From Somerset Wills - First Series - Brown, p. 53
Library of Congress, Washington, D.C.

John Langton md. Eliz. Bridges. In his will in Brown's Somerset Wills - 4th Series, he refers to Henry Symes, son of his brother-in-law, Thomas Symes.

"Eliz. Langton of Doynton, Co., Glouc. widow. Will 1696, Codicil 1699 prob. Apr. 24, 1703, by Charles Symes & Amy Meridth. Names nephew Harry Bridges bro. Sir Thomas Bridges, nephews Harry & Geo. Bridges, nieces Ann Powell & Eliz. Orange, cousin Arabella Bridges dau. of Harry Bridges, cousin William Bridges, cousin Edw. Symes, cousins Harry Symes, Geo. Symes, Charles Symes, Wm. Guise; Nephew John Symes, to his son John Symes & each of his two daus.; To Wm. Symes, Thomas Symes, & Richard Symes sons of Nephew Wm. Symes....to their sister Amy Symes. Mary, wife of nephew Richard Symes, Ann, wife of nephew Charles Symes; to poor of Almeshouse erected by my bro.

Sir Thomas Bridges; to Mary wife of Nephew Wm. Symes; To Charles Symes & Amy Meredith heirs of Tenement now in the possession of Deborah Mathew; to Amy Symes, dau. of Nephew William, articles that belonged to my sister Katherine Bridges; to niece Amy Powell my silver "Bason that hath my own Coat of Arms ingraved on it'; my niece Ann Still; Eliz. Symes, dau. of my Nephew Charles Symes; Cousin Matthew Huntley of Boxwell London." Pro. Apr. 24, 1703.

THOMAS SYMES (son of John of Poundsford by Amy Horner) and his wife Amy Bridges had issue:

1. GEORGE SYMES, b. circa 1643, of whom later.
2. Richard, d. in 1723 (Will in Brown's Fourth Series p. 71), leaving his estate to his nephew Richard, son of his late bro., Wm., for life, remainder to his great-nephew Richard, son of his nephew Thomas, remainder to the elder son of said Thomas, remainder to said Thomas's bro., Wm. Symes, a clergyman.
3. John d. before 1696, leaving a son John & 2 daughters.
4. Edw. m. Susanna Champion "Edw. Symes of Bridgewater & Susanna Champion widow, Oct. 12, 1676", from "Marriage Licenses in Bath & Wells Before 1755" in N.Y. Library page 7 - note.
5. Charles m. Ann Creed "June 21, 1686, Charles Symes, Rector of Compton Martyn, County Somerset, Bachelor 36, and Ann Creed of the Close of Salsbury Spinster 28".
6. Henry, of Island of Antigua, West Indies. He had sons John & Edw. in 1713 (Will of Wm. Phillippes, Brown's 4th Ed. p. 84)
7. Thomas, b. 1642; d. without issue; m. Merriel.

GEORGE SYMES (born 1743), son of Thomas Symes & wife Amy Bridges, was of West Indies. He md. Dorothy, only child of Thomas Everard of Island of Antigua in West Indies Gent. and his wife was Eliz. Geo. Symes d. 1687 leaving his bro. Henry with others as guardian of his children, Geo., John, Eliz., Christopher, & Henry but leaving hardly any estate.

Although very young Geo. Symes' sons were forced to earn their living. When old enough, Henry, the youngest, went to sea. In 1687, the year of his father's death, Geo. Symes made his way to Va. where he found work in Surry Co. with Thomas Matthews and others. But in 1698 he left Va. for Antigua.

GEORGE SYMES, son of THOMAS SYMES and his wife AMY BRIDGES, was b. c 1643 in Somerset, England, d. 1687, in Island of Antigua in West Indies; m. Dorothy, d. after Apr. 30, 1705-6, dau. of Thomas Everard, Gent. & his wife Eliz. Issue:

1. George of whom later.
2. John, d. unmarried before 1699
3. Eliz., married Ulysses Athey
4. Christopher
5. Henry

GEORGE SYMES, son of George Symes and his wife Dorothy Everard, emigrated 1687 (the year of his father's death) from Antigua to Surry Co., Va. d. Hanover Co., Va. circa 1718-1723; 1698 gave John Sheltonnergen power of attorney, and returned to Antigua to collect his legacy; had issue Adam & George, and was the kinsman if not the father of John, Matthew and Edward.

LINEAGE

Arms of Wm. Symes of Charde (granted 1591; Azure, three scallops, or; crest, a demi-hand, rampant, and erased, or. See arleian Publications for Somerset, 1623, p. 110. Berry's Encyclopedia gives the crest, but does not say when it was granted.

Wm. Symes of Charde, d. 1597; m. Eliz. Hill; their son
John, heir of Poundsford, d. 1661; m. Amy Horner, their son
Thomas, d. before 1676; m. Amy Bridges, their son
George, d. 1687; m. Dorothy Everard; their son
George, d. 1718-23; wife unknown; emigrated to Va. 1687; his son
Adam, d. 1733; m. Mary Isham, their son
George, d. 1763; m. Martha Walton; their son
Zachariah, d. circa 1800;m. Mary Bridges; their son
Briggs, d. 1832 in Tennessee; m. Fanny Duke

SIMMS

It is my belief that our Richard Simms of Orange is not the one mentioned in the Will of Thomas Madison, Rappahannock County 1674, in which he mentions his God-Child Rebecca, daughter of Robert Pettie, and land sold to Richard Simms. This would appear to connect up the William Simms crowd of Richmond county, with the family name Richard Simms, since they intermarried with the Petty's of Richmond County. At any rate this is not a documented genealogy, but a collection of documents, as a basis for study by students of genealogy. The connection between the Madisons and the Simms and the Brockmans extend over several generations and it may have well started back with Thomas Madison, and there is evidence that James Madison, father of the President and John Madison his father, lived together in the lower counties and went up to King and Queen and that the Madison family were responsible for Samuel Brockman and his mother when they came to Virginia and they may have intermarried. One Richard Simms left a Will at Rappahannock naming no children, and we assume that he is the one mentioned in the Will of Thomas Madison. On Thomas Madison was in King and Queen by 1696, imported by Sir William Skipwith.

"Wills of Rappahannock County, Va., 1656-1692", by William Montgomery Sweeny. Page 30

Maddison, Thomas 19 October, 1674
4 November, 1674

Sick & weake but of perfect sense & memory.

To wife Catherine Maddison all my movable goods within dores and without that are mine or that belongeth or appertaineth to me the sd. Thomas Maddison, I do also give and bequeath unto the said Katherine Maddison my wife all cattle in general both young & old and hoggs likewise both young & old that are running within my plantation or without or wheresoever else that belongeth or appertaineth properly unto me the sd. Thomas Maddison furthermore I the sd. Thomas Maddison doe leave my plantation and all my land to cleere and discharge all my debts which I owe onely 300 acres which I sould to Richard White and a parcel of land which I sold to Richard Simms and all the rest of my land I doe leave to discharge my debts which belong to my patent or patents and if there bee anything left over and above more than shall pay my debts then it shall return to Katherine Maddison my wife further more I doe leave my loving friends and neighbors Richard White and Thomas Bryant Executors of this my will and Testament to be assistant to Katherine Maddison my wife and I doe allso give my long gun to Thomas Bryant and my short gun to Richard White. I doe also give to my Godchild Rebecka Pettie the daughter of Robert Pettie one heifer of two years old and furthermore I do give and leave unto Katherine Maddison my wife my money which I have in England with my brother Leonard Maddison which is the sume of seaventy pounds Sterling.

Wit: Peter Calvin, jJohn Biforest.

A probate hereon is granted to Coll Wm. Travers in behalfe of Anne Maddison by order of court. Page 167.

"Wills of Rappahannock Co., Va. 1656-1692." by Wm. M. Sweeny Page 42.

Simms, Richard 22 January 1672-3
2 May 1677

To John Penn should I die without wife or issue all my reall and personall estate that is lands goods and chattels as well moveables as unmoveables to his heirs and assigns forever. Executor John Penn.

Wit: Thomas Harware, aged 34 years or thereabouts.
Henry Williamson, aged 34 years or thereabouts. Page 205.

In Va. in 1812, the James Coleman heirs sued the Penn Heirs over land allotted out by Ambrose Madison in his will 1732. It seems that this destroyed name on Ambrose Madison's will was George Penn. He was a will witness. (St. Mark's Parish.)

In the lawsuit of 1812 (later dismissed) the following Penns were named by Coleman heirs.

Joseph Penn, deceased and his children and heirs

Most of these other Penn heirs named are called descendents of Moses Penn and his wife Catherine Taylor. Moses and Joseph were bros. who m. sisters.

Gabriel Penn d. 1798 Amherst---wife Sarah living in 1812.
Geo. Penn (brother to Gabriel)
James Penn
Edmund Penn
Elizabeth Penn, wife of 2nd husband Wm. Long, 1st husband was Jas. Galloway
Sophia Penn, wife of Wm. S. Crawford
Permelia Penn, wife of Thos. Haskins
Matilda Penn, wife of Abner Nash
Frances Penn, wife of Wm. White
Nancy Penn, wife of John McCredie (1st husband Alex Brydie)
Sarah Penn, wife of Thos. Crowe
Catherine Penn, wife of Holder
John Penn
Sarah (widow of Gabriel)
Francis Lee and Chn: Wm. and Geo. Jr.
Seaton M. Penn
Chas. B. Penn, Elizabeth, Polly and Jos. Penn

End of Penn names in Coleman lawsuit. Presumbly these were all the heirs of George Penn b. 1696. Got a land grant in 1728 (Sept. 28) St. Mark's Parish (Spots. Co.)

(Richard Simms, father of Capt. William died intestate Orange County, 1746, Widow Joanne, named administrator.)

Copy of the Inventory of Richard Simms deceased, 1746. Pursuant to an order of Orange County Court we the subscribers being first sworn, have inventoried and appraised the estate of Richard Simms dece'd. money as followeth viz......

	L.	S.	D.
To a white mare and a two year old colt	4:	0:	0:
To a gray horse	3:	0:	0:
To a Bay Mare three years old	2:	5:	0:
To two old Horses	3:	5:	0:
To 3 Cows and a Calf	3:	5:	0:
To Two fifty gallon Casks	0:	5:	0:
To a parcel of Unwrote Flax	0:	5:	0:
To 1 old Saddle and Bridle	0:	15:	0:
To 1 old Saddle Bridle To 1 old Saddle Bridle, Coller & Hames)	10:	1:	0:
To 1 old Loome	0:	10:	0:
To 4 old Casks with one head in each	0:	5:	0:
To 1 Powdering Tub	0:	2:	0:
To Parcel of Feathers about 20	1:	0:	0:
To 2 Beds Bedsteads Covering and Hides	9:	10:	0:
To 3 old Guns	2:	10:	0:
To 3 Potts and two pr. Pott Hooks	0:	18:	0:
To 1 Gridiron & Frying Pan	0:	8:	0:
To a Parcel of Old Iron Hoes, Axes, etc.	0:	13:	3:
To 17 Pewter Spoons and about 5 pewter	0:	7:	0:
To a Parcel of Old Earthen Ware	0:	2:	6:
To 6 old Flag Chairs, 5 old Pails & a Tub	0:	15:	0:
To 2 old Meal sifters and two old Chests	0:	9:	0:
To 1 Old Spinning Wheel and 10 Cotten	0:	15:	0:
To 2 good meal bags and 1 old Meal Bagg	0:	8:	0:
To 2 Bibles and a Prayer Book	0:	8:	6:
To a Parcel of Old Baskets Boxes and Trays	0:	7:	6:
To 1 Earthen Pott and Two Gimblets	0:	2:	4:
To 1 old Tables	0:	9:	3:

March 16th, 1746-1747
Charles Curtis
Zach. Taylor
Wm Goldin
Peter Rucker

Returned into Orange County Court the 28th day of May, 1747 and Ordered to be recorded
Teste: John Nicholas, Cl. Crt.

Recorded in Orange County Will Book 2, page 110

Richmond County, Wills and Inventories, 1709-1717. Will of WILLIAM SIMMS, page 279.

In the name of God Amen, I William Sims of Sittenburn Parish in Richmond County Planter being of perfect mind and memory aforeseeing ye approved of Death, do make this my last Will and Testament annulling all former Wills bequeathing my Soul to God and my Body to the Earth and for my worldly Estate, I dispose of in manner following viz;

First I will and bequeath to my son, Thomas Sims and his heirs, forever, all my Lands and reall Estate lying in Richmond County; and in case my said son, Thomas, dies without heirs it is my Will and I accordingly give and bequeath ye said Lands to the Church Wardens of the Parish of Sittenburn for ye time being and their successors to be (build??) A Glebe for ye said Parish to ye use of a Minister of ye said Parish forever. Secondly, I give and bequeath to my Son, Thomas, after ye payment - of my just debts and funerall expenses, all my personal Estate of all kind or nature soever. Thirdly, I appoint and Constitute Capt. Nicholas Smith and George White both of ye Parish of Sittenburn my whole and Sole Executors of this my last will and Testament. Fourthly, it is my will yl Capt. Smith taken under his care and tuition my Son Thomas until he comes to the age of twenty years, and if ye sd. Smith dye yl then my other Executor shall do ye same. In witness where of I have here to affixed my seal this twenty eight day of April on thousand seven hundred and sixteen.

his hand
William X Sims Seal
& mark

Signed, Sealed and declared to be his last Will & Testament and their successors being first interlined.

John Bagge
Witt L. Jison
Edward Hinkley

This will was proved in Richmond County Court the first Day of August 1716 by the Oath of Edward Hinkley one of the Witnesses thereto, and admitted to record.

Teste: M. Beckwith, Cl. of Crt.

Page 81-82
p. 111, Settlement of Estate of William Sims deceased, 30 June, 1719.

Total 8792 lb. total includes:	Total
To pd. Mary Jefferys	400
To pd. John Molton for plank for Coffin	50
To pd. Mr. Ingol	90
To pd. Mr. Jno Bagg	312
To pd. Mr. Charles Bruce by Ord'r of Court	339
To pd. Capt. Walter King	509
To pd. Martin Kemp per Ord'r of Court	186
To pd. Dan'll Jefferys	45

Errors Excepted by Niche Smith (Rec. 4 Nov., 1719)

FINES - page 94. p. 3 - At a Court held 3 May, 1711.

present

Samuel Peachey	Charles Barber)	
Alexander Donaphaw	William Woodbridge)	Gent. Justices
John Tarpley	William Thornton)	

Dowing, etc., fined

George Downing, William Seale and William Sims being by order brought before this Court to answer to what should be objected against them relating to the breaking open the Prison of this County and Rich'd Clathermiks making his escape from thence; on hearing the evidence of James Ingo, James Wilson, Samuel Short, Elizabeth and Martha Hoyton in this behalfe, and the said George Downing, William Serle and William Sims being seperately examined and offering nothing materall in barr of what was laid to their charge in this matter are of opinion that they are guilty of the fact aforesaid; It is therefore ordered that they be each of them fined one thousand pounds of tobacco to Our Sovereign Lady, the Queen, and that each of them give good and sufficient security for their good behavior one year.

p. 3, Geo. Downing with Henry Berry bound in L 10 sterling to keep the peace.
p. 4, William Seale with William Berry bound as above.
p. 4, William Sims with Thomas Dickenson bound as above.

Culpeper County Deed Book E. 1765-1769. P. 191 - Sims to Scott, D.D. to Wm. Scott

This Indenture made the Eighteenth day of September in the year of our Lord Christ, One Thousand Seven Hundred & Sixty Six, between Thomas Sims of the Parish of Brumfield and County of Culpeper Planter of the one part, and William Scott of the County of Orange of the other part, Witnesseth that the said Thomas Sims & Rebecca, his wife, for and inconsideration of the sum of twenty Pounds, Current money of Virginia, to the Thomas Sims in Hand paid the receipt whereof he doth hereby acknowledge hath granted Bargained & sold Enfeoffed & Confirmed and by these presents Doth Grant Bargain Sell Enfeoff and Confirm unto the said William Scott his Heirs & Assigns all that Tract or parcell of Land containing Sixty Acres be, the same more or less, Situate Lying & being in the parish and County aforesaid being part of a patent granted to Michael Wilhoit, bearing date the twenty eight day of September, 1728, for two hundred eighty nine acres and is bounded as followeth to wit. Beginning at two Maples on the West side of Muddy Run in Adam Waylands Line thence with the said Line North eighty five East Eighty poles to a Red Oak White Oak & Spanish Oak a corner to the said Wayland in the said Wilhoits Line of the Patent thence with that Line North five West one hundred Poles to a red Oak and White Oak saplins in the said Line thence South eighty five degrees West Eighty poles to a pine, in a branch of the said Run, thence down several Courses thereof to the Beginning. Together with all Houses Buildings, Orchards ----- Improvements, Trees, Wood Underwood Watercourses Profits Commodities Hereditaments and Appurtenances Whosoever to the same belonging or in any wise appertaining, and also all the Estate, Title Claim or Demand - Whatsoever of the said Thomas Sims of in and to the same To have and to hold, the said Sixty Acres of Land be the same more or less according to the bounds above Specified together with the appurtenances unto the said William Scott his Hiers and Assigns To the only proper use and Behoof of said William Scott his Heirs and assigns forever, and the said Thomas Sims for himself his Heirs Executors & Administrators and Assigns Doth Covenant & Agree with the said William Scott his Heirs Executors Administrators and Assigns that the said Thomas Sims at the time of Ensealing and Delivering of these presents is and stands Lawfully seized in his Demesne as Fee in the said Tract of Lands and Premises with the appurtenances and hath good Right and Lawful Authority to sell and Convey the same to the said William Scott his Heirs and Assigns forever and that he will Warrant and forever Defend the said tract of Land and Premises with the appurtenances unto the said William Scott his Hiers and Assigns forever free and clear from all manner of incumbrances of what nature or Kindsoever, and against the Lawful Title or Claims of him the said Thomas Sims and Rebecca his wife or his Heirs or any Person Claiming under them or either of them against, the Lawful Claim of all and every other person and persons whatsoever. In Witness Whereof the Parties to these presents their hands and Seals hereunto to have Interchangeably set the Day and Year first within written.

Thos. Sims L S

Rebecca her + mark Sims L S

In presence of us: John Flynt
Thos. Sims Jun.
William his + mark Clark

At a Court held for the County of Culpeper on Thursday the 18th day of September 1766. This Indenture of Bargain & Sale from Thomas Sims and Rebecca his wife to William Scott was acknowledged by the said Thomas & ordered to be Recorded.

TESTE: Roger Dixon, Cl. Crt.

CULPEPER COUNTY

Will Book C. Pages, 129-131.

Will of THOMAS SIMMS, SR., son of William.

In the name of God Amen, & Thomas Sims, Sr., of Brumfield Parish and County of Culpeper being sick and weak in body but of perfect mind and memory, thanks be given to God. Therefore calling to mind the mortality of my body and knowing that it is Appointedffor all men once to die do make and ordain this my last Will and Testament that is to say principally and first of all. I do give and recommend by soul be buried in a decent Christian Burial at the discretion of my Executors nothing doubting but at the General Resurrection, I shall receive the same again by the Mighty Power of God and as touching such Worldly Estate wherewith it hath pleased God to bless me in this life. I give demise and dispose of the same in the following manner and form imprints.

ITEM.
First of all I do give and bequeath and bequeath to my eldest son, Thomas Sims, Jr., that part of my estate that fell to him by division, and likewise, I do give and bequeath to my son, Thomas Sims, my Negro woman by name, Milley, and child, to him and his heirs lawfully begotten forever. Likewise, my son, Thomas Sims, Jr., is to pay thirty pounds in gold or silver to my son, William Sims' deceased children, six pounds to each child as they come of age and other little debts comeing against me.

ITEM.
Secondly, I do give and bequeath to my son, James Sims, my Negro man Peter, and all that fell to him by division to him and his Heirs lawfully begotten forever. Likewise I do give and bequeath to Elizabeth Sims, wife of James, my Great Looking Glass and I desire at her Death that one of their sons may have it.

ITEM.
Thirdly, I do give and bequeath to my son, Elijah Sims, the land he lives on, the Garden Excepted and likewise Negro boy by name Abraham and all that fell to him by

Division to him and his heirs sons of his first wife lawfully begotten forever.

ITEM.
Fourthly, I do give and bequeath to my daughter, Amy Bobo, a Negro woman by name Cate, and all her children and I desire if John Sims lives with Absalom Bobo and his wife until he comes of age they may give him one of negro children if they see proper. This Negro woman Cate and all her children, and all that fell to her by Division is to her, her and her heirs lawfully begotten forever.

ITEM.
Fifthly, I do give and bequeath to my two granddaughters, Lucy and Anna Jones, daughters of my daughter Sarah Jones, deceased, a Negro woman by name Rose and a boy name Peter and all that part that fell to my said daughter Sarah Jones, by division to them and their heirs lawfully begotten forever. This estate they are to Receive at the day of marriage or coming to lawful age.

ITEM.
Sixthly, I do give and Bequeath to my son, Zachariah Sims, a Negro man by name Moses and all that fell to him by division to him and his heirs lawfully begotten forever.

ITEM.
Seventhly, I do give and Bequeath to my son, Richard Sims, a Negro woman by name Daphnie, and likewise thirty odd acres of Land and all that fell to him by Division to him and his heirs lawfully begotten forever.

ITEM.
Eightly, I do give and Bequeath Ann Graves an Negro woman by name Winney and her child and all that fell to her by Division to her and her heirs lawfully Begotten forever.

ITEM.
Ninthly, I do desire that my feather bed and furniture and what other things I possess may be sold to the highest bider in the Family and the money rising there from be equally divided amongst all my children, and lastly I do appoint my sons, Thomas and James Sims, my hole and sole Executors of this my last Will and Testament hereby revoking all former Wills and Declaring this to be my my last Will and Testament. In witness whereof I have here unto Set my hand and Seal this the 21st Day of April, 1784.

Thos. Sims (L.S.)

Sealed and Declared before us:
Jas. Sims
Edw'd Sims
William Mason

At a Court held for Culpeper County the 18th day of July 1785.

This last Will and Testament of Thomas Sims dec'd. was exhibited to the Court by Thomas Sims, one of the Exors therein named, and was proved by the Oaths by Edw'd Sims and William Mason two of the Witnesses thereto and Ordered to be recorded and on the motion of the said Executor Certificate is granted Him for Obtaining a probate thereof in due form. He having made Oath thereto and given bond and Security according to Law Liberty being reserved for the other Exor therein name to qualify when he may think fit.

TESTE: John Jameson, Cl. Crt. Virginia: In Culpeper County Circuit Court Clerk's Office.

I.C.T. Guinn, Clerk of the Circuit Court in and for the county and State aforesaid, do hereby Certify that the foregoing and attached is a true Copy of the last Will and Testament of Thomas Sims, Sr.; which is recorded in this office in Will Book C, Pages 129-131.

Given under my hand and the seal of the Court this 22nd day of March, 1957.

TESTE: "C. T. Guinn," Clerk by Margaret Brown, "Deputy Clerk."

According to the Will of Thomas Sims, Sr., he and wife Rebecca had the following children:

1. Thomas Sims, Jr.
2. William Sims (Died 1769 - wife Mathew (Martha??). Wm. was deceased when his father made his will.
3. James Sims (Sr.) wife Elizabeth Nalle.
4. Elijah Sims (according to his father's will, Elijah Sims was married twice).
5. Amy Bobo.
6. Sarah Jones (Deceased when Thomas, Sr., made his will).
7. Zachariah Sims.
8. Richard Sims.
9. John Sims and Ann Graves were mentioned in Thomas Sims, Sr.'s, Will. He did not say they were children, or grandchildren, but from the wording of the legacies willed to them they certainly had some legal claim to Thomas Sims, Sr., Estate.

Culpeper County Will Book D., 1791-1803, page 389, JAMES SIMS WILL

In the name of God, Amen.

I James Sims of Culpeper County and State of Virginia do make this my Last Will and Testament.

I lend to my Dear Wife Betty Sims during her natural life my tract of Land in Madison County which purchased of William Taylor and is adjoining the Land of Beverley and Robberts and George Sims. I also lend to my said wife during her natural life two slaves called and known by the names of Jacob and Poll. I also lend my said wife one third part of my personal Estate (other than slaves) and allow her to take her choice according to appraisement and at the death of my wife, I give and bequeath the Land Slaves and personal estate herein lent to her to be equally divided between all my children.

In case one or more of my children should depart this Life before my wife and if such child or children should leave issue in such case my will and desire is that such issue should have the part that their parents would have been entitled to, but if one or more of my children should depart this life before my wife without issue, then such child or children part shall be divided between my other children or their Legal Representatives - Whereas I have formerly given to my son Martin Simms a small male slave called George and to my Daughter Salley Jones Simms a small male slave called Gidion and a doubt may arise whether a legal title is vested in my said son and daughter of the said slaves to prevent any doubt concerning the title of the said slaves, I hereby give and Bequeath to my said son Martin Simms his heirs and assigns forever the said slave called George and also give and bequeath to my said daughter Salley Jones Simms her heirs and assigns forever, Gidion, the slave aforementioned.

In case I should depart this life before I build a dwelling house on the land which I have herein lent to my wife, in that case my Executors hereafter named and hereby (two words I could not make out. P.H.B.) and required to build for my wife a dwelling house and other necessary outhouses, I give and Bequeath to my Executors, hereafter named, in trust for the benefit of my daughter, Nancy Wilhitt and her children, one tenth part of my estate not before directed and do hereby require my said Executors or the surviors of them to apply the profit of the same in the support and maintainence of my said daughter and the children she now has or may have during the life of my said daughter and at the death of my said daughter I give and Bequeath the same to be equally divided between the children of my said daughter which she now has or may have but in case any other children should depart this life before their mother and such children should have issue, in that case the issue of such children shall have the part their parents would have been entitled to.

I give and bequeath to my other nine children the remainder of my estate, both real and personal to be equally divided between them in the following manner that my Executors, hereafter named, shall divide my estate in as equal manner as possible and then determined by Lott the particular part of each child and that my said Executors shall cause the same to be publicly divided and then return an account thereof to Court to be recorded and I do hereby give each of my said children the part so allotted to them to their heirs and assigns forever provided nevertheless that any child to whom I have acknowledged land such lands shall be considered in their part according to the value of such land exclusive of the improvements and any of my children who are settled on my lands shall have their part of my land laid off in such manner as to include the part which they at present possess.

I nominate and appoint my two sons George Simms and Edward Simms, Executors of this my Last Will and Testament in Witness here of I have here unto set my hand and affixed my seal this eighteenth day of February, One thousand and eight hundred and two.

James Simms (S.S.)

Sealed and Published as his Last Will and Testament in presence of
Benjamin Leavell +
Edmund Willis +
John Walker +

At a Court held for Culpeper County the 18th day of October, 1802.

This Last Will and Testament of James Simms deceased exhibited to the Court by the Executors therein named, and was proved by the oaths of Benjamin Leavell, Edmund Willis and John Walker, three of the witnesses thereto, and ordered to be recorded and on motion of the said Executors Certificate is granted them for obtaining a probate thereof in due form they having made oath thereto and given bond and security according to Law.

TESTE: Janeson C. Cur.

Dr. Edward Sims, Exor. of Estate of James Sims, dec.

1803	To Cash received for tobacco and wheat	L 89	17	4
	To Cash received of Coleman Thud on sale of personal estate	8	8	4
	To Cash received of Gabriel Wallock do.	20	3	7
	To Cash received of Delaney on do.	15	3	7
1804	To Cash received of William Hollaway on do.	5	3	6
	To Cash received of George Sims --- on do.	13	16	6
1806	To Cash received of Martin Sims --- on do.	25	16	6
		L177	8	5

CR.

1803				
Sept. 18	By Cash paid Daniel Field on proved acct.	L 24	5	8
	By Cash paid Charles Urquart	8	5	6
	By Cash paid Robert Patton	17	5	2
	By Cash paid Timothy Green on proved acct.	3	5	2
	By Cash paid Richard I. Tutt Still Tax	1	3	3
	By Cash paid Martin Sims as overseer	9	3	3
	By Cash paid William Ward Taxes	4	2	3
	By Cash paid James Colvin in part for building a dwelling house for widow	15	2	3
	By Cash paid William Newton	15	19	3
	By Cash paid Clerk fee	2	15	3
	By Cash for hauling wheat	L 1	7	3
	By Cash paid John Gop (Goss?) tax on land	L 1	2	11-1/2
	By Cash paid Joseph Roberts as Leyatee	5	3	6
	By Cash retained in my hand as balance of legacy due Amy Sims, Orphan of William Sims	10	16	6
	By Cash paid Betty Sims for her part of tob.	7	15	3
	By Cash paid for wheat	7	18	3
	By Cash paid Daniel Smith land tax	7	3	3
	By Cash paid Charles Major on legacy in part	9	4	3
	By Cash paid Sally I. Sims on do.	22	4	3
1803				
Sept. 18	By Cash paid John Walker, attorney	L 3	4	3
		146	9	8-1/2
	By balance due the Estate from said Sims	30	18	8-1/2
		L177	8	5

Dr. George Sims, Exor. of the Estate of James Sims, dec.

1804				
Jan. 2	To balance Martin Sims, bond	L 31	16	10
	To balance Eliab Delancys bond	21	14	6
	To William Newton bond	10	10	11
	To Edward Leavell bond	6	15	6
	To George Foushee bond	6	10	6
	To Michael Willhort bond	6	7	6
	To Isiah Bishop bond	6	2	6
	To John Roberts bond	28	5	4
	To Clarke Wise bond	21	19	4
	To James Sims bond	48	13	2
	To Gabrial Colvin bond	7	12	2
	To Robert Reaves bond	6	5	2
	To James G. Jones bond	13	9	3
	To Philip Graves and William Ere bond	18	2	6
	Suit brought according to law and debt acct.			
		L216	1	0

CR.

By Cash paid James G. Jones as legatee	28	15	8
By Cash paid Edward Sims as do.	7	16	0
By Cash paid Joseph Roberts ad do.	28	18	6

By cash paid Charles Major as do.	16	16	1-3/4
By Cash paid Clerks fee	6	13	4
By Cash paid William Tatum for work done for the widow	2	14	4
By Cash paid Doct. Clagett	L 2	2	4
By Cash paid Edward Sims	6	2	4
By Material and Labor furnished about the widow's house	8	6	3
	108	1	10-3/4
By balance due the Estate from said Sims	107	19	1-1/4
	L216	1	1-1/4

Pursuant to an order from the County Court of Culpeper to us directing, we the subscribers this day settled the accounts of George Sims and Edward Sims, Exors. of the Estate of James Sims, dec., and find the sum of one hundred and seven pounds, nineteen shillings and 1-3/4 due from George Sims to said Estate and sum of thirty pounds, eighteen shillings and eight pence, 1/2 due from Edward Sims to said Estate, Vouchers being produced to us for the greater part of the items and the balance we have good reason to believe to be correct - Certified by us this 2nd day of October, 1811.

Robert Hill
Daniel James
William Newton

At a Court held for Culpeper County the 21st day of Oct., 1811.

This settlement of the Exors. account of James Sims dec. was returned into Court and ordered to be recorded.

TESTE: William Broadus, Jr., C.C.

Virginia - In Culpeper County Circuit Court Clerk's Office

I, C. T. Guinn, Clerk of the Circuit Court inaand for the County aforesaid in the State of Virginia, do hereby certify that the foregoing is a true copy of the Executor account of the estate of James Sims, recorded in this office in Will Book F, page 283.

Given under my hand and Seal this 11th day of March, 1958.

TESTE: "C. T. Guinn", Clerk
By: "Nellie M. ByWaters", Deputy Clerk.

The following legatees were named in the Exors. account of James Sims, Sr.

1. George Sims (son)
2. Martin Sims (son - Elizabeth Nalle Sims had a brother named Martin Nalle.)
3. Joseph Roberts
4. Charles Major
5. Sally I. Sims (I think this was Sally Jones Sims, dau of James and Elizabeth Nalle Sims - This Sally Jones Sims was probably named for her Aunt Sarah Sims Jones).
6. James G. Jones
7. Edward Sims (son)

Legacy due Amy Sims, Orphan of William Sims - (I believe this Amy Sims was a niece of James Sims, Sr. James Sims witnessed his brother, William's Estate. I sent you a copy of William Sims will. I believe William Sims had five children. The following, is my reason: In the will of Thomas Sims, Sr., (father of the above Wm.) a part of the will reads - "Likewise my son Thomas Sims, Juner, is to pay thirty pounds in gold or silver to my son William Sims, deceased - children six pounds to each child as they come of age" etc.

According to Miss Wilson's records, James Sims, Sr., and wife Elizabeth, had the following children:

1. John
2. Robert
3. Bartlett
4. George
5. Edward
6. Martin
7. James Jr.
8. Nancy
9. Sarah
10. Daughter

1. Father (James Sims, Sr.) Culpeper Co., deeded land as a gift to son, John D 268 15 Sept. 1763.
2. Father (James Sims, Sr.) Culpeper Co., deeded land as a gift to son Robert D. 726 17 July, 1765
3. Father Culpeper Co. deeded land as a gift to son Bartlett D. 729 - 17 July, 1765.
4. Father Culpeper Co., deeded land as a gift to son George E. 658 - 20 Aug., 1768.
5. Father Culpeper Co., deeded land as a gift to son Edward.

P. 122 Pages 466-67 Will of Jeremiah Sims, dated 24 March, 1768.

Jeremiah Sims of the County of Culpeper being sick and weak.

Unto my beloved wife, Agatha Sims, one half of my estate both real and personal.

If my son James Sims should die without heir, my wife have the use of my whole estate during her natural life and then to be equally divided between my two nephews Thomas Graves and Jonathan Sims.

I do constitute and appoint my beloved wife, Agatha Sims, executrix, and my loving friends Edward Sims, John Nalle, Junr. and Henry Pendleton, executors.

Jeremiah Sims

Wit: Thomas Griffin
Moses (X) Spicer
Henry Pendleton
John Nalle Junr.

18 Aug. 1768. Exhibited to the court by Edward Sims and John Nalle, Junr. Proved by the oaths of Thomas Griffin, Moses Spicer and Henry Pendleton. Henry Pendleton made oath that he was desired by the testator to write the said will

----

(I copied the following will just as it was written. P.H.B.)

From "Culpeper County, Virginia, Will Book A" by Dorman 1749-1770, page 125 - Pages 477 - 78 Will of William Sims dated 29 May, 1768.

William Sims of the County of Culpeper being and low in body. To my well beloved wife, Mathew Sims all my worldly goods and chattles both within my house as well as wtout (sic) exception during hir natural life or widowhood for to raise my children on till they all come of age. My wife now with child, if it lives to have an equal part.

If my wife marries before children comes of age, I appoint Thomas Sims and James executors.

Wm. Sims.

Wit: James Sims
Ela. Sims
Jas. Steward

18,May, 1769. Exhibited to the court by Thomas Sims and Joseph Steward. James Sims the other executor refused to take upon himself the burthen of the exon. thereof."

From "Culpeper County" by Green - Page 52 (part II)

Jno: Nalle. Sept. 16, 1780: Children: Richard; Jno.; Wm.; Francis; Jas.; Agatha m. Hill; Mary m. Sims; Ann m. Burke; Gressel m. Parker; Amie m. Wm. Morris; Elizabeth m. Sims and Martin, whose whereabouts were not know. Aug. 19, 1782.

From - "William and Mary Quarterly" Vol. 19 - series 1 - page 289.

"John Jones (Abraham^3, Peter^2, Peter^1) was known as "Col. John Jones." He married in 1769, Elizabeth Crawley, daughter of William Crawley, sen., of Amelia County, and had issue:

1. Alexander Jones
2. David C. Jones
3. John Jones, Jr.
4. Daughter, who married Thomas Simms
5. Daughter, who married Peter Winston

(See wills of Col. John Jones 1805, and the latter 1802; also wills of William Crawley, Sr., and John Crawley.)"

From "Rucker Genealogy" by S. R. Wood

James Rucker and wife, Margaret of Culpeper, sold to James Griffin of Orange, 120 Acres land in Culpeper, part of a patent of John Powell, dated 1749, Land on top of the mountain running North, Sept. 16th, 1756. (D. B. B. page 488, Culpeper)

The same day, same book, page 500, he and Margaret "Sold 250 Acres to William Sims of Orange, for 400 pounds of tobacco, between the Stanton and Conway River.

The following is some Jones data that a cousin sent me -

"I went to see Virgie Johns. She said old Jones place where they (the Johns family) lived all the time at Burnleys had an old graveyard between the house and Burnleys for her brothers brought a rock from it and Mrs. Preston Douglas saw it and made them take it back, so it must have been some of her Jones." I do not know the exact location of this Jones - Johns place, but it either joins our place at Burnleys or it is near our place. Probably near the Roy Brockman place. Evidently Mrs. Preston Douglass was a Jones.

I have an old store bill 1827 from Thos. A. Robinson to Bluford Brockman. A Robinson family must have lived near the Brockmans at that date.

By Pauline Brandt (Mrs. M. A. Brandt 111)
Norfolk, Virginia

My great-grandparents, George and Sarah M. Payne Howard, had a son named Stephen Howard. He could have been named for the Stephen Howard mentioned in your notes. My immigrant ancestor, Matthew Howard and his wife Anne, (possibly Hall) lived in Lower Norfolk County, Va. Matthew Howard patented land on the Western Branch of the Elizabeth River in Lower Norfolk County, May, 1638. In 1645, Richard Hall of Lower Norfolk Co., in his will leaves legacies to the children of Matthew and Anne Howard. Matthew Howard was executor of Richard Hall's will. The children of Matthew and Anne Howard went to Maryland. Corneluis Howard, son of Matthew and Anne Howard, married 1st, Anne Dorsey of Ann Arundel Co., Md. (They are my direct line.) David Howard, son of Corneluis and Anne Dorsey Howard, married Eliza Allen, dau. of William Allen, of Talbot Co., Md. David and Eliza Allen Howard migrated to Goochland Co., Va. Their son, Allen Howard, died in Goochland in 1732. He was the father of Major Allen Howard (of Goochland & Albemarle Counties) and David Howard. William Howard of Alb. Co., was the son of this David Howard of Goochland Co. William Howard married Judith Allegre Amos (a widow) dau. of Dr. Giles and Judith Cox Allegre of Alb. Co. The son of William and Judith Allegre Amos Howard was George Howard. George Howard married Sarah M. Payne, dau. of Daniel Payne of Fluvanna Co., Va. William W. Howard, son of George and Sarah M. Payne Howard, married Sarah Ann Hudgins, dau. of Col. A. M. Hudgins of "Elk Hill" Fluvanna Co., Va. My father, Napoleon Bonaparte Howard, was the son of William W. and Sarah Ann Hudgins Howard. I have copies of deeds, wills and marriage bonds of all the above mentioned Howards.

The following is from "The Howard Lineage" by Gustine, Courson Weaver - page 34.

"The Howards of Baltimore, Maryland, in the United States of America trace their descent very clearly from Joshua Howard*, who in 1699, was granted a large tract of land in Baltimore County; and there formerly was in their possession an Armorial Shield painted on copper and inscribed "Howard Earl of Arundel." A reproduction of this shield is on the tomb of Corneluis Howard, a son of Joshua; it is, however, a modification of the Howard Shield differing in many respects. Etc."

*This Joshua Howard was a brother of my Corneluis Howard. They were sons of Matthew and Anne Howard of Lower Norfolk County, Va.

Feb. 6, 1959

Dear Mr. Brockman: I am truly behind. I have been helping copy Bible records for our chapter of DAR and haven't been able to do a thing for myself in four months.

I thought I had the entire will of John Petty of Orange County, who died in 1770. But all I can find is an abstract.

Will of John Petty, 27 Sept., 1770, Will Book 2; p. 422. Orange Co., Va., gives wife Rebecca; first son Thomas Petty, daughters: Sarah Corley; Tabitha Edwards; son Luke Petty in Carolina; grand-daughter Ann Ford which is my life and she was the dau. of John Petty's daughter Abfaer (Apphia) and a lot of other spellings who married John Ford; then there was son in law William Ransdell, son Francis Petty, son Abner Petty, son George Petty, son John Petty, son Zachariah Petty, Ann Ransdell, dau., Rebecca Boston, dau. Susannah Hawkins, dau. Jemima Boston. Here are all the children:

1. Thomas
2. Sarah Corley, N.C.
3. Tabitha Edwards, N.C.

4. Luke, Carolina
5. Apphia m. John Ford
6. Ann m. Wm. Ransdell, Sr.
7. Francis, son
8. Abner
9. George
10. Zachariah, will prob. 1796 in Culpeper Co.
11. Rebecca m. Boston
12. Susanna Hawkins m. Joseph Hawkins
13. John
14. Jemima Boston

Executors of will wife, Rebecca and son Thomas, and son-in-law William Ransdell. Wit. by Alexander Waugh and Cattey Petty. One girl married Joseph Boston and one married Yovel Boston, but I haven't determined which m. which.

In Orange Co., Va., Will Book 3, page 231. Sale and settlement Oct. 14, 1790, by William Ransdell Sr., admr. of John Pettey's will. One feather bed and furniture to Abfier Ford. Purchasers at Sale: James Sleet who was husband of my Ann Ford, mentioned in will and daughter of Abfer Petty who m. John Ford, Reuben Moore, Francis Moore, John Boston, Thomas Bryant, James Clark, Jr. Heirs in estate settlement were given here as: Abfier Ford, John Petty, George Petty, Yovel Boston, Zachariah Petty, Joseph Boston, Joseph Hawkins.

The proof I have that John Petty married Rebecca Simms is from Alice K. Houts, Genealogical records chairman, DAR, 230 West 61st St., Kansas City 13, Mo. She has worked out a line for Mrs. Harts to join Colonial Dames of American and she gives the following: I paid her for this information on the whole Colonial line.

Zachariah Petty son of John Petty, b. Orange Co., Va. D. Orange Co., Va. Will 9-27-1770. Married Rebecca Simms who died after 1770.

This John Petty was the son of Thomas Petty, b. Essex Co., Va. D. Orange Co., Va. Will 1750. Married Catherine Carton who died prior to 1748. This Thomas Petty was son of Capt. Thomas Petty, b. Essex Co., Va., April or May, 1664, died Essex Co., Va., Will 1720, wife Rachel Wilson. Member of the council James City Council Virginia. Captain of Colonial Militia (Dragoon) Sheriff of King and Queen Co., Va., 1714.

The children I have for Thomas Petty, will prob. May 24, 1750, wife Catherine Garton, are as follows:

John m. Rebecca Simms
Thomas m. Elizabeth Moore
Christopher
William
James
Rebecca m. Thomas Simms, which is also my line
Mary m. Knight
George
Martha

So John Petty m. Rebecca Simms and Rebecca Petty m. Thomas Simms; and both of these are my lines.

I also have Capt. Thomas Petty, wife Rachel Wilson, will 1720, Exxex Co., Va., to be son of Thomas Petty, wife Katherine Morris, will made Sept. 20, 1662, pro. Jan. 7, 1663 in Rappah. Co., Va.

I will be glad to have anything on the Simms and Pettys that I don't have. My sister, Mrs. Thomas of Bowling Green, Ky., and I are working on a book on our family lineage, Gilmore-Carter and mean to supply as many allied lines as possible. I am truly sorry that I have been so long answering you. Sincerely, Dolly Barmann
(Mrs. Paul Barmann)

March 8, 1959

Dear Mr. Brockman: I have Rebecca Simms, wife of John Petty, listed as daughter of Thomas Simms of Richmond Co., Va., wife, Rebecca Harrelson, will Culp. Co., Va.
Children: Thomas Sims Jr., m. Mary Nalle
James Simms m. Elizabeth Nalle
Rebecca Simms m. John Petty

Then Rebecca Harrelson Simms was mentioned in Will of Paul Harrelson, Hanover Co., as his granddaughter. The children of Paul Harrelson and wife Rebecckah were:

1. Peter
2. Paul Harrelson, Jr.
3. Ann Harrelson m. Henry Chiles
4. Judith Harrelson
5. Joanne, m. Richard Simms (conjecture by W.E.B.) Or Rebecca, m. Thomas Sims.

So Rebecca Harrelson Sims could have been the daughter of either 1. Peter or 2. Paul, Jr.

Then Thomas Simms above is listed as son of William Simms will 1716, in Richmond Co., Va., wife Amy? Issue mentioned - 1. Thomas Simms, not 21, in 1716 m. Rebecca Petty. 2. Mary Simms m. Mathew Beans, 3. girl child m. Thomas Scott.

John Petty was the son of Thomas Petty of Richmond Co., Va., will 1716, in Richmond Co., Va., will prob. May 24, 1750, Orange Co., Va., wife Catherine Garton. Will mentions children

1. John Petty, b. x. 1708, d. 1770, m. Rebecca Simms
2. Thomas Petty b. x. 1710 m. Elizabeth Moore
3. Christopher b.c. 1711
4. William
5. James
6. Rebecca Petty m. by 1725, Thomas Simms
7. Mary Petty m. Knight
8. George Petty
9. Martha Petty.

Then Catherine Garton is dau. of John Garton of Richmond Co., wife Martha, he made will June 17, 1698, Martha alive in 1698. Issue:
Richard Garton was dead in 1798; John Garton; Matthew; Catherine m. Thomas Petty; Ruth.

Thomas Petty was the son of Capt. Thomas Petty. Born April or May 1664, m. 1685, Rachel Wilson, she was sister of Abraham Wilson. Capt. Thomas Petty d. will 1720, Essex Co., Va. South Farnham Parish, written 1719, Essex Co., Va. This Capt. Thomas Petty is assigned as son of Thomas Petty, Rappahannock Co., Va., died, will made Sept. 20, 1662, proved Jan.,7, 1663, Rappa. Co., wife Katherine Morric, Issue: 1. Dorothy

Petty m. 1st, James Fugett; 2nd, Godfrey Stanton. 2. Capt. Thomas Petty born in April or May of 1664, d. 1720, in Essex Co.

After Thomas Petty died in 1663, his wife Katherine Morris Petty m. John Long of King and Queen Co., Va. Issue: Catherine Long who married first, Edward Tunstall; 2nd, Richard Wyatt; Capt.

John Long died and Katherine Morris Petty Long m. 3rd, Thomas Gaines. m. 1671-1676; don't know if they had children.

Katherine Morris Petty Long Gaines was the dau. of Major George Morris of New Kent Co., Va., who died in 1685 and wife Elenaor: Issue was Katherine who m. Thômas Petty.

I have received Simms and Petty data from every corner of Va., and some from Ky. See if this ties in with your information. Mrs. R. M. Anderson, Route 3, Chatham, Va., has given me a lot of information and I do not have all of it cataloged properly. However, here is from the Petty side.

I, like you, am interested in straightening out all of these lines. My connection with the Petty-Simms lines is this. My Ann Ford m. James Sleet in Spotsylvania Co., Va., 1752; her father was John Ford and her mother Apphia, (Abfaer) Petty, he died in 1791 Culp. Co., and she was alive in 1806. Apphia Petty was the dau. of John Petty of Orange County, Va., and wife Rebecca Simms. John Petty's will prob. Sept. 27, 1770, in Orange Co., and it named wife Rebecca and 14 children and grandchild, Ann Ford.

My sister and I are preparing to publish a book on Gilmore-Carter and Allied Lines, but we will not publish anything we are not sure of. We have nine lines proved by DAR presently. I'll be glad to exchange help anwhere possible.

Yours truly, Dolly Barmann
(Mrs. Paul V. Barmann)

January 21, 1959

Inquiry 5388(A) Adams-Chiles-Harrelson.- Paul Harrelson left Will New Kent, Aug. 15, 1718, probated April 5, 1734, naming wife Rebecka, sons Peter and Paul, daughters Ann Chiles and Judith, granddaughter Rebecka Sims, the latter apparently being daughter of deceased daughter married to a Sims. Since Joanna, widow of Richard Sims was a widow at Orange 1746, it could not have been this Sims. I cannot place your Henry Chiles. One Henry Chiles and brother John were sons of John Chiles and wife Eleanor Webber, daughter of Henry Webber and wife Jane of King William. Proven by Deed of Henry Webber, June 2, 1724, Spottsylvania at which time John Chiles was deceased and his wife Eleanor had married Edwin Hickman. Henry Chiles, son of John and Eleanor married first Mercy Carr, and second Susanna, widow of John Graves (Will 1747 Spotts). Henry Chiles left a will at Spottsylvania probated Aug. 1, 1763, naming wife and sons Walto, John, Henry, William, James, Thomas Carr, Benjamin, daughters Sarah, Elizabeth and Ann Chiles and daughter Susannah Harley (Haley) who had two daughters who apparently her husband was deceased. John Chiles left a Will at Louisa Oct. 10, 1774, Will Book 2, page 198, and one of the witnesses was Susannah Haley. One Susannah Haley left Will in Kentucky. These Chiles, Haleys and Simms all came up to Louisa, Orange and Albemarle, and some went to Pittsylvania and some to Cambell County, hence probably of the same family. Susanna Chiles, widow of Henry left Will at Culpeper. Also James, son left Will in one of these counties.

W.E. Brockman

TERRETT

While Terrett is not strictly an Orange County family, marriage relationships with the Dades and Brockmans bring them into this area. Details of their English and Scotch ancestry has not been documented, but we know that Margaret Stuart great, great, daughter of Rev. David Stuart and wife Jane Gibbon, identify them with the Scotch Royal family of the Stewarts. Robert Bruce 1, King of Scotland had a daughter Princess Margery, who married Walter, Lor Stewart and this so far as I know is the beginnihg of the lineage of the American Stuarts. The second husband of Mary, Queen of Scotts, was of the Stuart family, and during her stormy career, a presbyterian clergyman by the name of David Stuart was much in the limelight of history. Darnby, known as Lord Bothby, the third husband of Queen Mary was also of the Stuart line and his clashes with Rev. Stuart take up much space in the history. Only one child was born to Mary, Queen of Scotts and he was James 1, of England, and history implies, if not accused, him of being born out of wedlock and that his real father was Darnby, a man who was typical of the politicians in those days and has been accused of many crimes, typical of the early rulers of that age. Frances Dade of one of the real prominent families of lower Virginia, married Chas. Stuart, son of Rev. David and Jane Gibbon. His son, Colonel Charles Stuart, married Helen Wray, and had Jacob whose daughter Margaret, married Colonel George Hunter Terrett, the officer who went on the Flagship Mississippi with Commodore Peary to open up Japan. William Henry Terrett, the immigrant, was born in England, 1707, and his wife was Margaret Pearson, daughter of Simon, whose family for nearly three hundred years was prominent in Alexandria County, Va. Henry Terrett was in Spottsylvania and his name is shown as witness to Wills there. Nathaniel Terrett, one of the family, arrived in Orange County, 1752, from Ireland, but apparently was a native of England. Captain George Hunter Terrett, son of Capt. W. H. Terrett and grandson of the immigrant was the founder of the Terrett home Oakland, near Alexandria and I went out there with Catherine Terrett Parsons in 1957, and examined the graveyard and found one stone with initials G. T. The graveyard is being preserved altho the property is now in the hands of non-relatives. The present house is on the old foundation, the house having being burned by the Northern Armies, 1864. George Hunter Terrett, father of Marguerite Terrett, wife of W. E. Brockman, the compiler of this record, was born there and attended the Episcopal school nearby. There is much data available on this family and I am in hopes that some of the Eastern relatives will compile it. William Henry Terrett, 1707-1758, was deputy clerk of Fairfax County at its origin, and he acquired 982 acres in 1741, and two tracts of 127 and 300 acres in 1746. His wife was Margaret Pearson. William Henry Terrett, the immigrant it was, made a Will dated February 7, 1755, in which he names Pearon, William H., Jr., Nathaniel and others. He gave son W. H. 1,000 acres. His widow married John West, and in her Will in 1798, she named Son William Henry, Nathaniel, Constance Washington, Susanna, and Roger West, apparently her own son. William Henry, the second married Amelia Hunter, daughter of Dr. John Hunter and Elizabeth Chapman, and granddaughter of Nathaniel Chapman and Constance Pearson. Captain George Hunter Terrett, the first to bear the middle name Hunter, was son of Capt. William Henry Terrett, 1752-1726, and his wife was Hannah Butler Ashton. He served in the War of 1812 and was pushed back by the British at Bladensburg, just out of Washington on the Baltimore Road.

George Hunter Terrett, 1807-1875, whose wife was Margaret Stuart had an eventful life and a sad ending. His granddaughter, Mrs. W. E. Brockman has a beautiful ivory miniature picutre of Margaret Stuart, with her father, George Hunter 11, made in Italy. Colonel George Hunter Terrett, a career military man was commissioned Second Lieutenant in the United States Marine Corps April 1, 1830. He continued in the

Marine Corps until April 1861, when he resigned to enter the Confederate States Navy. It is no doubt that the action of Robert E. Lee another Army officer in resigning to become a Confederate Officer, influenced his action. It was a step that brought to him and his family poverty, after living near Washington where he entertained for the Political and Military Leaders of the time. His career as senior Marine Officer of Commodore Peary's Flagship, the Mississippi was the high point in his military career. In 1844, he was senior Marine Officer on board the Flagship Cumberland in the Mediterrean. He was commissioned Major by Brevet to rank from September 13, 1847, "for gallant and meritorious conduct at the storming of the Castle of Chapultepec and his advance upon San Cosme Gate." A marker in the middle of a field between Junction City and Stockton, Texas, reads "Ft. Terrett in honor of Major George Terrett." The autobiography of Commodore Peary states that he left on the Mississippi, a United States Frigate on November 24, 1852. His picture in Oil by Pietro Graucivinia, Naples, 1851, was during his Mediterrean assignment. One of the Peary books shows a chart of some thirteen vessels anchored in Yokohoma Bay and locates the Flagship, Mississippi. February 13, 1854, the fleet under the Navy Command of Commander Henry Adams approached Edo where it anchored. A complete ship's log is available showing the location of the fleet from 1852 to its arrival in Japan, March 8, 1854. Much conversation and bickering went on as to the Protocol of meeting and receiving the Japanese on board ship, which is mindful of the recent Geneva conference. The treaty with Japan was signed March 21, 1854, the "Treaty of Kanajawa". The book "Bluejackets with Peary in Japan", by John R. C. Lewis is interesting. Peary mentions very few names of those associated with him. It looked as if he was reluctant to have any credit reflect on those who gave him several years of support in this historical venture. Subsequently a book written by a Japanese on the return visit to America is revealing and interesting as well as humorous.

Because of the limited Navy in the Confederate States, George Hunter Terrett was transferred as a Colonel in the Army where he rendered distinguished service, and after his capture at Charlotte Courthouse in 1865 and his imprisonment at the Old Capitol Prison in Washington, he took the oath of allegiance. His career as a military man was over--the South which he chose had lost carrying men and fortunes with it. Nearly a hundred years later, it has not yet recovered, physically or morally, as the minds of the olders are still bitter over an unwarranted attack by over zealous men of the North. Col. Terrett died in Washington in 1875, a disillusioned and unhappy man.

The genealogy of Margaret Stuart, who married Colonel George H. Terrett, is proven in the account given by Douglas Southall Freeman, Volume 1, on the life of George Washington. In his discussion of Chotank, a Washington plantation in King George County, south of the Potomac, he says "upstream from Chotank was first Cedar Grove, residence of Rev. David Stuart, he had come to Virginia in 1715 after the defeat of the Old Pretender, and had married Jane Gibbons, daughter of Sir John Gibbons, Governor of Barbados, and from 1731, has been Rector of St. Paul's** overlooking the valley was Litchfield, where the Dade family lived "Frances Dade, married Charles, son of Rev. David Stuart. James Stuart was son of James II. James I was son of Henry Stuart, Lord Darnley and Mary, Queen of Scotts, and he was King of England from 1603 to 1625. James II was son of Charles I and grandson of James I and he reigned from 1685 to 1688. He tried to restore Catholicism which angered the English and forced James to flee to France where he died in 1701. His son was proclaimed by the French to be "James III, King of England and Scotland", but his attempt to gain the throne of England ended in his defeat in Scotland in 1715, and then many of his supporters in England and Scotland including presumably his son Rev. David, a protestant sought refuge in Virginia. Two daughters, Mary and Anne, by his first wife of James II, were protestants and Mary had married William of Orange and the two came to England as ruling heads.

Again from Freeman: "The Ashtons of Nominy plantation, besides their link with the Tubervilles, were blended with the Lees, the Ayletts and many others. "The Ashton descent was thru Col. Henry Ashton, 1671-1731, son of John Ashton. A description of the Nominy plantation will be found in Eubank, page 47." Burditt Ashton, married Ann, daughter of Aug. Washington, and Hannah Butler Ashton married Captain George H. Terrett, and he was a descendant of Simon Pearson and Nathaniel Chapman, prominent men of the Potomac area.

HUNTER TERRETT FAMILIES OF FAIRFAX OR PRINCE WILLIAM COUNTIES OF VIRGINIA

Copied from the family Bible in the possession of Mrs. Leo C. Lloyd (Amelia Hunter) of Arlington, Va.

William Henry Terrett, born in England 4-19-1707 - died in Virginia
Married in Virginia January 27, 1735
Margaret Pearson - born in Virginia 3-5-1720.

	BORN	DIED	MARRIED
Pearson	5-21-1737	1-17-1755	
Mary	2-10-1739	8-18-1748	
Constant	12-26-1742		
Margaret	7-01-1745		
Susanna Maria Diana	11-15-1747		
Nancy	2-20-175-		
William Henry	11-21-1752		Amelia Hunter 7-25-1775
Thomas	8-26-175-	Sunday following	
Amelia	4-14-175-		
Nathaniel	3-04-1758		

William Henry Terrett born in Virginia 11-21-1752 died at Oakland about 1829.
Married in Virginia July 25, 1775.
Amelia Hunter born in Virginia (about) 1754, died about 1830.

	BORN	DIED	MARRIED
William Henry Hunter	5-13-1776		
George Hunter Terrett	3-13-1778	About 1844	Hannah Butler Ashton, 1801
Elizabeth Hunter	10-30-1780		
Peggy Hunter	11-8-1781		
Nathaniel	6-03-1784		
William Henry Hunter	1-04-1787	4-11-1790	
John Hunter	3-04-1790	About 1831	Julia Dade about 1812
Nancy Douglas	5-31-1794	About 1857	Allan Macrea about 1815
Nathaniel Chapman	11-26-17--		
Washington	4-11-1799		

George Hunter Terrett, born at "Oakland" 3-13-1778, died at "Oakland" about 1844.
Married 1801.
Hannah Butler Ashton of King George County, Va., born 11-2-1785, died 1860.

ISSUE	BORN	DIED	MARRIED
Wm. Henry	10-22-1803	8-11-1863	Susan Bushby
Mary Ashton	8-25-1805		Orris S. Payne
George Hunter	10-15-1807	1875	Margaret Stuart

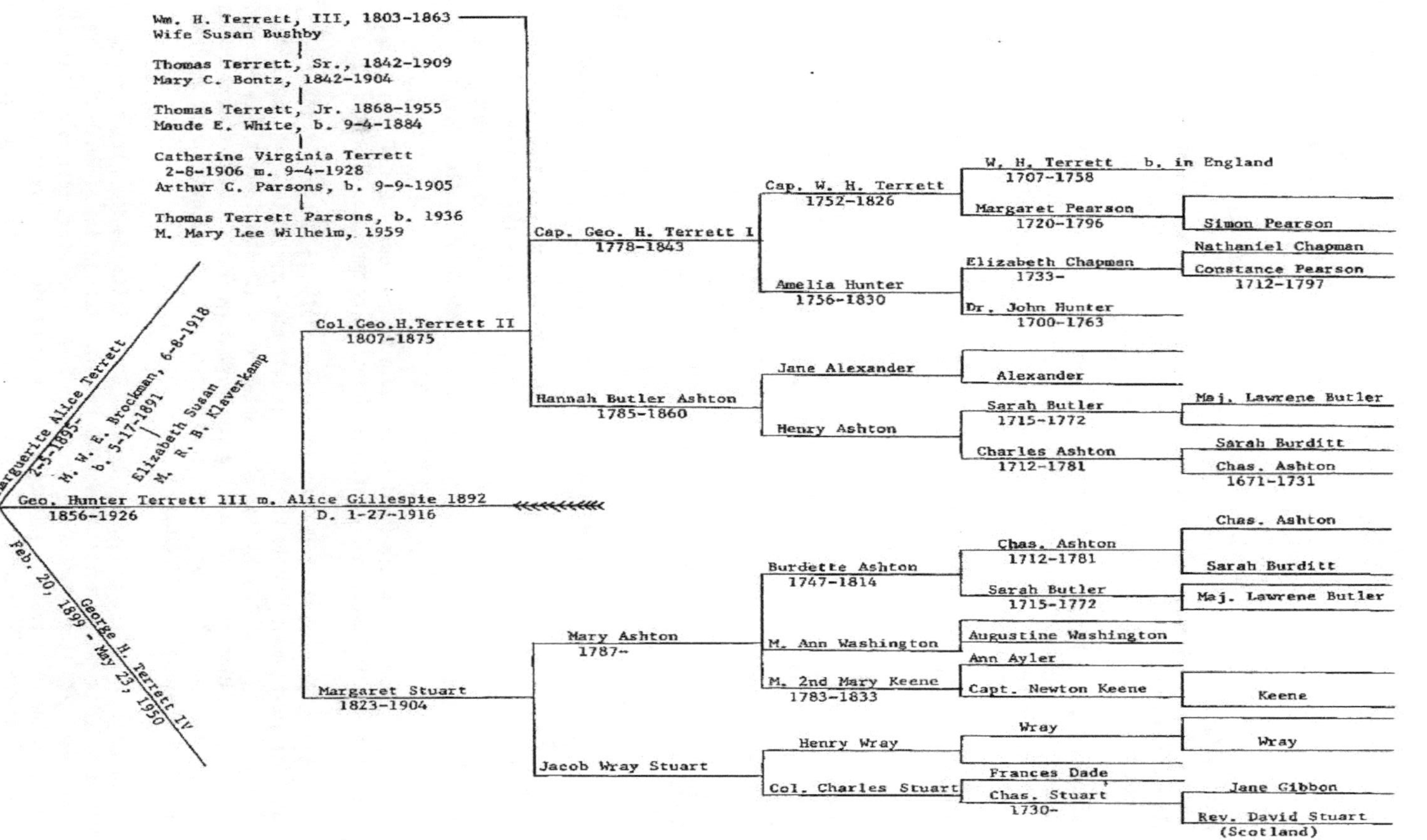

Wm. H. Terrett, III, 1803-1863
Wife Susan Bushby
Thomas Terrett, Sr., 1842-1909
Mary C. Bontz, 1842-1904
Thomas Terrett, Jr. 1868-1955
Maude E. White, b. 9-4-1884
Catherine Virginia Terrett
2-8-1906 m. 9-4-1928
Arthur C. Parsons, b. 9-9-1905
Thomas Terrett Parsons, b. 1936
M. Mary Lee Wilhelm, 1959
Marguerite Alice Terrett
2-5-1895-
M. W. E. Brockman, 6-8-1918
b. 5-17-1891
Elizabeth Susan
M. R. B. Klaverkamp
Geo. Hunter Terrett III m. Alice Gillespie 1892
1856-1926
D. 1-27-1916
George H. Terrett IV
Feb. 20, 1899 - May 23, 1950
Col.Geo.H.Terrett II
1807-1875
Margaret Stuart
1823-1904
Cap. Geo. H. Terrett I
1778-1843
Hannah Butler Ashton
1785-1860
Mary Ashton
1787-
Jacob Wray Stuart
Cap. W. H. Terrett
1752-1826
Amelia Hunter
1756-1830
Jane Alexander
Henry Ashton
Burdette Ashton
1747-1814
M. Ann Washington
M. 2nd Mary Keene
1783-1833
Henry Wray
Col. Charles Stuart
W. H. Terrett b. in England
1707-1758
Margaret Pearson
1720-1796
Elizabeth Chapman
1733-
Dr. John Hunter
1700-1763
Alexander
Sarah Butler
1715-1772
Charles Ashton
1712-1781
Chas. Ashton
1712-1781
Sarah Butler
1715-1772
Augustine Washington
Ann Ayler
Capt. Newton Keene
Wray
Frances Dade
Chas. Stuart
1730-
Simon Pearson
Nathaniel Chapman
Constance Pearson
1712-1797
Maj. Lawrene Butler
Sarah Burditt
Chas. Ashton
1671-1731
Chas. Ashton
Sarah Burditt
Maj. Lawrene Butler
Keene
Wray
Jane Gibbon
Rev. David Stuart
(Scotland)

ISSUE	BORN	DIED	MARRIED
Amelia Hunter	6-19-1810	9-17-1887	Nathaniel Chapman Hunter 5-25-1848
Burdette Ashton	8-21-1812	3-17-1845	Marion Bludworth 18--
Nathaniel Hunter	3-25-1815	9- -1901	Jane McCabe 12-4-1850
John Chapman	12-10-1817	9-21-1846	Unmarried
Washington	9-24-1820	1855	Unmarried
James Wallace	9-23-1822	18--	Unmarried
Frederic Augustus Chapman	10-28-1824	4-3-1895	Mary Wray Stuart 11-11-1851
Alexander Hunter	7-22-1827	2- -1885	Unmarried
Gibson Andrew	5-15-1830	2-10-1907	Victoria Teresa Young 6-3-1857.

Nathaniel Chapman H7nter, born at "Contemplation", Va., 1808, d. Washington, 9-13-1883.
Married at "Oakland", Va., May 25, 1848.
Amelia Hunter Terrett, born "Oakland", 5-9-1810, died Fiarfax County, Va., 1887.

ISSUE	BORN	DIED	MARRIED
Nathaniel Burdette	6-21-1885		Mabel Marshaw Hamer at Buffalo Dec. 14, 1911.
Hubert Chapman	8-15-1886	6-28-1887	
Melville Talbott	7-07-1888		
Amelia Lauretta	2-11-1892		Leo C. Lloyd, Sept. 23, 1915

ISSUE
Edith Amelia Lloyd married Charles Preston Scott, Cot. 1940.

ISSUE
Donna Amelia
Marcia Day

This is a true copy of the family Bible in the possession of Mrs. Amelia Hunter Lloyd of Arlington, Virginia:

(Signed) Anita Howard, State Chairman
Geneological Records, Virginia
Daughters of the American Rev.
5-25-1953 - Alex. Virginia

Several loose sheets were found in the Bible in the handwriting of Lida N. Hunter containing the following family records: (dictated by Nathaniel C. Hunter, Jr.)

After the death of Wm. Henry Terrett (b. 4-19-1707) his widow married John West, Jr., his first cousin, and by this marriage left one daughter (or maybe other children). On May 1, 1773, John West, Jr., and Margaret (Pearson Terrett) his wife deeded lands to Nathaniel Terrett. Our ancestor, William Henry Terrett, died therefore between 1757 and 1773. Margaret Pearson Terrett West was the daughter of Simon Pearson of Stafford County, Virginia.

In June, 1777, William Fairfax, agent of Lord Fairfax, deeded a tract of land to "Capt." William Henry Terrett of Fairfax Co., Va., heir at law of Wm. Henry Terrett, "deceased". It is my opinion that Wm. Henry Terrett must have settled at "Oakland" early in the 40's, possibly as soon as married. He seems to have purchased it in 1741. The second William Henry Terrett was doubtless born there, and there he died.

Chapman	10-11-1853	12-31-1916	Lida F. Newlon 10-1-1884

Nathaniel Chapman Hunter, Jr., born at "Oakland", Va., 10-11-1853.
Married at Falls Church, Va., Oct. 1, 1884.
Lida Florence Newlon, born at Bloomfield, Va., 2-5-1861.

George Hunter Terrett and Hannah Ashton were your grandparents and John Hunter Terrett and Julia Dade were mine.

(Signed) Anita Howard.

William Henry Terrett, b. "Oakland", Va., 10-22-1803, d. 8-11-1863, Virginia.
Married Susan Bushby of Wash. D. C.

ISSUE	BORN	DIED	MARRIED
William		about 1861	Unmarried
Thomas	1-21-1842	1-6-1909	Mary Catherine Bontz
Rebecca			John Jost
Charles			Unmarried
Chapman G.) twins			?
Susan E.)			Jerome Dorman

Thomas Terrett, Sr., b. Alex., Va., 1-21-1842, d. 1-6-1909.
Married Mary Catherine Bontz, b. 3-15-1842, d. 10-6-1904.

ISSUE	BORN	DIED	MARRIED
William Lee	9-02-1864	2-03-1946	Mae Dorman
Alice Rebecca	9-28-1865	4-21-1870	Unmarried
Thomas	8-10-1868	8-08-1955	Maude Emily White 1900
Hattie Virginia	2-03-1871	9-25-1891	Unmarried
Martha A.	9-26-1873		Vernon Rector
Henry Bontz	2-06-1876	5- -1938	Dora Bailey
Nettie L.	7-11-1878		Howard Clapp
Eva E.	11-19-1880		Thomas Row
Mary Grace	1-23-1884		Ollie Pearson
Frank P.	4-17-1887		Unmarried
Nellie R.	8-17-1889		Edward McCoy

Thomas Terrett, Jr., b. 8-10-1868, Fairfax Co., Va., d. 8-8-1955, Wash. D. C.
Married 2-27-1900, Fairfax Co., Virginia.
Maude Emily White b. 9-4-1884, Wash. D. C.

ISSUE	BORN	DIED	MARRIED
Thomas VErnon	11-18-1900		Mary Louise Hall (Va.)
Ruth Louise	7-10-1904		Sherod Leophart Earle II
Catherine Virginia	2-28-1906		Arthur Charles Parsons (Pa.)
Robert Walton	4-16-1907		Evelyn Madison Gooding (Md.)

Catherine Virginia Terrett, b. Fairfax Co., Va., 2-28-1906.
Married at Epiphany Episcopal Church 9-4-1928 at 8 P.M. to
Arthur Charles Parsons, b. Ormsby, Pa., 9-9-1905.

ISSUE	BORN	DIED	MARRIED
Charles Joshua II	5-27-1935	5-27-1935	
Thomas Terrett	12-15-1936		Mary Lee Wilhelm 6-13-1959
Arthur Charles Jr.	11-29-1942	11-29-1942	

After the War between the States, the Sons and Daughters of the Southland had little, left but their heritage. Many left the country and settled in South America. Others came West. George Hunter Terrett, son of Col George H. Terett, came to the middle west, finally settling in St. Paul, Minnesota, where he married and lived until his death in 1926. He was educated at the Episcopal Seminary at Alexandria with the idea of a ministerial career. Loss of the homestead and other factors caused him to change his career and he entered business with zest and enthusiasm where he was sucessful but continued his studious life up to the few monts prior to his death. His curiosity as to the origin and purpose of man and his relations with God are reflected in his writings. His library was replete with books by those considered the greatest thinkers and philosophers of our time. George Hunter Terett III, chose as his wife Alice Gilespie, a native of Wisconsin, who died in January, 1916. There were two surviving children, Marguerite Allice, wife of William Everett Brockman, and George Hunter Terrett IV, who died May 23, 1950, at Santa Monica, California, leaving a widow, Louise Frances Terrett. The Brockmans have one daughter Elizabeth Susan, born December 9, 1933. She was educated at Northrup Collegiate School, the Christian College, Columbia, Missouri, and graduated from the University of Minnesota in 1956, with a Bachelor of Arts degree as an Art Major. On August 24, 1957, she married Robert Bruce Klaverkamp, a native of Mankato, who was a graduate of Minnesota in Journalism. The couple now live in Tokyo, Japan, where Robert is connected with the United Press International.

From the ALEXANDRIA GAZETTE, 1909 - THOMAS TERRETT

Mr. Thomas Terrett, a popular and well known resident of Fairfax County, died at the Alexandria Hospital this morning. The deceased was about 67 years old. He leaves nine children, four sons and five daughters. His wife died about four years ago. From his frequent visits to Alexandria he became a familiar figure on our streets. Mr. Terrett was above the average in intelligence, having been studious throughout life. He was a close student of Shakespeare. Many of those who knew him best attest to his thoughtfulness and charity towards those who needed help. He always took an active part in the affairs of his native county and his counsel was valued by all.

(Thomas Terett, son of William Henry Terrett and wife Susan Bushby. William Henry was brother of Colonel George Hunter Terrett, 1807-1875).

TOWLES - CLARK - SMOOT

By Jeannette Wasson Gray.

STOCKELEY TOWLES

Stockeley Towles was the son of Henry and Ann Stockeley Towles. The Towles and Stockeley families were neighbors in Accomac Co. Stockeley was living in Middlesex Co., when he married Ann Vallott, daughter of Claude and Ann (Jenkinson) Vallott, on Oct. 21st, 1700, according to Christ Church Parish Records.

Children of Stockeley and Ann (Vallott) Towles

1. Oliver
2. John born April 5, 1712
3. Henry (First)
4. Elizabeth born Dec. 7, 1716

5. Ann born April 23, 1719
6. Catherine born July 5, 1721
7. Mary (first) born Nov. 1, 1723
8. Jane born Feb. 20, 1726
9. Joseph born Feb. 23, 1728
10. Frances born May 8, 1730
11. Stockeley
12. Judith born April 13, 1735
13. Lucy

Sometime after 1735, Stockeley removed from Middlesex County with his family to what was then Orange County, in a portion which in 1748 became Culpeper County.

He married secondly, Jane Sparks who at the time of her marriage was the Widow Wharton. Children of Stockeley and Jane Towles:

1. Mary (second) born April 12, 1749
2. Henry (second) born March 15, 1756

At the time of his death in 1757, Stockeley lived in Brumfield Parish of Culpeper County which in 1792 was organized into what is now Madison County. His will, dated January 15, 1757, was probated in Culpeper County on Dec. 15, 1757.

A law suit in chancery dated 1845 "Clarks Administrator vs. Towles' Executors", presumable filed in Madison County, Virginia, proves a list of his children, several marriages and some grandchildren.

WILLIAM CLARK

William Clark in 1736 married Ann James in Orange Co., Va. where he had settled with his brother, John, at the base of Clark's Mt. In 1745, William bought a plantation on Robinson River extending back to the base of Thoroughfare Mt. where his immediate neighbor was Stockeley Towles who had been a neighbor in Middlesex Co., of Edward Clark/

William's descendants are not in agreement concerning his parents. One group says he was the son of Edward Clark and his 3rd wife, Ann Christopher who were married in Middlesex Co., in 1706. In the "Parish Register of Christ Church, Middlesex Co., Va." 1653-1812 is this entry:

"William, son of Edward and Ann Clark, born April 26, bapt. June 10, 1716". Ref.: Folio 94. This William had brothers James, John and Bartholomew.

One descendant of this William Clark has had accepted colonial service for William Clark (49) in the Militia of Augusta Co., 1742, George Robinson, Capt. This birthdate of William would then be 1693. Virginia Magazine of History and Biography, Vol. VIII, 1900-1901, p. 33.

By 1752, Ann Clark had died and William had married Martha Foster. Children of William and Ann (James) Clark:

1. James Clark, born 1737, married Mary Marston
2. William Clark, Jr., born 1739, d. 1815, married Sarah Wharton

3. John Clark, born Feb. 19, 1741. Married Mary Towles
4. Reuben Clark, married Bathsheba Sampson
5. Ann Clark, married Zachariah Griffin
6. Lucy Clark, married Andrew Beck

Children of William and Martha (Foster) Clark:
1. Joseph Clark, born April 12, 1752, m. 1774 (1) Ann Haynes, (2) Catherine Canady - no issue
2. Robert (Robin) Clark, born 1754, d. 1855 in Orange. m. Joanna Jones
3. Larkin Clark, born in Elbert Ct. Ga., 1820, married Lucy Welch
4. Ambrose Clark, d. 1812, married 1796, Mary Thomas, Orange Co. prob.
5. George Clark, to Elbert Co., Ga., married Mary Thomas
6. Sarah Clark married Elisha W. Beckman

In 1739, John Taliaferro conveyed to William Clark for three lives "the said William, his wife Ann and his son James" land adjoining that which he patented in 1735 to John Clark and Joseph Fisher.

17 Feb., 1763, William Clark was paid 0.5.3 due him from the estate of the Reverend John Beckett, dec., Joseph James, administrator. Culpeper Co.

16 March, 1769, William Clark helped Robert Terrill and Thomas Piner appraise the estate of Benj. Powell.

18 May, 1769, William with Jasper Haines and William Sparks gave an inventory of the estate of Daniel Phillips.

17 May, 1770, Wm (x) Clark, Wm. (x) Sparks and Thomas Piner appraised the estate of Henry Sparks.

William Clark was an express rider in the Revolutionary War (Record of payment to Mary Bell for rider and horse stationed t her house in Orange by H. Young, Quartermaster, State Volunteers.

William Clark furnished supplies (bacon and rye) to the army and was paid in 1780. Public Service Claims Certificates 121-1,2. Culpeper Co. C 5290.

By his will, dated Oct. 20, 1787, probated Dec. 17, 1787, Culpeper Co., William Clark, Sr., "old ind infirm" left his land to his son Joseph and personal estate to some of his children. In Boughan et al v. Beckham et al, the Chancery suit, 1820 gives names of other children.

JAMES CLARK

James Clark, son of William and Ann (James) Clark was born in 1737 and died in 1789. He married Mary Marston, daughter of Hugh and Elizabeth (Towles) Marston. Said Elizabeth Towles was the daughter of Stokeley Towles and his first wife, Ann Vallott. Children of James Clark and Mary Marston Clark:
1. Elizabeth Clark married Thomas Boughon
2. James died young
3. Lucy b. about 1760 married Henry Sparks in 1776 in Culpeper Co., Va.
4. Ann (Nancy) Clark b. 1777, married James C. Garton (Gordon)
5. John Clark, born 1767, died 1852. Married 1st, Mildred Gibbs, 1786; 2nd, Mary Gaines, Culpeper Co., Va., St. Marks Parish.
6. Thomas Manson Clark, 1773-1836, married 1st, Mary Jones; 2nd, Catherine Robertson Jameson
7. Susanna Clark married William Marston, July 24, 1794
8. Frances (Fanny) Clark married Reed Smoot, May 31, 1796, Madison Co.
9. Mary (Molly) Clark married Moses Hudson, 1789, Culpeper Co.

10. Reuben Clark
11. Joanna Clark married Benjamin Hancock, Aug. 30, 1796
12. Joseph Clark married Mildred Smith Jameson
13. Rhoda Clark, married Lewis Willis, Feb. 2, 1801, died 1820.
14. Ambrose Clark married Ann Booten May 25, 1818.

All the foregoing signed a deed Jan. 25, 1823, to Joseph Hume, conveying land they had inherited from their Uncle Ambrose, and seem to have left Virginia, en masse except Thomas, who died not long after in Orange Co., Va.

James Clark's will is in Book C., p. 342, Culpeper Co., Va., date June 7, 1789, proven Sept. 21, 1789. In this will he lends to wife for 10 years a tract of land in Orange Co., Va., and "This tract of land I now live on in Culpeper Co." He appointed his wife and brothers William and Joseph executors. The plantation in Orange Co., was about three miles from the town of Orange on the road to Madison Mills; the other in Culpeper Co., now Madison, on the south side of the Robertson River, and apparently including the present village of Locustdale. Immediately south of this Madison Plantation was that of his brother, William; Rueben's plantation was near Culpeper. John was south of the Rapidan, east of the present village of Rapidan.

Capt. James Clark served in the Revolution from Culpeper Co.

WILLIAM READ SMOOT

William Read Smoot, the son of George and Anne (Beale) Smoot, was born in St. Mary's County, Maryland about 1767. He went to Virginia with his brothers and on May 31, 1796 in Madison County he secured a license to marry Frances Clark, the daughter of Capt. James and Mary (Marston) Clark.

The 1810 census for Franklin County, Kentucky shows William Read Smoot as head of a family with a wife, six young children and five slaves. In 1820, he had ten children at home, but had no slaves, and was engaged in agriculture. In 1840, he was listed for the first time as Reed Smoot. Children of William Read (Reed) and Frances (Clark) Smoot:

1. William Smoot, 1800-1843, married Martha Marston, daughter of William Marston, in Owen County, Kentucky on June 23, 1826.
2. George Smoot, 1801-1883, married Dorothy Dennis, 2nd wife Jane Goodrich.
3. Letitia Smoot, born 1805, married John Clements Nov. 16, 1821, Owen Co.
4. Mary Smoot married Ebenezer Wallace Aug. 12, 1824.
5. Reed Smoot, 1811-1873, married Harriett Claxon, Jan. 10, 1835, in Owen Co. To Pope County, Illinois in 1840's.
6. Nancy Smoot married 1. Noel Smither; 2. __?__ Hall.
7. Daniel Smoot
8. John Smoot
9. Druzilla Smoot married Pleasant Bush, May 29, 1839, Owen Co.
10. Thomas Smoot, born 1822, married 1st, Mary Smoot, daughter of William and Vianna (Moore) Smoot of Henry Co. Ky. His 2nd wife was Lucy Sparks, widow of Dr. F. Jones of Shelby County, Ky.

REED SMOOT

Reed Smoot (1811-1873) son of William Read and Frances (Clark) Smoot, married Harriett Claxon, daughter of Cassius Claxon II, and Harriet Henderson (?). They had five daughters, all born in Pope County, Illinois.

1. Nancy married 1. Willy Rose; 2. Washington Jackson.
2. Sarah (Sally) married 1. L. D. Webster; 2. W. T. Downey.
3. Elizabeth married Thomas Chipp.
4. Mary Amanda married Alexander Wasson.
5. Jane married John Franklin Wasson, brother of Alex.

Harry Wright Newman in The Smoots of Maryland and Virginia has traced the Smoots from the pioneer settler.

WILLIS FAMILY of Orange County, Virginia

Contributed by Kathrine Cox Gottschalk,
650 East Capitol St., N.E., Washington 3, D.C.

John Willis who died testate in Orange County, Virginia in 1762, married in 1735, in King George Co., Va. Elizabeth Plunkett. (Ref. St. Paul's Parish Reg.) He was born about 1710, and was the son of William and Sarah Willis of Richmond & King George Co., Va. His mother as the young widow of William Willis married a 2nd time to Henry Wood by whom she had one son, Henry Wood. As her third husband Rush Hudson, she had other children, named in her will. This Sarah maiden name unknown married a fourth time, as his 2nd wife, Mr. Edward Turberville. Edward Turberville had one daughter by his first wife, who married Walter Shropshire of King George Co., Va. In the settlement of the estate of Edward Tuberville in Orange Co., Va., the widow, Mrs. Sarah Turberville, received one third of his estate and Walter Shropshire received the other two thirds in right of his wife. The will of Sarah Turberville is recorded in Book 2, page 310, Orange Co., Va., dated June 18, 1760, and probated May 28, 1761. She named her children as follows, My son John Willis 1 shilling; my son, William Willis, 10 shillings; my son, Henry Wood, 1 shilling; my son David Hudson, 1 shilling; my son, Joshua Hudson, 1 shilling. To my daughter, Sarah Hawkins, all my wearing clothes. To Ruch Hudson's daughter, Sarah, 1 sheet; to Rush Hudson's daughter, 1 trunk. My son, Rush Hudson to be Executor of my estate. Wit: Benj. Hawkins, Moses Harwood, Kezia Rosser.

John Willis appears on the records of King George Co., Va., and also in Orange County. His will recorded in Book 2, page 323, Orange Co., Va., dated November 23, 1761, and probated November 25, 1762, devises as follows: To my son, Wm. Willis, Negroes, Thomas & Judith, and a lot of land in Culpeper Co., Va. To Edmund Terrell, two Negroes. To Walter Shropshire, 1 shilling, 3 pence. To each one of my children viz: John, Benjamin, Joshua, James, Reuben, Francis, Lewis, Moses and Mary, all of my estate to be equally divided after the death of my wife (Elizabeth). The place I own, formerly belonging to Mr. Marks, belongs to my son Benjamin Willis. The place that I live on to go to my son, John Willis. My son, John, and Edmund Terrell and my wife to be executors of my estate.

The son Benjamin of the above John and Elizabeth (Plunkett) Willis was a rich bachelor. He died testate July 16, 1810, at the age of 70 years, naming all of his brothers and sisters, also some of their children. The estate accounts give details about these heirs as follows: The marriages are taken from Orange Co., etc, where dates are given.

1. Reuben Willis, residing 1815 in Orange Co., Va., married Ann Garrett in 1776.
2. Joshua Willis, in Orange Co., Va., 1815. (Married Sarah ? . D. 1820 in Madison Co., Va.)

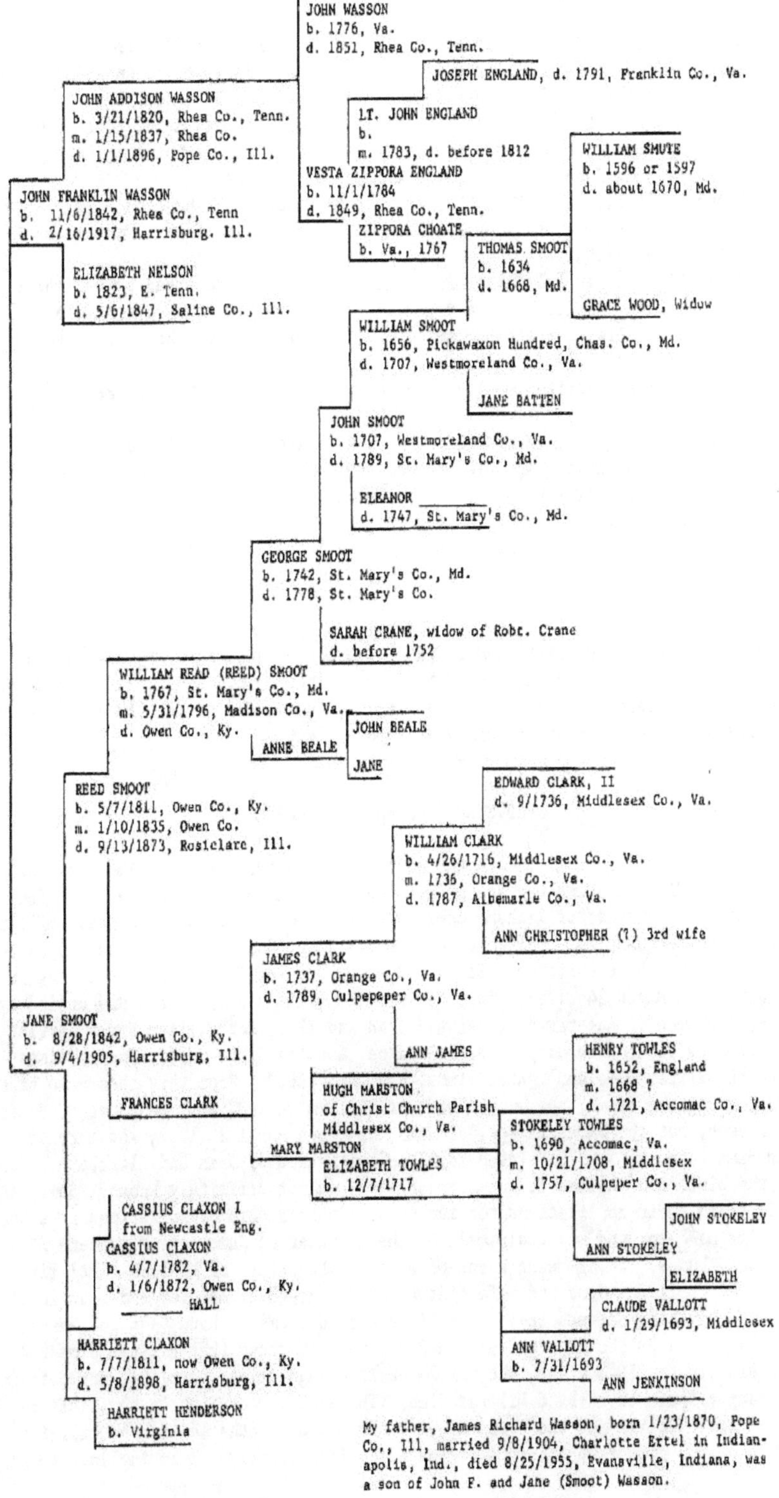

My father, James Richard Wasson, born 1/23/1870, Pope Co., Ill, married 9/8/1904, Charlotte Ertel in Indianapolis, Ind., died 8/25/1955, Evansville, Indiana, was a son of John F. and Jane (Smoot) Wasson.

Jeannette Wasson Gray
626 McKinley, Harrisburg, Illinois

3. William Willis, in 1816 was in Ky. He was born February 22, 1742, married and left issue: Issac, of Orange Co., Va.; William, Jr., of Ky. in 1816; Benjamin Jr., named for his uncle Benjamin, living 1816 in Louisa Co., Va.
4. Lewis Willis, living in 1816 in Georgia. (His wife was named Edna Tilman.) They signed deeds in Orange and in Culpeper Co., before going to Georgia. He was listed as an heir of his brother Benjamin's estate.
5. Frances Willis, m. 1. Thos. Morston; 2. Mr. Camp. Her husband died before 1815 and she, as a widow, was living in Culpeper Co., 1815. Heir of her brother, Benjamin.
6. Sarah Willis, married Walter Shropshire. Both were deceased by 6-4-1816.
7. Mary Willis, married Richard Price and was living in Kentucky in 1816.
8. Margaret Willis, married Edmund Terrell who pre-deceased her. She was deceased after 1810, and before June 14, 1816.
9. Moses Willis, married 1. Elizabeth Thomas; 2. Susannah White. He died in 1806 left heirs.
10. John Willis, (Jr.), married Sarah _?_. He died before 1810 leaving issue.
11. James Willis, living in 1810 married and left at least two sons, James and George Willis, living in Georgia in 1816.
12. Benjamin Willis, who died in 1810 unmarried, leaving as his heirs brothers and sisters and the heirs of his deceased brothers and sisters when his estate was settled in 1816.

Other records of the Willis family name in Orange and Culpeper belong to Henry Willis, Gentleman, of Spotsylvania Co. No relationship or connection has been discovered in our research between this Henry Willis, Gent., and the family of the above John Willis or his parents or his grand parents. (K.C.G.)

STEP-STAP-STEPP-STAPP-STEEP

Interest in this name is due to the marriage of Captain William Simms to Anestar Step in 1751. William Simms was son of Richard Simms and wife Joanna, and the family lived in Orange County after Richard came up from one of the lower counties. William Simms was born February 25, 1731, married Anestar Step, daughter of Joshua, August 6, 1751. There were three children: Elizabeth, born Dec. 3, 1752; James, born May 10, 1755; Lucy, born March 24, 1758. This is from the William Simms Bible and copied by me (W. E. Brockman). Anestar died between 1758 and 1760, for William Simms married as his second wife, on February 2, 1761, Agatha, and the Bible reads "Joanna Simms, daughter of William Sims and Agatha Simms, was born 1762". From this record we have assumed that Agatha Simms, the second wife of William was a Simms, daughter of James and Elizabeth, but the James is spelled JAMS, was born April 2, 1737, and married William Sims February 2, 1761" (died 1812). The surname of Jams and Elizabeth is torn out of the Bible and whether it was Step or Sims, is not definitely known. Some of the descendants in their applications for membership in Patriotic organizations give her name as Agatha Step, and she could well be the daughter of James and Elizabeth Step, (dau of John Lucas), James being a son of Joshua, the father of William Sims' first wife Anestar. William Sims and wife Agatha named a daughter Anester and I am inclined to believe that her name was Step. The Bible record seems to have been deliberately torn out and perhaps the grandchildren did not want it known that William Sims had married his first wife's niece, who was 24 years of age at her marriage, and but six years younger than her husband William Sims. The spelling of Sims in the Bible record as the name of William and the spelling with two M's of Agatha led to the belief that they were of two different branches of the Sims, Simms family. I am inclined to go along with the D.A.R. relatives and accept Agatha as a daughter of James and Elizabeth Step and she named her fifth child Anestar after her predecessor and perhaps Aunt Anestar Step Sims. The Bible is confused and written all over some of the printed pages and in one place there appears "---------(I omit the name) died today by his own hand". In another William Sims Bible the family known as the Madison Sims, one sons name is erased because he had displeased his father. Much on the Sims family appears in my previous books so I will not repeat here. Capt. William Sims had thirteen children, and their names appear in two deeds in Albemarle County in the transfer of the home place in part to Samuel Brockman who married Anester Sims. James Step that we accept as father of Agatha Sims, is believed to have been a son of Joshua Step, and he is shown as a resident of Orange in 1758, with three tithables. His father is Joshua shown in 1755, with nine, but he was guardian for five children of his brother, John, and perhaps they had reached 21 and had remained with him. The name Step first appears in my research in the Will of Robert Moss, Essex, August 8, 1685, and probated April 3, 1689. Half of his estate goes to his wife Rebecca and legacies to daughter Dorothy, wife of Abraham Step (Stapp) and to Rebecca and Martha Stapp, daughters of Abraham. Elizabeth, widow of Thomas, brother of Robert Moss, married second Edmund Crask, and her Will, 1683, leaves legacies to Martha Stapp. Abraham Stapp left a Will at Essex Oct. 20, 1710, naming wife Dorothy. His son, Abraham, February 17, 1718, conveys to John Jones the plantation where his father Abraham dwelt prior to his death. Dec. 8, 1719, William Step and brother Joshua, appoint John Foster, attorney, to acknowledge deed which was witnessed by William Mason, the latter appearing in Culpeper later. The Will of Joshua Step at Orange mentions only his grandchildren, but Dec. 23, 1775, Joshua gives to granddaughter Elizabeth Sims, a Negro, Ben, and to son James, four Negroes. Grandson Achilles mentioned in Joshua's Will, served in the State Militia Revolutionary War and married Margaret Vawter, Nov. 27, 1782, and removed to Scott County, Kentucky. His brother Thomas married Betsy Burbage, 1776. Somewhere in my records there is a record of James Step and wife Elizabeth, but I fail to locate them at this time. It took me three trips to Albemarle County to the home "Aspen Grove" bought by the Sims family from the Ruckers to find the Sims Bible in the attic which present owners could not locate. Getting data is not easy. A valuable diary of Robert Ellis is to be found on Micro-film at the Virginia State Library, but the holders of it have not been willing for me to reprint it, apparently preferring to have people travel to Charlottesville and ruin their eyes looking thru a projector, which I myself did. The Steps and Sims intermarried much. November 16, 1753, Henry Gains reports as administrator of John Step at Culpeper and makes allowances for five children who are under the Guardianship of Joshua Step and then says "paid to me one third of the estate due my wife". So he had married the relict of John Step. Joshua is also guardian to Thomas and Elizabeth Lucas, orphans of Thomas Lucas at Orange. Frances Sims, daughter of Thomas, Jr., at Culpeper, married Joshua Morris, whose mother was Elizabeth Step. The name Rebecca is all thru the Sims and Step families and it is my opinion that Samuel Brockman II, married Rebecca, sister of Capt. William Sims. Equal candidates however are Graves, sister of Thomas, and Step, daughter of Joshua.

In April, 1958, I took a trip thru the lower counties of Virginia and spent some time at the library in Richmond. As I drove thru King and Queen Co., past the York and the Pamunkey Rivers through King William I felt like a homing pigeon as I went over Port Tobago Road where Samuel Brockman had his plantation on 1731, and perhaps a long time before. Right near Newtown I saw a sign reading Greenway which is the name of the Brockman homeplace in Orange where Samuel Brockman first built the White House. In Charlottesville, I saw the land survey of John Robinson, November 17, 1746. It was in the Engineers Book and located the Robinson land on the Rivanna just north of the bend and a island in the stream. It was next to Samuel Brock(man), and Samuel must have gotten his land somewhere around 1744 when William Marshall was transferring land to legatees of the Marshall family and perhaps Betty Brockman, wife of William got the land that way. In 1775, William, son of Samuel, transferred along with Richard Durrett and Thomas Jones, 370 acres which is also presumed to come from the Marshalls and the Durretts and just the connection with the Brockmans is confusing to say the least. I believe Elizabeth or Betty, wife of William Brockman was Elizabeth Mason, born in St. Peters Parish 1729, but just which Brockman, Samuel or son William, married a Mason and which a Marshall is unknown by this writer. I found the Bible of Captain William Simms and saw that "Agga Simms, daughter of Jams and Elizabeth (then torn) was born April 2, 1737, and married William Sims, February 2, 1761." She could have been the daughter of James Simms and wife Elizabeth (Will Culpeper 1802) who had a daughter Agatha or she could have been a daughter of James and Elizabeth Step. There is some indication that Rebecca wife of Samuel Brockman II, was a sister of Capt. William Simms but this is not certain. Several descendants of Captain William Simms have joined the D.A.R. on data that his wife was Agatha Step, but the record is not entirely correct, but does show that William Simms was born Feb. 25, 1732, but most likely in Orange as I have not known of any Sims that lived in Fairfax, however, in genealogy anthing is possible and always probable.

A lawsuit at Albemarle, 1799, proves that Frances, wife of Thomas Brockman was a daughter of Henry Shelton and she was dead at the time of the suit.

A Note of Thanks to

Mary Pauline Howard who has been the largest Single Contributor to the history of the Albemarle County Families recorded in this Book.

Mary Pauline Howard, daughter of Napoleon Bonaparte and Sarah Mildred Mitchell Howard, born July 14, 1904, on a farm (part of the Brockman "Bleake Hill" tract) Burnleys, Virginia. Granddaughter of Lucetta Elizabeth Brockman Mitchell. Attended public schools of Albemarle and Amherst Counties. Graduated from St. Vincent de Paul (now De Paul) Hospital School of Nursing Class of 1924. Married Maurice Adolph Brandt II, Oct. 3, 1928. Residence - Old Brandt Home, 627 Boissevain Ave., Norfolk, Virginia.

T The Will of Robert Moss, Essex Co., August 8, 1685, proved April 3, 1689, mentions wife Rebecca and children:

1. Robert.
2. Dorothy, married Abraham Step.
   a. Rebecca
   b. Martha
   c. Joshua, whose daughter married William Simms, 1751.
3. Daughter married Jeremiah Parker, son of Thomas.

The Will also mentions brother Thomas, and his children Elizabeth and Frances. Will of Thomas Moss, March 3, 1678, proved June 13, 1678, mentions wife Elizabeth, children Elizabeth and Frances. Elizabeth, the widow of Thomas married Edward Crask. Thomas also mentioned brother William and his son and daughter but not by name.

The name of the wife of Joshua Step is not known for certain. She was apparently deceased when he wrote his Will. He is thought to have had atleast sex children:

1. Anester, married William Simms. (deceased when father made will)
2. Son, who had son Achilles. Revolutionary Soldier, married 1786.
3. Daughter married Wilhout, daughter Lucy.

4. Daughter, married Creel, daughter Sarah.
5. Daughter, married Hubbard, daughter Martha.
6. James Step, married Elizabeth Lucas.

From "Virginia Colonial Abstracts" by Fleet, Vol. 8, Essex Co., Wills - Deeds.
Page 81 (p. 234) - Will of Abraham Stapp of Essex Co., dated 20 Oct, 1710 - probated April 8, 1714.

To son Abraham Stapp, all land on N. side of Road of "my now dwelling plantation". To son William all land on S. side of Road. To son Jacob Stapp, upper part of land bought of Edward Moseley, and to son Joshua Stapp, the lower part bordering on Mr. Robt. Brooke. To young Joseph Stapp and James Stapp, 25 acres each of lower land. Jacob and Joshua to buy them 100 acres each elsewhere. To wife Dorothy, all property during life time. To daughter Ruth Stapp, cattle. To daughters Rebecca and Martha Stapp, a shilling each.

Signed - Abraham Stapp

Wit: Robert Moss
Peter Hollon
Will Harte - his mark -

P. 234 - Bonds - 8 April, 1714, L 300. Sterling
Dorothy Step (Sic)
Extx. Abra. Step
Wit: John Prickett — Dan'll Hayes
Daniel Bronn — John Hart
Rec. 8 Apr. 1714.

Orange County Will Book 3, 1778-1801.

Copy of the WILL OF JOSHUA STAPP

"In the name of God, Amen. I, Joshua Stapp, of the County of Orange, being in perfect health and sound sence and memory and mindfull of the uncertainty of this life do make and ordain this my last will and testament in manner and form following: First I give my soul to Almighty God who gave it me trusting in Jesus Christ for the remission of my sins and as for what worldly goods it hath pleased God to bestow me, I give in manner and form following viz:

ITEM
My will and desire is that my Negro man and Negro woman, BM be both free and at their own disposal and if there should be any charges required by the Court towards their being legally set free from bondage, then my will is that such charge be paid out of my Estate.

ITEM
My will is that my grandson, Achilles Stapp, have my Negro woman, Cate.

ITEM
I give the residue of my estate not already mentioned to be divided between the persons whose names I hereafter mention (viz.) my grandson, Achilles Stapp; my granddaughter, Lucy Willhort; my granddaughter, Sarah Creel; andy my granddaughter, Martha Hubbard, to them and their heirs forever.

ITEM
My will is that my Estate be not sold but be appraised and divided according to appraisement.

ITEM
Lastley, I constitute and appoint my grandson, Achilles Stapp, Executor to this my last will and testament revoking all former wills by me made acknowledging this to be my last will and testament in witness whereof I have hereinto set my hand and seal this 19th day of December, one thousand seven hundred and eighty two.

Signed, Sealed and Published in presence of:

John Payne
John Wayt
William Wayt

Joshua his x mark Stapp (Sg)

At a Court held for Orange County on Thursday, March 27th, 1783, this last will and testament of Joshua Stapp, deceased, being presented into Court by Achillis Stapp, Executor, therein named and proved by the oaths of John Wait and William Wait two of the witnesses thereto and ordered to be recorded and on the motion of the said Executor who made oath acording to law Certificate is granted him for obtaining Probate thereof in due form whereupon he with Robert Miller his security, entered into Bond for the same in the sum of two hundred, fifty pounds.

TESTE: James Taylor, C.D.C."

Orang County Record, D.B. 13, page 297 - Nov., 1762.

John Lucas, son of John Lucas deceased to Eliz. Step, aunt of said John Lucas, 200 A. and one Negro "accoding to the will 1758 of William Lucas deceased, grandfather of said John Lucas". John Lucas Exec., Wit: Zach. Taylor, Zach. Burnley and Wm. Lucas.

D. B. 14, page 288, April 26, 1769.

Wm. Lucas and Mary his wife and Thomas Stapp to Joseph Holladay, 107 A. for 70 lb. on Marsh Run - part of Wm. Lucas land. Wm Lucas
Mary Lucas
Thomas Stapp

One Thomas Stapp married Betsy Barbage, January 4, 1779. I believe he was a grandson of Joshua. (P.H.B.) I think he moved to Woodford Co., Kentucky.

From "Virginia Soldiers of 1776" by Burgess. Vol. page 1443.
Achilles Stapp served in State Line in Rev. War. Achilles married Margaret Vawter November 27, 1782, and removed to Scott County, Kentucky. His brother, Thomas also of Orange County, Virginia married Betsy Burbage, 1776.

From "Marriage Records of Brunswick County" by Augusta B. Fothergill. Page 112.
November, 1774 - Step, Thomas, Susanna Clark, dau. of Joshua. (W. B. IV - 244)

"In Orange County Deed Book 16, page 393, is recorded a deed conveying from Joshua Stapp to his son, James, four Negroes. One of the witnesses was William Sims. On the same day, December 23, 1775, Joshua Stapp coveyed to his granddaughter, Elizabeth Sims of Albemarle, a Negro boy named Ben. Witnesses included William Sims."

BROCKMAN

The genealogy of this family has been treated in previous books compiled by me, and the most recent two, the "Brockman Scrapbook" and Orange County Virginia Families Volume II". These two books and my book on the Hume and Kennedy Families are at this writing available, the former books are now out of print. This chapter is to supplement and correct previous books. The Offical records of Cheriton, Kent County, England, recently confirmed, show the birth of Henry Brockman November 8, 1623, and since Sir William Brockman had lost a son Henry in 1622, three years of age, speculation has existed as to this Henry being a son, as it was the custom of the family to name new children after those deceased. The Drake-Brockman family, who inherited the Kent property through a female line, believe that Henry, the emigrant to Maryland was a son of Thomas, cousin to Sir William. A brother Zouch had a son William and a grandson Henry, and his will is of record at Cheriton, June 2, 1696. Zouch whose will at Cheriton was proved November 27, 1680, was father of William. Our best calculations are that Henry of Maryland was grandson of Thomas, and second cousin to Sir William. It must be remembered that several generations lived in the same household in early days of England and such homesteads had forty to fifty rooms, and the record of a birth, does not always indicate the parentage, and this was the case of Henry Brockman, born 1623. Henry son of William of Cheriton, was married in 1714, but the marriage record does not indicate the name of the bride, but by that time, Samuel Brockman of Virginia, presumably the son of another Henry was already married and had offspring. All of the Virginia Brockmans with the exception of Aaron of Louisa have been identified, and no descendants can be found of John Brookman (two o's instead of a c) buried from Bruton Church, 1696, or of John Brocke, who came with Francis Osborne to the York area in 1637, and he was deceased by 1664.

Richard Osborne was custodian of Charles I, the first being at Osborne House, Isle of Wight, with Charles at Garisbroke Castle. Richard Hamone was officer in charge of Charles I, and Gen. Mainwarring Hammond, Royalist, under Cromwell, was awarded 4,000 acres on which he built the White House near West Point, Virginia, later passing into the hands of the Bassetts, and then to the Curtis Family. During 1636, 64 new settlers went to St. Michaels, Barbados, to escape the turbulent conditions in England. There we found Thomas Brookman and Henry Brockman was picked up there and brought to Maryland.

The Following Letter from Mr. Leonardo Andrea, a famous Authority on Genealogical Research is interesting.

4204 Devine Street
Columbia 55, S.C.
9 October 1950

Dear Mr. Brockman,

Your letter came just after my return from Greer, S.C. where I had gone to make a talk before the local DAR Chapter.

I do not have that chart of which you spoke as being from Frankfort, Ky. If I had had the chart, I would long before have sent it to you.

My references were made from an old scrap book of clippings which a friend of mine had and which she had taken from all sorts of odds and ends of miscellany taken from old genealogical pages of magazines and newspapers. Some of the clippings were so old and yellowed and all were cut close without date or newspaper. Many however were from a Memphis newspaper and many from an Atlanta Ga. newspaper, the extinct Georgian.

I called Miss Annie Locke of the Richland County Library who is a native of Alabama. She has some of the clippings from the Georgian but her scrap book does not have the Brockman one.

Miss Bertie Smith, a first cousin of my stepmother, had this old scrap book. She died long ago and I was at the home of her mother, the late Mrs. Ella Holtzclaw Smith of Greer and got the data from her scrap book. Aunt Ella was a sort of a hermit after Bertie died. I tried to get her to give to me all the trunk full of papers that Bertie had collected, but she would not. After Aunt Ella died some two years ago, I wrote to Mr. Murray Hughes of Greer, S.C., who was executor of her estate and asked Mr. Hughes if he would allow me to have that old trunk or its contents. He replied that he would let me know what the heirs wanted.

I understand that there was a general and wholesale burning of the old papers. I do know that mother's brother, Lee Green Smith did salvage some of the old photographs and I saw them recently and saw these. Uncle Lee said that Aunt Ella's nieces who were her heirs came from out of state and burned in a bon fire, all the old papers, scrap books and other data.

You may write to Mr. Hughes in Greer, and ask him if he has any idea as to what became of all these valuable papers. I had suggested to him that all the old papers ect be given to the S.C. Society Library......That old paper gave descent of John Brockman (Bertie joined DAR thru his service) thru Henry Brockman of Barbadoes and wife was Rebecca and a Rebecca Salmon I am sure the scrap book said. Any way, Rebecca Salmon was wife of one of them...It also said that the Brockman's of Barbadoes were Catholic and joined the Catholic colony of Maryland under Lord Baltimore and that the Brockmans had left England after the Protestants took over there and refused to allow Catholic services and his father came to Barbadoes.

There was much in that old clipping said based on a chart or old paper of much age owned by some of the Brockmans in Kentucky.

At the time, I was not much interested in genealogy, but I did make some notes on it......Henry Brockman to Maryland was son of Thomas and Amey......Henry Brockman wed Rebecca Salmon and had a son Samuel who was only heir...This Samuel was Protestant and b. Maryland but when small to Virginia, is how it seemed to run.

Perhaps Mr. Hughes of Greer can let you know what became of the trunkful of old papers. He has never told me, but may tell you. All that I know is that Uncle Lee Smith told me they were all burned in a bon fire......Anyway that Brockman chart was in one of Bertie's scrap books, pasted in and clipped from some paper.

I made sure that you had already had access to this paper.

I was in Greenville and Pickens Counties in S.C. making a study of Hunt records and many times I noted Brockman intermarriages as well as Groce and then Groce and Hunt and Brockman.

I am now making a study of Haley data in S.C. for a client, but find very little. The first Haleys in S.C. were from Va. and settled down Sumter Co. way among the Collins-Bashaw set. Tisdales were among them and old John Tisdale named a son, Haley Tisdale and one Sherwood...I am inclined to think that John Tisdale (b. 1731) married a Haley or a James. The James came down also and were neighbors of Tisdale and Haley as well as Ridgeway and one Ridgeway wed a widow Haley it seemed.

I am sorry that I can be of so little help on this so-called chart. I presumed that you had it since I knew that many years ago you had had some correspondence with Cousin Bertie Smith. In fact it was not a chart she had, but a clipping based on an old chart owned by some Brockman in Kentucky......As to Eleanor, it did not say chart prepared by her....At the time, I did not know exactly how to abstract records and my notes are crude compared to what I would have made now.

Yours sincerely,

P.S. By the way many Salmon-Sammon records in S.C. and mainly in Laurens-Spartanburg-Greenville where a George Salmon came early. This George knew the Brockmans as noted by his name as witness and surveyor for the first Brockmans in S.C.........L.A.

BROCKMANS DESCENDED FROM ESSEX COUNTY FAMILY,
ENGLAND, DATING BACK TO JOHN BROKEMAN WHO RECEIVED AN ESTATE AND COAT OF ARMS
WITH THE CRUSADERS CROSS FOR THE FAMILY SERVICE DURING
THE CRUSADES - ESSEX ESTATE GRANTED UNDER RICHARD II.

Thomas Brookman, wife Amy buried in the Barbadoes 1678

Henry Brockman in Maryland 1674

Samuel Brockman of King and Queen County, Virginia, Planter, 1731
Believed to be living on Estate of his In-Laws, 1704

-1-

Children of Samuel Brockman and wife Mary, Will Orange, 1766. (She died 1776.)

1. Samuel, m. Rebecker by 1744; died 1790. Wife died 1814.
2. William of Albemarle, m. Elizabeth Mason by 1748. Will 1809.
3. John, m. Mary Collins by 1734, died 1756. Widow married Kelly Jennings.
*4. Mary, m. Richard Hunt Singleton. He died 1774, Williamsburg.
*5. Elizabeth, m. Anthony Street.
*6. Rachael, m. John Rogers.
*7. Dau. (Susanna) m. Haley, John Haley, legatee.

* children given in preceding books.

-2-

Children of Samuel Brockman and wife Rebecker:

*1. Mary, m. Jacob Crossthwaite, Oct. 11, 1764.
2. William, m. Mary Lindsay.
3. John, m. Elizabeth Burrus by 1776.
4. Sallie, m. Thomas Bell.
5. Jemima, m. William Hancock.
6. Susan (Sukey) m. Thomas Garnett.

-3-

Children of William Brockman of Albemarle and wife Elizabeth Mason:

1. John, (Rev. Express Rider) m. Elizabeth Smith, died 1795. Widow married W. W. Embre.
2. Thomas, (Rev. Soldier) m. Frances Shelton.
3. William Mason, m. Mary B. Smith, 1784.
4. Ambrose, m. 1st, Nancy Simms; 2nd, Franky Johnson.
5. Samuel, m. Ann (Anestar) Simms, Jan. 14, 1790.
6. Frances, m. James Taylor (See Will).

7. Elizabeth, m. William Brockman of Orange.
8. Margaret (Peggy), m. Richard I. Henderson.
9. Catherine (Caty), m. Roger Bell, Dec. 25, 1789.
10. Nancy, m. Thomas Wells, dau., Nancy.

-4-

Children of John Brockman and wife Mary Collins:
1. Samuel, m. Mary Bell; 2nd, Christian Woolfolk, c. 1778, widow of Joseph.
2. John, (Rev. Soldier) m. Amelia Martin, after 1757.
3. Joseph, m. Mary Page, April 15, 1773.
4. Susannah, m. John Atkins. c 1752.
5. Sarah, may have married Joseph Atkins.
6. Elizabeth, may have married Aaron Bledsoe, Jr.
7. William, (Rev. Lieut., 1777) m. Elizabeth Brockman of Albemarle.
8. Hannah, m. William Toler of Goochland.
9. Mary, m.
10. Rachael, m. Robert Page.
11. Major, (Rev. Soldier) m. Elizabeth Patterson, d. 1823, Caswell, N. C.

-5-

Children of William Brockman and wife Mary Lindsay:
1. Caleb Lindsay Brockman, b. 1781, d. by 1814.
2. Joshua Lindsay, b. 1783, d. 1837.
*3. Samuel Lindsay, m. Frances Ann Graves, b. 1799. M. 11-23-1825.
4. William Lindsay, m. Elizabeth Catherine Graves.
5. Curtis Lindsay, m. Nancy Quisenberry, Oct. 28, 1811; 2nd, Sarah Elanore Daniel, widow, 7-28-184-.
6. Lindsay Ellis, m. Susan Jemima Graves, Feb. 4, 1839. Moved to Mo., d. 1860.
7. Elizabeth Lindsay, m. 1st, C. B. Bronaugh; 2nd, Mason of Ky.

-6-

Children of John Brockman (Appt. Lieut. Feb. 1777) and wife Elizabeth Burrus:*
1. Samuel Burrus, m. Nancy Durrett, 1791.
2. Eleanor, m. 1st, Aaron Croosthwait; 2nd, John Ireland.
*3. Elyjah, m. Sally Tomlinson.
4. Molly, m. James Mallory.
5. Jacob Burrus, m. Jane Burrus, 1810.
6. Stephen, m. Elizabeth Embree (See Vol. 2)
7. John, m. Ann Minor Meriwether; Mary Kenneth Estes; Catherine Jenkins.
8. Rebecca, m. Brockman Bell, 1810.
9. Asa, m. Lucy Ellis Quisenberry, 1819.
10. Oswald, m. Mary Frances Shisler, 1830.
11. Thomas, died unmarried.

-7-

Children of John Brockman and wife Elizabeth Smith:
1. Elyjah, m. Fanny Harrison, Oct. 22, 1795.
2. Polly, m. Jasper Franklin, Oct. 27, 1796.
*3. William, m. Elizabeth Henderson, Feb. 15, 1813.
4. Elizabeth, m. Overton Harris, Dec. 18, 1806.
5. Frances.
6. Vallatilda.
7. Sally, m. Alexander Marr; 2nd, John Smith.

-8-

Children of Thomas Brockman, Rev. Soldier and wife Frances Shelton: (He died intestate 1838; buried in Montgomery County, Ill., body later removed to Missouri. Wife died by 1799.)
*1. Thomas, b. 1806, m. Mahla Turner, Feb. 4, 1830.

2. Samuel, b. Feb. 26, 1808, d. Jan. 12, 1881. M. 2nd, Charlotte L. Brown, dau. of Richard and Sarah Womack Brown, whose brother married a daughter of Thomas, Sr. Charlotte died 1866.
3. Ambrose, m. Maria, d. Johnson County, Mo., 1847. See Miscel. Brockman notes.
4. Shelton of Kentucky.
5. John, wife Mary Jane (d. 1873).
6. Mahala, m. Richard Scaggs, March 6, 1835.
7. Daughter married Brown.

-9-

Children of William Mason Brockman and wife Mary B. Smith:

1. Sarah, m. Robert Brockman, son of Joseph., June 16, 1826.
2. James, m. Jane Marshall, June 3, 1833.
3. Catherine, m. Dabney Spicer, April 2, 1817; d. by 1831. M. 2nd, John Lewis, January 25, 1833. See Brockman Miscel.
4. Elizabeth, m. Harris, parents of Overton; 2nd. Mahannes, Nov. 20, 1802. See Brockman Miscel.
5. Mary, m. Thomas Rhodes, April 5, 1813.
6. Frances, m. James McCallester also McAlister, June 4, 1821.

-10-

Children of Ambrose Brockman and wives, Nancy Simms and Frankey Johnson. Ambrose born June 28, 1764, died Oct. 4, 1823, m. Nancy Simms, born Feb. 9, 1765, died Sept. 16, 1821, m. Franky Johnson, 1823.

1. John Mason, b. April 8, 1795, wife Maria Watson, b. 1797.
2. William Mason, b. April 2, 1798, m. Mary Jones, 1818.
3. Willis Mason, b. July 29, 1800, m. Harriet Clemens, 1820.
4. Frances, b. Dec. 29, 1802, m. Alex McCandless, 1818.
5. Ann, b. Dec. 20, 1805, m. 1st, Flint; 2nd, Joseph Falston, 1823.
6. Drucilla, m. Lewis Mahannes, Dec. 29, 1808.
7. Peggy, over 14, 1823, guardian, David Thompson.
8. Lucy Simms, b. Jan. 18, 1787, d. Jan. 24, 1852. M. Feb. 17, 1806, William Brockman, Jr., of Orange, b. Jan. 18, 1777, died June 5, 1844.

-11-

Children of Samuel Brockman of Albemarle and wife Ann Simms. He died 1807 and buried at Green Plains on Highway 20 near Charlottesville. Wife born February 14, 1768. Married June 14, 1790.

1. Richard Simms Brockman, m. Martha (Patsy) Dickerson, 1812.
2. Tandy Brockman, m. Katherine Leake, 1819.
3. Bluford, m. Elizabeth Catterton, Dec. 17, 1822.
4. Tazewell, m. Sarah Salmon, Nov. 11, 1847.
5. Julia A., m. Anderson B. Carr, May 6, 1808.
6. Agatha, m. Thomas Edwards, 1815.
7. Simpson, unmarried.

-12-

Children of Samuel Brockman and wives, Mary Bell and Christian Woolfolk:

1. Sarah, m. Thomas Bibb, Sept. 14, 1785.
2. Elizabeth, m. David Thompson, Nov. 23, 1784.
3. Mary, m. William White, Sept. 10, 1782.
4. Lewis, m. Betsie Bledsoe, March 3, 1779. (Rev. Soldier)
5. James, m. Nancy Bledsoe, Dec. 6, 1790.
6. Susan, m. Moses Perry, March 23, 1786.
7. Job, m--- Dau. Alice one of three children.
   (Aaron Brockman m. Lydia Porter at Louisa, may have been son)
8. John Brockman, married Nancy Long, 12-2-1788. Believed to be widow, and daughter of John Durrett.

-13-

Children of John Brockman (Rev. Soldier) and wife Amelia Martin:

*1. Major Brockman, m. Mary Patterson, b. Dec. 18, 1760; Rev. Soldier. Children James and Mary. "Major deceased by 1800."
2. Jesse, Rev. Soldier, died 1778.
3. Henry, m. Susannah Patterson.
4. Anne, m. Thomas Parks.
5. Mary, m. Joel Dean.
6. Frances, m. Thomas Mullins.
7. Lucy, m. John Owens.

-14-

Children of Joseph Brockman, Rev. Soldier, and wife Mary Page:

1. Robert, b. 7-8-1775, Albemarle Miller, m. Sarah Brockman, 1826. Son, Robert.
2. Charles, Road Supervisor Rev. War. No further record.
3. Joseph, Jr., probably 21 in 1804, per tax list.
4. James, m. Nancy Harris, Dec. 18, 1805.

-15-

Children of William Brockman of Orange and wife Elizabeth Brockman of Albemarle:

1. Jane, m. William Dollins.
2. Nelly (Eleanor) m. Moses Brockman, 1796. (See German Brockmans)
3. Nancy, m. Elijah Lucas, Aug. 24, 1801.
4. Mildred (Amelia) m. Andrew Brockman, April 22, 1793.
5. Sally, m. Benjamin Ball.
6. Catherine, m. John Rogers.
7. John, m. Lucy Delaney.
8. William, m. Lucy Simms Brockman, Feb. 5, 1806.
9. Elizabeth, m. Samuel Mahannes, son Tandy.

-16-

Children of Major B. Brockman, Rev. Soldier, son of John and Mary. Will at Caswell Co., N. C., 1825. B. Oct. 13, 1755; wife Elizabeth. May have been married 1st to Jessie Jones.

1. John.
2. Barney, married Telitha Landrum.
3. Mary.
4. Susanna.

*Note by the Compiler: The first few generations are given to correct errors in preceding books. For details of later generations see Brockman Scrapbook in leading libraries. W. E. Brockman.

THE WHITE HOUSE, Home of Samuel Brockman, and Greenway, later Home of his Grandsons was on this property.

THIS INDENTURE made the sixth Day of June MDCCXXXII In the third year of the reign of our Sovereign Lord Goerge the Second by the grace of God of Great Brittain, France & Ireland King Defender of the faith and in the year of our Lord Christ MDCCXXXII BETWEEN John Henderson of Spotsylvania County planter of the one part and Samuell Brockman of King & Queen County planter of the other part WITNESSETH that the said John Henderson for and in consideration of the sum of five Shillings Current money of Virginia to him in hand paid by the said Samuell Brockman the receipt whereof he doth hereby acknowledge hath Bargained & Sold and by these presents doth bargain, & Sell unto the said Samuell Brockman all that messuage plantation tract or Devident of Land containing three hundred acres lying & being in the County of Spotsylvania and bounded as followeth (to wit) Begining at a spanish oak and beach standing just below the mouth of a small branch on the North side the Northanna thence North forty two Degrees East two hundred & Ninty Eight poles to four pines in John Hendersons back line, thence North west one hundred and Seventy poles to a pine in John Cooks line Thence South thirty two Degrees West three hundred & thirty Eight poles to a small white oak and Juniper tree standing on the North side of Northanna, thence Down the Northanna the severall courses to the begining; and there reveision and Reveisions Remainder and Remainders together with the rents & profits of the premises and Every part and parcell thereof TO HAVE AND TO HOLD the said messauge plantation tract or Divedend of land & all & Singular other the premises before mentioned & intended to be hereby bargained and sould with there & Every of their appurtenances unto the said Saml. Brockman his Exrs. & assigns from the Day before ------ be heretofor & During--- ------------ one whole year from thence next Ensueing & fully to be compleat and ended yeilding and paying therefore the yearly rent of one Ear of Indian corn at ye feast of St. Michael the Arch Angel only if the same be demanded to the Intent & by virture of these presents & of the ------------------------into possession the said Samuell Brockman may ----------- of the premises and be ------------------------ and inheritance thereof to ----------------- whereof the said John Henderson hath hereunto Sett his hand and seal the day and year first above written -

John Henderson (SEAL)
Sarrah Henderson (SEAL)

Signed Seal'd & Deliver'd
In presence of

Recorded in Deed Book "B" at page 294.

William Henderson
Benja. Cave
Robert Bickers

THIS INDENTURE made the Seaventh Day of June in the third year of the reign of our Sovereign Lord George the Second by the Grace of God of Great Britten, France & Ireland King Defender of the faith etc and in the year of our Lord Christ MDCCXXXII Between John Henderson of the county of Spotsylvania planter of the one part and Samuel Brockman of the County of King & Queen planter of the other part WITNESSETH that for & in consideration of the sum of twelve hundred pounds of lawfull tobacco to the said John Henderson In hand well & truly paid by the said Samuel Brockman at and before the Ensealing and Delivery of these presents the said John Henderson hath granted alien'd released and Confirmed and by these presents Doth Grant alien release and confirm unto the sd. Samuel Brockman in his actual possession Now being by virtue of a bargain and sale to him thereof made for one whole year by Indenture bearing Date of the Day before the date hereof & by force of the Statute for transferring Uses uses into possession and to his heirs & assigns all that Messuage plantation tract or Devidend of land containing three hundred acres lying and being in the aforesaid County of Spotsylvania and bounded as followeth (to witt) -*******together with all the Estate right title Interest reversion Claime and Demand whatsoever of him the said John Henderson for and unto the premises and Every part and parcell thereof and the reversions and remainders and premises -----------------& other rents & Profits of the premises and of Every ------- parcell thereof TO HAVE AND TO HOLD the said messuage plantation tract or Dwelling --------- & all & singular other the premises herein before mentioned & Intended to be hereby granted with the appurtenances unto the said Samuell Brockman & his heirs to the only proper use of the said Samuell Brockman his heirs & assigns forever and the said John Henderson for himself his heirs Executors and administrators Doth Covenant and Grant to and with the said Samuell Brockman his heirs and assigns by these presents that it shall & may be lawfull to and for the said Samuell Brockman his heirs & assigns from time to time and at all times forever hereafter peaceably & quietly TO HAVE HOLD possess and enjoy the said Massuage plantation tract or Devidend of land & premises with the appurtenances without the lawfull lot suits trouble or Interruption of him the said John Henderson his heirs or assigns or any of them or any other person or persons whatsoever Lawfully claiming or to claim in by from or under him and the said John Henderson for himself his heirs and said messuage plantation tract or Devidend of land & other the premises with their appurtenances unto the said Samuell Brockman & his heirs against him the sd. John Henderson his heirs shall will warrent & forever defend by these presents IN WITNESS whereof the said John Henderson hath herunto set his hand and seal the Day & year first above written -

John Henderson (SEAL)
Sarrah Henderson (SEAL)

William Henderson
Robert Bickers
Benja. Cave

At a Court held for Spotsylvania County on Tuesday June the Sixth 1732.

John Henderson acknowledged this his Deed of release for land unto Samuell Brockman Like wise Sarah the wife of the said John acknowledged her right of Dower of the said land unto the sd. Brockman at whose motion the same is admitted to record -

TESTE: John Waller Clerk Court.

A copy,

TESTE: , Deputy Clerk.
Circuit Court of Spotsylvania County, Va.

Recorded in Deed Book "B" at page 295.

It is astounding that no early record of Samuel Brockman can be found prior to 1731, when he lived in King and Queen, for he certainly grew up in the lower part of Virginia, married and raised a family there, and the only conclusion I come to is that he was attached to the house of John Madison, who is recorded as having sponsored a Brockman to Virginia (Southern Planter), and his father Henry being dead, he does not appear on the 1704 Quit Rent Rolls. Acquiring land in Spotsylvania (Orange) in 1732, he moved there with his family, except those already married. Samuel also had land in what is now Albemarle County. A survey of the land of John Robinson in Albemarle, 1746 showed that it was North of the Rivanna and next to Samuel Brock (Brockman) and we know the latter had 350 acres which he disposed of in his Will probated in Orange on September 25, 1766. A law suit in Albemarle 1799, shows that the wife of Thomas Brockman, Revolutionary soldier and son of William, was Frances, a daughter of Henry Shelton, and she was dead at that time. At Williamsburg last Easter, I attended Bruton Church where Mary Brockman Singleton, daughter of Samuel and wife of Richard Hunt Singleton baptized their children in the 1740's and saw the old Sarah Coke house, now reconstructed, where her husband kept a boarding house for young men up to the time of his death in 1774, when his widow after settling the estate, moved to the home of her daughter Mary who had married John Crittenden Webb and lived in Orange. One of the most proplexing problems has been the identity of Major Brockman. In fact two of them. There were two and I reached this decision in 1914, when I wrote my first Brockman book, however the confusion arose over the fact that the father of the second Major did not mention him in his Will, as this often happened when their children were deceased, or provision had been made for the children in some other way. Even the paymasters in the Revolutionary War left mixed records and it has taken many years to bring the facts to light.

TWO MAJOR BROCKMANS

The identity of the first Major Brockman, came through Revolutionary War files which record Major B. Brockman and Major B. Brock, the two surnames used interchangably as serving and receiving pay from Louisa County, Va. Major B. Brockman had moved to Guilford County, North Carolina with his older brother John, who had sold his land in Orange, September 25, 1760.

Mary Collins Brockman, widow of John and parent of Major and John, had married Kelly Jennings in 1758, since November 24, 1758, Kelly Jennings was named guardian of the minor children of Mary. They must have moved to Goochland by May 24, 1759, since Samuel the brother of Major and John had been named guardian in place of Kelly Jennings. Major probably stayed with his mother for a time, however by October 13, 1776, he had come of age and he sold his interest in his Louisa land, left him by his father, to brother Samuel and he is then of Guilford County, North Carolina. He is referred to in his father's Will, John Brockman, of Orange, dated August 8, 1755, as an unborn child, and the guardianship papers identify his son as Major as well as the 1776 deed. He was therefore born about October 13, 1755. He is recorded in the files of the National Archives, Washington, D.C. as having enlisted December 1, 1777, and on February 13, re-enlisted with Jesse Brockman, the latter recorded as having died May 30-31, 1778, and Jesse was likely a son of John and Amelia Martin Brockman. He received pay for several succeeding months as Major B. Brockman and Major B. Brock. Furthur records of his military service will be given. He is thought to have married Jessie Jones, but there is no proof. The division of his property in his will suggests an earlier marriage. We know that his wife at the time of his death was Elizabeth, and the home place Caswell County, North Carolina.

The second Major Brockman is recorded in the National Archives also as Major Brock, apparently starting when he enlisted in May or June 1778, in the 7th Infantry, where his uncle Major was already serving. He was assigned to duty as a waggoner. This Major Brockman was son of John and Amelia Martin Brockman, born according to family data passed down on December 18, 1760, but not mentioned by his father in his Will at Greenville, S.C., 1801. John, the father was a Revolutionary soldier and his record is with the Historical Commission at Columbia, S.C. And since there has been much contention among D.A.R. officials, it might be well to point out that John Brockman (wife Elizabeth Burrus) was appointed Lieutenant in the State Militia at Orange, February 1777, Order Book, page 61. William Brockman, son of John and Mary Collins Brockman, also Lieutenant, 1777. Other Revolutionary Soldiers by the name of Brockman were: Joseph of Orange and Albemarle; John of Albemarle, (wife Elizabeth Smith) Express Rider, died 1795, Amherst; Thomas of Albemarle; Lewis of Georgia (born in Louisa, lived in Orange); Major B. Brockman and Major Brockman; Jesse, son of John and Amelia Martin Brockman, killed in service. Major B. Brockman, son of John and Mary Collins Brockman served in the 3rd., 5th., and 7th Infantries and nephew Major, son of John and Amelia Martin Brockman, joined the 7th where he was recorded as Major Brock. When Jesse and Major B. enlisted in the 7th, it was under command of Captain Joseph Spencer.

Record of Pay of two Major Brockmans

Major B. Brockman (Major B. Brock)

February 2, 1778 - 2 months, 13 days, 6 2/3 pounds. Enlisted Dec. 1, 1777. Re-enlisted Feb. 13, 1778. No record of pay for March, but for April, May, June, July, August, September, October, November, December, 1778. January and February, 1779.

DISCHARGED FEBRUARY 16, 1779.

Major Brockman (Major Brock)

Major Brockman (Major Brock) May, 1778; then June with 7th Infantry (joined since Muster) Then Pay for June, 1778 to February, 1779.

DISCHARGED FEBRUARY 16, 1779.

FINAL PAYMENT RECEIVED MAY 1779, AND IT IS NOT CLEAR WHETHER RECEIVED BY MAJOR B. OR MAJOR BROCKMAN.

The second Major Brockman, born December 18, 1760, son of John and Amelia Martin Brockman, after serving in the Revolutionary War, married Mary Patterson in Goochland, but license at Orange. Presumably he was married at the home of his grandmother Mary Brockman Jennings. The Jennings were an old English Family. One William Mason left John Jennings of Orange all of his estate. Sarah Jennings was wife of John Churchill, son of Winston, (See the Duchess of Marlborough). Two children were born to the union of Major Brockman and Mary Patterson. James married first Mary Burroughs and had two children and then he married his first cousin Lucy Brockman, daughter of Henry. Mary, the second child, left no traceable record. The children of James by his first wife brought suit to gain some of the property James got thru his wife Lucy, but they were not successful. Major left no will and relatives say that widow Mary moved to Illinois. "See page 154 for confirming documents of three Major Brockmans."

1101 West Second St.
Arlington, Texas
April 11, 1959

Dear Mr. Brockman:

I received your letter of Mar. 31, and also one today, containing the will of Major Brockman. I surely do appreciate you sending me the will - that should help in establishing my line for D.A.R.

In Jan., 1958, I had a letter from a Mr. Robert B. Brockman. His mother, Mrs. James Major Brockman, had been given a letter that I had written to the Major of Woodruff, S.C. She was ill so her son wrote me a nice letter, saying he'd be glad to help me as he had access to some old family records. I wrote him immediately but no answer - and I wrote him again this January - in case he had lost my address, but still no answer. The son's address is 1017 Woodlawn Ave., Columbia, S.C. Another son, Herbert Brockman, lives on Route 1, Greer, S.C. (NOTE: Regret to say I have not been able to contact these Brockmans. W.E. Brockman)

I will try to find out where the D.A.R. obtained the date of Major's birth, Dec. 18, 1760.

Sincerely - Gussie Brockman Lebo

(Also from Mrs. Lebo.)

My dear Cousin: I had a letter recently from the D.A.R. in regard to their statement that Major Brockman was the son of John and Amelia Martin Brockman. I'll quote from their letter -

"According to two genealogies, "Hume, Kennedy and Brockman Families" by Brockman, and the Clark, Parks, Brockman and other Families by H. W. Clark, Major, who married Mary Patterson, was the son of John and Amelia (Martin) Brockman. This John was born in 1739, and died 1801. Major and his wife Mary had a son James, born March 17, 1782, who married Lucy Brockman. James is the only child known for Major and Mary Brockman."

Mrs. Barney B. Brockman, 207 Newell Drive, Ferguson, Missouri, writes that she thought her husband's ancestors lived in New York and owned a part of the land on which Trinity Church was located, but that records were destroyed by fire and claim to the property could not be proven. Barney, Sr., was born May 13, 1865 and married Mary S. Cloles at Goodellsville, Tennessee December 7, 1880. They had seven children and moved to Colorado and then returned to Tennessee.

WILL OF MAJOR BROCKMAN, SON OF JOHN AND MARY COLLINS BROCKMAN

NORTH CAROLINA IN THE SUPERIOR COURT

CASWELL COUNTY OFFICE OF THE CLERK

I, G. M. HARRIS, Clerk of the Superior Court of Caswell County, State of North Carolina, which is a Court of Record, having an official seal, which is affixed, do hereby certify that the foregoing and attached (2) sheets to be a true copy of the Will of Major Brockman as the same is taken from record in Will Book K, page 100 in so far as I can read the writing of that period.
as the same is taken from and compared with the original now on file in this office.

In witness whereof, I have hereunto set my hand and affixed the seal of the Superior Court of Caswell County at my office in the city of Yanceyville, North Carolina, this the 24 day of March, 1959.

G.M. Harris, Clerk Superior Court
Caswell County, North Carolina
By: Ceare Matlock, Asst. C.S.C.

WILL OF MAJOR BROCKMAN -----October Court 1825.

I Major Brockman of the County of Caswell and State of North Carolina, being sick but thank God of sound mind & memory, desire to make this my last will & testament in manner & form as follows-- After my death and burial and all my just debts paid, I lend to my wife Elizabeth Brockman during her natural life, part of the tract of land whereon I now live including the house & plantation whereon I now live to the spring branch and down the said Spring Branch strait accross the Creek a West course to Grants line, to be laid off down said branch so as to include the spring on her part, and at her decease, I give the said land and plantation to my three youngest children, viz: Barney Brockman, Susanna Brockman, and Mary Brockman to them and their heirs forever to be equally divided between them also I lend to my wife Elizabeth Brockman all my stock of horses, cattle, sheep & hogs together with all my household and kitchen furniture during her life, and at her decease to be equally divided between my three youngest children before men ioned to them and their heirs forever-- and further, it is my will that my wife shall have all the crop of every description, that is now on hand together with all my plantation utensils & tools for the support of her and her children--

Item, I give to my son John Brockman the balance of the tract of land I now live on, not before willed to my wife & children to him and his heirs forever--
Item, I give to my son John Brockman my land joining Williamson Price, Obriant & others to him and his heirs forever- and lastly I appoint my son John Brockman Executor of this my last will to have it executed.
In Testimony whereof I have hereunto set my hand & affixed my seal this 21 day of September in the year of our Lord 1825.

his
Major X Brockman (Seal)
mark

Test: James Rawley

Yelverton D. Rawley

State of North Carolina

Caswell County ---- October Court 1825

The Execution of the last Will and Testament of Major Brockman was duly proved in open by the Oath of James Rawley one of the subscribing witnesses thereto and on motion ordered to be recorded. At the same time John Brockman appeared in open Court and duly qualified to Execute the same and letters testamentary were ordered to be issued to him which did issue accordingly.

Test: Paul A. Haralson Clk.

Book K, page 100.

WILL OF JAMES BROCKMAN, SON OF MAJOR AND MARY PATTERSON BROCKMAN

The State of South Carolina }
Spartanburgh District }
In the Name of God Amen-

I James Brockman of the State & district above mentioned being of sound & disposing mind, do make and ordain this my last Will & Testament, revoking all former Wills which I may already have made -

1st I desire all my just debts to be paid by my Executors hereinafter named out of the proceeds of the sale of my property already made. If the said amount is not sufficeint when collected to pay all my just debts then-in that case the balance due after exhausting the said funds to be paid by my children John Holland, S. R. Westmoreland, Mark Bennett, William Brockman & James F. Brockman in whose hand I have placed funds for that purpose-

2nd I have already disposed of all or nearly all my property & which I now confirm as a part of this my last Will & Testaments- My object in this division was to give equally to all of my children the property which I had made or accumulated by myself & to divide out amongst my last set of children. The children of my present wife all the property that came to me by & through their mother my present wife Lucy Brockman. I have given to William H. Mahaffey & Polly Mahaffey his wife Two Hundred & Twelve dollars which is their proportion of my estate on the principles above stated. I have given to John B. Brockman one Hundred dollars & there is now due due him one hundred & Twelve dollars which my five sons & sons in Law first above mentioned are to pay - And if they do not pay it in my life time they are to pay it after my death- To John Holland and wife Susan Holland I have given Twenty two Hundred & six dollars & sixty cents their proportion of my said estate - To S. R. Westmoreland and wife Elizabeth Westmoreland I have given the same amount their like destributive share of my said estate- To Mark Bennett & Lucitta Bennett his wife, to William T. Brockman & to James F. Brockman I have given each the sum of Twenty Two Hundred & six dollars & sixty cents. To Henry Brockman I have given in his life time Four Hundred & forty four dollars and I have reserved out of his childrens share Five Hundred dollars for my support & placed it in the hands of my five sons in Laws first above named. There is now due the said children of the said Henry Brockman Four Hundred & seventy eight dollars & Eighty-three cents which my said son & sons in Laws have in their hands & which they are to pay over to them at my death if they do not do before-

3rd My five sons & sons in Laws first above mentioned have given me their obligation to support me & my wife Lucy Brockman during out lives & in the division of my property I have already compensated them for the same-

4th In case I should die possessed of any other property than that already mentioned I wish the same to be divided equally amongst all of my children & their representatives according to the Statute of distributions.

5th I do hereby nominate constitute and appoint my five sons & sons in laws already mentioned Viz John Holland, S. R. Westmoreland, Mark Bennett, William T. Brockman & James F. Brockman my Executors of this my last Will & Testament & to see that the same is executed in good faith according to the principles herein set forth-

In Testimony whereof I ha ve hereunto set my hand & seal & declared this to be my last Will & Testament in the presence of the subscribing witnesses, who have subscribed the same in my presence This February Eighteenth in the year of our Lord one Thousand Eight-Hundred & Fifty six- & in the Eighteenth year of the Sovereignty & Independence of the United States of America.

Signed, sealed & published as)
the last Will & Testament of)
the Testator in the presence)
of the subscribing witnesses)
who subscribed their names) s/ James Brockman (Seal)
thereto in the presence of)
the said Testator & of each)
other the day & year above)
mentioned.)

s/ Robt. McKay
s/ D. Hoke
s/ B. J. Perry

WILL OF JAMES H. BROCKMAN

(Son of Col Thomas Patterson Brockman)

GREENVILLE DISTRICT)
) The Muncupative Will of James H. Brockman
SOUTH CAROLINA)

On the 12th day of September, 1844, we the undersigned were called on to witness the declarations of James H. Brockman, as to what disposition he wished make of his worldly effects, in case he did not recover from the bed of sickness on which he was then lying.

James H. Brockman then declared that if his wife (who was then supposed to be pregnant) had a child that lived he wished all his property divided equally between his wife Mary Elizabeth Brockman and the child. On the other hand if his wife did not have a child that lived, he wished his wife to have all his property that was hers before they were married and his father to have all that was left.

He wished the negroes to be divided without being sold.

Wm. F. Lester

James Kilgore

A. B. Crook

Probated the 28th day of July, 1845

Recorded in Will Book C Pages 177-181

SCATTERED BROCKMAN ITEMS

From Claude B. Adams, of Colorado Springs, Colorado. "I have a friend whose mother was a Brockman. She is Mrs. Ben (Mabel) Warren, daughter of Virginia Florence Brockman and Socrates Robertson. Virginia was the younger of a family of nine. Her parents were Lindsay Ellis Brockman, born Feb. 5, 1815, died July 27, 1860, and his wife was Susan Jemima Graves" (Son of William and Mary Lindsay Brockman of Orange). Mrs. Warren has a cousin Forest Brockman, Clifton Hill, Mo., whose parents were John G. and Mary Stamper Brockman. My great, great, grandmother was Susannah Burton Wallis, of Caswell, N.C. May Burton II, of Orange County, Va., served in the War of 1812, and he married Nancy, daughter of Lewis Woolfolk in 1819, in Scott, Kentucky.

From Harold H. Brockman, New Orleans, La.: My father's name was Roy Lee Brockman whose parents settled in Texas after leaving their home state Tennessee. They lived mostly in McKinney, Texas, and it was my impression that the family had its origin in Germany.

Brockman marriages in Montgomery Tennessee 1838 to 1854: Oswald, Samuel, Ann E., Margaret and Mary J. Brockman. No other data available.

Guilford, N.C., Matilda Loye Brockman, tombstone at Holis Chapel Cemetary, five miles from Greensboro, born August 6, 1859, died July 11, 1925.

Adair County, Kentucky Marriages:

May 15, 1815 - Thomas Brockman and Martha Allen.
February 12, 1817 - John Brockman and Sarah Phelps.
October 4, 1825 - William E. Brockman and Elizabeth Hays. Wit: C. W. Hays, Sr., and Robert Hays.
Shelby, Tenn., Louisa Brockman and John G. Stubernak, April 22, 1854.
Greenville, S.C. Mary Brockman Will January 1862. Children Nettie, Ellen, Jesse H. Executor B. T. Brockman.

Clay County, Missouri Marriages:

Feb. 15, 1835 - Fanny Brockman and William Oldacre.
June 26, 1849 - Louisa Brockman and Hiram Green.
May 17, 1849 - John Brockman and Margaret Ann Pence.
Oct. 9, 1856 - Elizabeth Brockman and Thomas Robertson.
June 4, 1855 - Mary Brockman and James C. Nichols.
May 18, 1854 - Margaret Ann Brockman and Thomas C. Easton.

In previous books I have referred to Stephen Brockman, son of John and Elizabeth Burrus Brockman. Marvin Brockman of Renick, Randolph C., Missouri states that Stephen Brockman was born 1785 and died 1825. His wife was Elizabeth Embree of Orange and Ky. where Stephen received a gift of land from his father John. Elizabeth, his wife was born 1793 and died 1860. The marriage was in 1809. Children of Stephen are given as Willis, Joe, Jacob, Stephen H., Mary, Mille, Emma and Gabriel. Stephen was born 1813 and died 1885, and he married Margaret Kimbrough, 1816-1867. Children Thomas, James H., John Wesley. Thomas, 1845-1916, married second Ada Elgin, 1866, their son Marvin, married Ina E. Ryther, their son James, b. 1916, Tabitha Margaret Brockman, dau. of John Wesley, and wife Sarah Elizabeth Hamilton, was born March 4, 1840 at Renick, Mo. and died at Atlantic, Mo., May 11, 1934. Her husband was Arthur B. Myers, wedding April 23, 1871. Sarah Elizabeth Brockman died May 4, 1918. Ruby Helen Myers, daughter of Arthur B. Myers, was born August 23, 1896, married McNeil.

From - "Lewises, Meriwethers and Their Kin" by Sarah Travers Lewis (Scott) Anderson.

Issue of Ann Minor Meriwether by second marriage (to John Brockman).

1. Virginia Brockman, married Joseph Fowlkes.
2. Francis Brockman married Margaret McDougal.
3. Emmet Brockman.
4. Hugh Brockman.
5. Charles James Brockman, M.D., married Margaret Terrell Cobb at "Music Hall", Va. She was daughter of Samuel Cobb and Mary Noel and was raised at "Music Hall" by James Hunter Terrill. Dr. Charles Brockman associated in practice with Dr. Gerraed at whose home in Kentucky he died. Issue:
   a. James Hunter Brockman.
   b. Garrett Meriwether Brockman.

ALBEMARLE CO. RECORDS

Dabney Spicer m. Catherine Brockman, daughter of William Brockman, Jr., and wife Mary Smith, April 2, 1817, by Rev. John Goss.

Will Book 1830-31 ---- Dabney Spicer - adm. accts.

John Lewis m. Mrs. Catherine Brockman Spicer, w dow, Jan. 25, 1833, by Rev. John Goss.

The above indicates that Catherine Lewis named in the division of property of her father, William Brockman Jr., was married twice. It is possible that Sarah Jane Spicer (my gr. grandmother) was a daughter of Dabney Spicer and Catherine Brockman Spicer. If this was proven correct then my gr. grandfather Horace Rhodes, and his wife, Sarah Jane Spicer were first cousins.

Signed - Mildred Marshall

Information from Goss Mahanen, Gordonsville, Va.

Elizabeth Brockman, daughter of William Brockman and wife, Mary, married Harris. Their children were:

1. James Harris - son Overton Harris
2. Calvin Harris
3. Mary (Polly) Harris m. Wm. Mahanes

Widow Harris married 2nd, Samuel Mahanes, father of Wm. Children were as follows:

2 daughters who married Leake's
1 daughter married Shepherd
Melvina m. Moore, moved to Lynchberg

Meredith ("Reddy") Mahanes (son of Samuel) married Sarah Payne. Children:

1. Fanny Mahanes, m. Addie Spicer as a second wife. Mrs. Fanny M. Spicer m. 2nd, John Calvin Harris, Jan. 21, 1904.
2. Lucy Ann Mahanes m. Nath. Lang, Dec. 21, 1861.
3. Rebecca Mahanes m. Cazwell, "Doc" Shotwell.
4. Mary I. Mahanes, m. Thos. F. Bruce, April 5, 1875.
5. Jim Mahanes, m. Bunchy Harris.
6. Charles E. Mahanes, m. Louise M. Salmon, Dec. 21, 1867.
7. W. Samuel Mahanes, m. Lucy Ann Salmon, Feb. 18, 1867.
8. George R. Mahanes, m. Frances C. Mundy, Dec. 2, 1878.

Alb. Co., Va., D. B. 17, page 31, 1810 (Jan).
Lewis Mahanes from Nancy Mahanes

"Whereas by the last will an testement of Merideth Mahanes of Lancester Co. and state of Va., a certain trach or parcel of land lying in said county was given to Nancy Mahanes his said wife with all it appentinancies during life then to be sold agreeable to will".

Deed Book 58, page 230, Feb., 1859.
Elizabeth Mahanes heirs to Thomas Gilbert.

"All of our respective rights titles and interest in a certain lot peice on parcel of land asigned to the heirs of Elizabeth Mahanes dec'd in the devision of the Dower land belonging to the estate of William Brockman dec'd and containing by survey thirty three acres and adjoining the land of the said Thomas Gilbert, Sarah Brockman, Walter Prickett and John H. Taylor and lying on the waters of Preddys Creek".

F. M. Leake (Seal)
Cornelia E. Leake (Seal)
C. P. Shepherd (Seal)
Mildred A. Shepherd (Seal)
Austin M. Leake (Seal)
Emily A. Leake (Seal)

Some Mahanes marriages recorded in Alb. Co., Va.

Samuel Mahanes m. Nancy Hamphrup, May 28, 1816.
Samuel Mahanes m. Elizabeth Harris, Dec. 22, 1818.
Wm Mahanes m. Martha Millway, Aug. 14, 1826.
Wm. Mahanes m. Polly B. Harris, Dec. 28, 1832.
George W. Moore m. Elizabeth M. Mahanes, May 22, 1841.

Charles R. Shepherd m. Amanda Mahanes, Oct. 26, 1841.
Austin Leake m. Ann Mahanes, March 3, 1847.
Frances M. Leake m. Cornelia Mahanes, May 20, 1850.
Taoner Mahanes m. Emily Salmon, Dec. 20, 1866.
Harris m. Elizabeth Brockman, Nov. 2, 1812.

By Mrs. Pauline Brandt

I obtained a photostat copy of the following will from the Virginia State Library.

TAYLOR JAMES WILL

"In the name of God Amen: I James Taylor here by make my last will and testament in manner and form following to wit:

ITEM 1

I lend to my beloved wife Franky (Brockman) Taylor for and during her natural life all my land and whatever crop may be at my death plantation, tools and utensils household furniture and kitchen utensils all my cattle and stock of every kind (she paying out of the same all my just debts) also I lend my said wife during her natural life the following Negroes Viz Nanny Alee Walker, John Jacob Lydin and Handy.

ITEM 2

I give to my son John Taylor a negro boy named Bob, to him and his heirs forever.

ITEM 3

I give to my daughter Betsy Cofer for and during her natural life a negro girl Jinny and her increase and at the death of my said daughter I give and bequeath the said girl Jinny and her increase to the children of my said daughter Betsy to them and their heirs forever.

ITEM 4

I give to my daughter Franky for and during her natural life a Negro woman named Fanny and her future increase in case my said daughter should have children then in that case at her death the said negro woman and her increase I give to said Frankys children otherwise I wish at her death the said Negro in value to be equally divided among the rest of my children.

ITEM 5

I give to my son Jonathan a negroe boy named Nelson to him and his heirs forever.

ITEM 6

I give to my son Brockman a negroe girl named Milly and her increase to him and his heirs forever.

ITEM 7th

I give my land at the death of my wife to my son Brockman and daughter Franky during the natural life of my said daughter Franky equally between them but after the death of my wife and daughter Franky I give and devise all my land to my said son Brockman and his heirs forever.

ITEM 8th

I wish at the death of my wife all her dower estate herein lent or given during her life in lieu of her dower (except the land which I have here in devised to my son Brockman Taylor and his heirs forever after the death of my daughter Franky) to be sold at the best bidder & the money equally divided among my following children and their heirs Viz John, Betsy, Franky, James, Jonathan & Brockman.

ITEM 9th

I hereby appoint my son Brockman Taylor & John Goss executors of this my last will hereby revokeing all former wills heretofore made by me In witness whereof I have here unto set my hand & seal this 2nd December 1819.

his
James x Taylor (Seal)
mark

TESTE: Samuel + (his mark) Elliot

William Brockman

At a Court held for Albemarle County the 9th day of May 1821, this Instrument of writing purporting to be the last will and testament of James Taylor deceased was produced into Court and proved by the oaths of Samuel Elliot and William Brockman two of the witnesses thereto and ordered to be recorded.

TESTE Alex Garrett C.A.C."

On the same page of the photostat copy of the will of James Taylor there was part of the will of one Wm. Hall of Albemarle Co., dated of this will Jan. 31st 1814. Witness to the Wm. Hall will were: B. (Buckner) Townley, Jonathan Munday, Abraham Munday. This will names the children of Wm. Hall as follows:

1. Ambrose Hall
2. Nicholas Hall
3. William Hall
4. Joseph Hall
5. John Hall
6. Mary Hall
7. Judy Hall
8. Sarah Hall
9. Betsy Elliot
10. Anna Munday
11. Patsy Dowell
12. Ginny Wilkerson

Page 41 - Orange Co., Va., Families, Vol. I, by W. E. Brockman, gives the names of Sarah Brockman's children:

1. Porterfield Brockman
2. Mary Ann Brockman married John A. Wilkerson Dec. 24, 1851. Min. Benj. Creel. They had one son, Eraus Wilkerson.

James P. (Porterfield, son of Sarah & Robert) Brockman married Elizabeth Flynt Dec. 21st, 1854. Their son was Jim Brockman. (A cousin from Richmond wrote me that he married Mary Lucy Wilkerson) but in "Marriages of Alb. Co. & Charlottesville, Va., 1781-1929" by W. L. Norford, page 18, I found the following: "Brockman, James R. and Molly Wilkerson Oct. 5th, 1882." (I do know that Jim Brockman and wife _?_ Wilkerson Brockman had the following children:

1. Willie Brockman (I do not know the name of his wife or if he ever married.) He died in Texas.
2. Oliver Brockman married Lillie Dudley. One Son, Fulton O. Brockman of Richmond, Va.
3. Mary J. Brockman m. _?_ Jeter.
4. Eula M. Brockman m. _?_ Gaines.

Oliver Brockman (age 73) died Oct. 22, 1956, in Richmond, Va.

The following records are copies of old family papers, Bible records etc., that a Catterton relative sent me recently.

"The Cattertons came over to the New World from England in 1665, and settled in Calvert County, Maryland. When they lived in England, they spelled the family name "Chatterton"; but when they settled in Maryland they dropped the "h" and spelled the name "Catterton". This is a list of Michael Catterton's children. The Michael Catterton that lived in Maryland and died in 1782. The names (of the children) are taken from Michael Catterton's will made in 1782. Michael (son of Michael Sr., of Calvert Co., Md.) and William and their sister, Gatwood Catterton came from Maryland to Nortonville about 1784-1785. Michael bought 515 acres of land and William bought 748 acres of land. Children of Michael Catterton (Sr.) of Maryland.

1. Elizabeth Catterton Owens
2. Mary Catterton
3. Gattwood Catterton m. Samuel Austin Dec. 2, 1791
4. Michael Catterton (Jr.)
5. William Catterton was born Oct. 29, 1765. Married 1st, Elizabeth Foster, Oct. 20, 1789. He married second, Agatha (Agnes) Simms Dec. 26, 1792. Agatha (Agnes) Simms was born March 25, 1769, died 1836. William died Nov. 4, 1843.
6. Frances Catterton
7. Sarah Catterton Hamsell. (Mr. Catterton wrote me that they had letters from John Hamsell written to his uncle, William Catterton, at Nortonsville, Va. Dates of the letters between 1825-1832. In one of the letters in 1825, he tells about the wagons crossing the river at Charleston, West Va. In an old letter that Michael Hamsell wrote back from Missouri to Wm. Catterton in 1838, he spoke of the company of Wagons, and said they were on the road 55 days going to Missouri).

----

116 Linden Drive - Forrest Hills
Danville, Virginia

Dear Mrs. Brandt-

I have been planning to write you for some months, but somehow get busy with other things and don't get around to writing. Mrs. J. W. Wyatt, who belongs to the same D.A.R. chapter I do, gave me your name and told me you had Brockman ancestors.

Here is all I know- my father was a son of Clement Walker Brockman of Charlottesville, born around 1855. Daddy had three aunts, Mattie and Lutie Brockman and Annie who married Henry Clifford Chaplin of Charlottesville. So far as I know my grandfather (Clement Walker) had no brothers. I have heard Daddy speak of his grandfather as Fountain Brockman and we have some coin spoons with "F M B" engraved on them that are supposed to have been a wedding present. We are related to the Terrills and Edwards too. My father was Leigh Chaplin Brockman.

This is not much to go on but I'm hoping you can help me- you seem to have so much information. Would appreciate hearing from you as soon as convenient, particularly since "The Brockman Scrapbook" is not in our local library and they borrowed it from the State Library for me for ten days.

I did't tell you about myself in my first letter- I was born in 1912- My mother was Lillie Oliver Mustain before marriage and I am the first of two children, however my brother died at the age of fourteen months. Daddy died in 1934.

Sincerely
(signed) Lillian Brockman McCollum
(Mrs. W. H.)

From Marvin Brockman of Renick, Randolph Co., Mo:

Stephen Brockman (son of John and Elizabeth Burrus Brockman-W.E.B.), born 1785, died 1825, wife Elizabeth Embree, 1793-1860, married 1809. Children: Willis, Joe, Jacob, Stephen H., Mary Mille, Emma, Gabriel.

Stephen Brockman born 1813, died 1885, married Margaret Kimbrough, 1816-1867. Children: Lucy, Cosgrove, Thomas, James H., Wesley.

Thomas Brockman, 1845-1916, married second Ada Elgin, in 1866. Children: Marvin Brockman, born 1894, married Ira E. Ryther, a son, James, born 1916. There may have been other children, but Marvin Brockman is just giving his own line.

The County Clerk of Scott Co. gave me the name of a Mrs. Golisborough who does research, here is her first report. June 27, 1958.

1815 - Fragments of a deed for a tract of land on Dry Runn, sold by Wm. Josiah, and Robert W. Gale. In the description was the phrase, "land adjoining Elijah Brockman -- to Johnson Gillespie's line". Wit: Dan'l B. White. Recorded 3-7-1822. Deed Book F, page 4.

7 May, 1832 - Elijah Brockman of Scott Co., from Sally and Wm. Ward all of Scott Co., Ky., for $120.00, 12 acres and 27 poles on Dry Run, beginning at Lewis Woolfolk's corner -- to a stake in Rogers line. Book L, page 435.

23-1835 - Sally Brockman and John Brockman, Jacob Brockman and Polly Brockman all of Scot Co., Ky., to Simeon Neal for $180.00, 12 acres and 27 poles on Dry Run, beginning at Lewis Woolfolk's corner -- to a stake in Roger's line. Wit: James Long, D. Bradford, J. W. Thompson. Book N, page 310.

2 Sept. 1839 - Wm. Tomlinson and Zerelda his wife to Sarah Brockman and her children for $170.93 1/2 "To them in hand paid by Elijah Brockman in his lifetime". Elijah Brockman was the husband of the said Sarah Brockman -- a tract of land on Dry Run, beginning at a Box Elder and Hackelberry corner to the said Brockman's original tract, thence West to a stake on the Cincinnatti Road, thence with said Road north 24, west 16 poles -- to a stake in Johnson Gillespie's line -- containing 36 acres and 20 poles. Wit: Ben B. Ford, Clerk, a Duvall, Deputy Clerk, p. 309.

17 Sept., 1844 - Sally Brockman and John Brockman, Polly Brockman and Jacob Brockman of Randolph Co., Mo., appoint Wm. Tomlinson of the said state and county as their attorney to collect from Simeon, Wm., and Asa Neal of Scott Co., Ky., the amount of all monies due to us on notes by them executed to us and dated 7th Sept., 1842. Wit: Chas H. Barron J. P. Thos. Egan J.P. Book S, page 381.

John R. and Elizabeth Brockman have land transactions during the year 1836.
4th Oct., 1836 - John Brockman and Elizabeth Brockman to James F. Shannon. n402.

The foregoing from research for me by Mrs. Goldsborough of Georgelsion, Ky.-July 1958- except the Tax Book records which are from Historical Society of Kentucky to a second cousin of mine who lives in Randolph Co.

My Great Grandfather Jacob Brockman, b. 7-10-1801, Scott Co., Ky., m. 2-26-1824, to Mary Polly Cobbler. He died 8-17-1873. Polly died 5-10-1844, Randolph Co. Jacob, son of Elijah and Sally Tomlin (Sarah Tomlinson) Brockman.

C. B. Adams --- Jacob and Polly to Randolph Co., Mo. in 1842.

Elijah and Sally Tomlin Brockman - a letter to Mary Brockman Cavanaugh in 1941 from Ky. State Historical society States:- Tax book of Scott Co., Ky., shows only Brockmans paying taxes was Elijah on 3 slaves and 2 horses in 1801. Also only Brockmans paying taxes in 1823 were:

Joseph Brockman - 1 slave
John Brockman - 1 horse
Jacob Brockman - 1 horse
Elijah Brockman - 123 a land on Dry Run, 2 slaves and 4 horses.

A report from Mrs. Goldsborough of Georgetown, Ky., dated Aug., 1958, on separate

Mary Brockman Cavanough, my second cousin on Brockman side, third cousin on our maternal side lives at Moberty, Randolph Co., Mo.

A more recent report from Mrs. Goldsborough, gives history of Joseph Tomlinson, b. 1802, Scott Co., Ky., and Fletcher, his brother, and a sister, Mrs. Stevenson, also Wm. Tomlinson who served on Jury in 1808 in Scott County.

History of Randolph Co. - Early Settlers

Isom Embree, (1816-1883) m. 1827.
Stephen H. Brockman came of age 14 (1827.
Isom Embre probably son of Caleb and Sally Burrus Embree in 1803.
John W. Brockman son of Stephen H, born 3-4-1840, m. Sarah E. Hamilton. Moved to Macon Co., Jan. 16, 1863. Children: Alice, Mary F., Tabitha M., Wilbur H., Stephen B., Ida May, Thomas and Nelly Pearl. John W. (deacon) Love Lake Baptist Church.
Isom Embree's son William Embree, b. 1-11-1828, Randolph Co., who m. Sallie Fray.
Stephen H. Brockman's post office Renick Randolph Co., Mo.
Wm. Embree had a store at same place, later 1884 had farm of 1040 A.

These records indicate that Stephen no doubt brother of Elijah and Asa.

Elizabeth relinquished her estate and listed living children: Jacob, Stephen, and Asa died before 1831, deeds Elijah bought land in 1832.

Liberty, Missouri Paper (Clay Co.) 11-27-44.

Ambrose Brockman, Believed to be the Son of Thomas Brockman of Albemarle Revolutionary Soldier.

J. Arch Nicholson of Holt, father of Mrs. Estil Hurt of Lexington, Mo., while visiting at the home of his daughter recently, took the office of the Lexington Advertiser-News two documents which are the original certificates for 640 acres of land located in Clay and Daviess counties, issued more than 100 years ago to his great grandfather, Ambrose Brockman, who lived north of Excelsior Springs.

One of the certificates, dated March 8, 1834, bears the signature of President Andrew Jackson, and the other, issued May 1, 1843, is signed by President John Tyler.

The claims on the land were filed by Mr. Brockman, a veteran of the War of 1812, in Lexington, where was located the nearest land office. The documents are of the finest parchment, and bear the seal of the United States government. They are perfectly legible, both as to printing and writing.

Mr. Nicholson has given the documents to Mrs. Hurt. They have been in the possession of his family since they were issued, and he received them from his father. The land, however, is no longer in the possession of his family, he said.

Mr. Nicholson's family has continued to reside in that section through the intervening years. His mother, Mrs. Sarah Louisa Samuel Nicholson, was a half-sister of Frank and Jesse James.

Besides Mrs. Hurt, Mr. Nicholson has another daughter, Pfc. Ella F. Nicholson, who has been in the Marine corps for sixteen months. She, also, has been visiting at the home of Mrs. Hurt here, making a stop-over on the way back to California from Chicago, where she completed a course in the school of aviation instruments. A son of Mr. Nicholson, John W. Nicholson, aviation ordnance machinist second class, is serving on an airplane carrier in the South Pacific.

Though their relationship to their great - great - grandfather, Ambrose Brockman, both Mrs. Hurt and Private Nicholson are members of the Daughters of the American Revolution, and Mrs. Hurt is a member of the United Daughters of the Confederacy.

Mrs. June Dewey, Route 4, Box 300 A, Port Orchard, Washington, writes that her Great grandmother Caroline Elizabeth Brockman, was born July 31, 1837, and died March 18, 1916, and married Henry Clay Peters September 1854.

NOTE: Caroline Elizabeth was daughter of Ambrose Brockman and wife Maria, son of Thomas of Albemarle and wife Frances Shelton, who moved to Illinois and some of the children, including Ambrose referred to in the article above moved to Missouri.

Applicant's Working Sheet

NATIONAL SOCIETY, DAUGHTERS OF THE AMERICAN REVOLUTION

(Miss or Mrs.) Erma Eleanor Keefer Farris, wife of Alton Boone Farris, descendant of John Brockman, Express Rider - Rev. Service

1. The daughter of Maxia Clarence Keefer born on 7-6-1877 at Madison Co., Tex. died at North Zulch, Texas on 1-26-1946 and his first wife Mary Ball born on 3-30-1878 at Wilson Co., Tex., died at Huntsville, Texas on 11-13-1957 married on 7-10-1895.

2. The said Maxia Clarence Keefer was the child of Bennett Keefer born on 4-1-1850 at Madison Co., Tex., died at Edge, BRazos Co., Tex., on 10-8-1879 and his first wife James Annie Mitchell born on 10-12-1859 at Mitchell's Prairie died at North Zulch, Texas on 9-26-1942 married on 10-15-1874.

3. The said James Annie Mitchell was the child of James Franklin Mitchell born on 3-17-1829 at Tennessee died at Mitchell's Prairie on c. 1871 and his first wife Mary A. (Annie) Martin born on 2-29-1832 at Madison Co., Tex., died at Madison County Texas on c. 1869 married on 11-22-1849.

4. The said James Franklin Mitchell was the child of James B. Mitchell born on 11-17-1795 at Bedford Co., Va., died at Mitchell's Prairie on 5-30-1870 and his first wife Calpernia Franklin born on 7-5-1802 at Franklin Co., Va., died at Mitchell's Prairie on 12-30-1863 married on 5-6-1819.

5. The said Calpernia Franklin was the child of Jasper Franklin born on 1776 at Amherst Co., Va., died at Franklin Co., Va., on .... and his first wife Polly Brockman born on 1780 at Albemarle Co., Va., died at Franklin Co., Va., on c. 1819. Married on 10-27-1796.

6. The said Polly Brockman was the child of John Brockman born on c. 1745 at Albemarle Co., Va., died at Amherst Co., Va., on July, 1795, and his first wife Elizabet (Betty) Smith born on c. 1749 at Albemarle Co., died at Kentucky. Married on c. 1767.

- 1 -

Children of John Brockman and Elizabeth Smith, dau. of Thomas. She married 2nd. W. W. Embre.

1. Elijah m. Fanny Harrison, Oct. 22, 1795.
2. Polly m. Jasper Franklin, Oct. 27, 1796.
3. William m. Elizabeth Henderson, Feb. 15, 1813.
4. Elizabeth m. Overton Harris, Dec. 19, 1806.
5. Frances
6. Vallatilda
7. Sally m. Alexander Marr; 2nd, John Smith.

- 2 -

Children of Jasper Franklin & Polly Brockman:

1. Reuben
2. Anthony
3. Calpernia m. James B. Mitchell
   -------- (possibly others)

- 3 -

Children of James B. Mitchell & Calpernia Franklin:

1. Thomas
2. Edwin
3. James F. m. Mary A. Martin
4. Mary
5. Nathaniel
6. Anthony Wayne m. (1) Susan Harms, (2) .... (3)............

- 4 -

Children of James F. Mitchell & Mary A. Martin:

1. Dicey Calpernia m. Jack Lennox
2. Edward
3. James Annie m. (1) Bennett Keefer, (2) Aaron Drake

- 5 -

Children of Bennett Keefer and James Annie Mitchell:

1. Maxia Clarence Keefer, b. 7-6-1877, d. 1-26-1946.

- 6 -

Children of Maxia Clarence Keefer & Mary Ball:

1. Elbert Olan, b. 3-24-1898, d. 7-19-1919. Elbert Olan passed away in his twent second year, unmarried.
2. Ruby Myrtle, born 5-10-1899. M. Bill McMahan.
3. Otha Frank, b. 7-26-1900. Otha m. (1) Sudie Isgitt, children: Elbert Olan 7-10-25, m. Bett -------. LaNell b. 3-25-28, m. Billy Phillips, 11-25-49, children: Brenda and Donald. Velia Marie b. 11-14-35, m. Robert Adair, (2) Alma Anders.
4. Clemence Oda, b. 12-10-1903, m. Olan Ford, 6-13-22.
5. Guy Lester, b. 2-18-1904, m. (1) Thelma Wilson. (2) Bertia McMahan, children: Mary Jean, b. 9-16-36; Clarence Lester, b. 5-1-42.
6. Thelma Claris, b. 9-26-1906, m. Pauline Black 6-3-32. Children: Ellen Annette, b. 2-16-39, m. Wm. Hill, 8-27-58; Fred Maxia, b. 3-22-47.
7. Erma Eleanor, b. 2-21-1908, m. Alton Boone Farris, 11-11-27.

- 7 -

Children of Alton Farris and Erma Keefer:

1. Maggie Mary, b. 8-18-1928, m. A. T. Ryden, Jr., of Stillwater, Minnesota. Children: Sandra Lynn, b. 9-12-54; Alan Theodore, b. 1-14-57.
2. Jack Truett Farris m. Saran ANN Terrell of Monroe, Ga., 7-9-1951.
3. Alton Keefer Farris m. Naomi Ruth Voyles of Idabel, Okla., 2-3-52. Children: Ruth Marie, b. 5-13-1954; Alton Keefer, Jr., b. 8-26-1955.
4. James Maxia Farris m. Rochelle Louise McCollum of Huntsville, Texas, 12-23-55. Children: Terry Harold, b. 5-3-58.

GERMAN BROCKMANS

In my Orange County Virginia Families, Volume 1, references as to the German Brockmans were given. Since the English family were awarded the Crusaders Cross for participation in the Crusades under Richard I, it is assumed that some members of the family stayed in Germany, (Bremen, Brockmanland County) and Holland, although I am inclined to think that the Holland branch arose from the Brockmans who fled to Holland with Charles II, after his father had been beheaded. Henry Brockman came to Maryland with a party of Hollanders, he having been picked up in the Barbados. The German family seemed to have settled and moved to the same areas in America where we find the English family and it is likely that they did so in seeking their blood relatives. John Valentine Brockman, also spelled Brukman arrived in Philadelphia November 7, 1754, on the "John and Elizabeth" under the command of Captain Ham, from Amsterdam. Their destination was New York, where their relatives were supposed to have an interest in lower New York including the present site of Trinity Church. We next find a V. Brockmann as a tenant of Pres. James Madison and a William Brockmann as a customer of the store run by Madison at Madison Mills just outside of Orange and Simms Brockman overseer of Madison and witness to his Will. John, a son of Valentine Brockman was married, October 3, 1822, in Montgomery County, Va., to Rebecca Peck, daughter of Jacob, and William married her sister November 20, 1827. Furthur than this I have been unable to trace the descendants of John Valentine Brockman. Moses and Andrew Brockman of Orange bought land in 1793 at age 21 and married Brockman sisters, and Aaron of Louisa left a Will in Ky. These three may have been sons of Valentine Brockman. C. T. Brockman of 302 Bluegrass Ave., Lexington, Ky., says that his great, great, grandfather John, came from Pennsylvania and married Frances Drake in 1814, and if this is true both Johns could not have been sons of Valentine Brockman, but perhaps first cousins. There were other German and Dutch Brockmans in the Carolinas, and other southern states and a drove of them located in Cincinnati and nearby points. Both groups, the English and Germans as well as the Dutch had christian names of John, Thomas, Richard. It may be a coincident that Thomas Drake, born in Virginia, 1770, married Rachael Peak (Peck) and a daughter Frances married John Brockman. Following data was prepared 50 years ago by seekers of the Drake fortune.

Thomas Drake born in Va., about the year 1770, moved to Scott Co., Kentucky, and married Rachal Peak, date unknown and died between 1812 and 1816. Buried on Dry Run about six miles from Georgetown in Scott Co., Ky. He lived and died on the old home place where he settled when he moved from Virginia and which afterward passed to his son-in-law, Thomas Wolf, who married his daughter Sally S. Drake. Sally S. Drake (Wolf) and Thomas .... both died at the same place.

Thomas Drake was the son of James Drake whose middle name was Francis, I think. James (Francis) Drake was born in England about 1750 and moved to the United States, first settling near Culpepper, Virginia and then moved to Scott Co., Ky., where he died (1818), about the last of the 18th or beginning of the 19th century, at his son Thomas Drakes, on the old home place. He also had one daughter, Polly, who married Isaac Foster and one daughter, Elizabeth, who married Lewis Valandingham.

Heirs of Rachel Peak and Thomas Drake: Daughters: Frances Drake born Sept. 19, 1800, married John Brockman in Sept, between the 1st and 19th in the year 1814, being not quite fourteen years of age, died Aug. 30, 1883, and she was buried on Dry Run about six miles from Georgetown in Scott Co., on her father Thomas Drakes' old home place.

Sallie S. Drake born Jan. 24, 1804, married Thomas Wolf Sept. 24, 1822, and died May 10, 1855. Was buried on the old home place of her father Thomas Drake on Dry Run about six miles from Georgetown in Scott Co., Ky.

Winniford Drake married George Chisna of Scott Co., Ky. Dates of birth, marriage and death unknown.

Mary E. (PollyO Drake born about 1807. Married Richard Peck. Died Sept. 16, 1881. No heirs.

Sons

Thomas Drake born Oct. 27, 1816, married Margaret Price, June 13, 1839 and died Dec. 15, 1892, and was buried on the home place of his father Thomas Drake on Dry Run in Scott Co., six miles from Georgetown in Scott Co., Ky.

James Presley Drake born July 8, 1805, married Katherine Wood and died Nov. 9, 1885, in DeKalb Co., Mo. Married in 1827.

Henry Bruce Drake born Jan. 14, 1810, and married Basheba Burgess of Scott Co., Ky., and died Mar. 9, 1846.

Washington Drake, date of birth and death unknown. No heirs.

Heirs of Francis Drake Brockman and John Brockman. (John is my great - great grandfather.. William T. Brockman is my great grandfather)

SONS:

William Thomas Brockman, born Oct 12, 1821, and married Elvira Wolf, his consiu Feb. 4, 1847 and died Oct. 30, 1885. Buried in Georgetown Ky.

Elijah I. Brockman born May 1, 1823, married Jane Dawson of Mo., and died Nov. 15, 1861.

John Asariah Brockman born Sept. 4, 1830, and died Mar. 7, 1850. No heirs.

Asa Tandy born Mar. 9, 1833, and died Nov. 18, 1845. No heirs.

Richard Pack Brockman born June 19, 1844, and died Nov. 17, 1845. No heirs.

DAUGHTERS:

Zerilda Emerine Brockman born July 9, 1815, married Bev Raugl in Scott Co., Ky., and died June 22, 1856.

Mary (called Pop) Brockman was born Sept. 25, 1817, and married Dave Sebastian in Scott Co., Ky., and died Apr. 14, 1854 and left ten heirs Ben Sebastian living and Cynthia Sebastian, dead, who married Harvey Pomll. Cynthia Sebastian Pomll left two heirs. Ida Pomll who married John Farmer and Lillie Pomll who married a Swimford.

Louisa Brockman born Dec. 3, 1819, married Wesley Lynn in Mo., and I do not know if she is living or dead.

Patsy Brockman born May 20, 1825, married Joseph Drake, her cousin (son of Henry Bruce Drake) in Scott Co., Ky., died in March, 1906. Both deceased. Left one heir, Leona Drake (deceased) who married A. J. Might and she left one heir, Iva Might, now living at Athens, Ky.

Josephine Brockman born Mar. 24, 1827, married James Drake, her cousin, in Scott Co., Ky., and died in Aug, 1908.

Vianna Brockman born Sept. 12, 1828, married James Wolf, her cousin in Scott Co., Ky. and died Feb. 8, 1884.

Asbrew S. Brockman and Irene L. Brockman (twins) born Aug. 5, 1836. Irene L. Brockman married Ben Sebastian in Scott Co., and died Jan 14, 1870. No heirs. Asbrew S. Brockman not married, died Mar. 4, 1850.

Sarah E. J. Brockman born Dec. 25, 1840, married William Mifford in Scott Co., Ky. She is living in Shelbyville, Indiana.

Children of Sallie S. Wolf (nee: Drake) and Thomas Wolf, both deceased.
SONS:
James Wolf, born Nov. 6, 18--, married Viann Brockman, her cousin, in Scott Co., Ky., and is now living in Lexington, Ky.
Thomas J. Wolf, born Nov. 8, 1826. Died in Scott Co., Ky., about 1894, unmarried.
William H. Wolf, born Apr. 22, 1828, married Jane Mullen in Scott Co., Ky., and both died about 1893. William Wolf having died in the spring and his wife the following fall of 1893. Left two heirs. One son, Chas. Wolf and one grand-daughter, Jennie B. Morgan, both now living in Georgetown, Ky.
Jacob Wolf born Aug. 10, 1837, not married, died in Scott Co., Ky., and was buried on the old home place six miles from Georgetown in Scott Co., Ky.
DAUGHTERS:
Elvira Wolf born July 15, 1823, married William T. Brockman, her cousin, on Feb. 4, 1847, and died April 4, ... Buried in Georgetown, Ky.
Sally Ann Wolf born Mar. 26, 1830, not married and died Aug. 3, 1849.
Mary Jane Wolf born Aug 8, 1832, married Cyrel Valanding born in Scott Co., and died in 1885. No heirs.
Elizabeth Wolf born May 30, 1835, married Thomas Mullen in Scott Co., Ky., and is now living in Scott Co., Ky.

Children of Elvira Brockman (nee: Wolf) and William T. Brockman:
Henry Buford Brockman born Jan. 20, 1848, and died July 16, 1855. No heirs.
Richard Thomas Brockman born July 31, 1849, married Margaret Angeline Vanse Dec. 22, 1870 and both are now living in Georgetown, Ky.
Alpheus Brockman born June 15, 1851, married Lavina Jane McFarland, Dec. 1870, and died Aug. 15, 1873. Left one heir William Alouza (called Low) Brockman.
Theodore Brockman born .... 18, 1854, not married, and died in Dec., 1863.
Martha Ann Brockman born Aug. 11, 1856, married G. D. Warnock, Dec. 18, 1906, now living in Georgetown Ky.
James Harvey Brockman born Oct. 14, 1854, married Carolina Sniclair in 1878, is now living at Connersville, Ind.
Sarah Francis Brockman born Aug. 20, 1861, married James H. Ellint, May 17, 1895, is now living in Georgetown, Ky.

Children of Margaret Drake (nee: Price) and Thomas Drake:
Thomas Drake born Sept. 17, 1840, married Laura C. Beatty, Jan, 1871 and died in 1907. Buried in Franklin Co., Ky. Leaves three heirs: James William Drake, born Oct. 11, 1871; Emil Rodes Drake, born Mar. 27, 1882; and one granddaughter, all living in Lexington, Ky.
Henry Bruce Drake born Oct y, 1843, married Emily Farmer now living on Perry St. in Covington, Ky.
James Wickliffe Drake, born Mar. 7, 1852, married Eunice Fightmaster and died in Kansas City, do not know when. Leaves one heir, Sidney Drake born June 16, 1880 and now lives in Franklin Co., Ky.
Emma Drake, born Feb. 13, 1857, married Wm. O. Nelson Jan. 29, 1878. Now living in Coriuth, Ky.
Mary Ellen Drake, born May 13, 1860, married Bud Mulberry Feb. 6, 1877. Now living at Sadieville, Ky.

Children of Vianna Wolf (nee: Brockman) and James Wolf.
John I. P. Dudley Wolf born May 6, 1851, and died Dec. 19, 1876. No heirs.
Sarah F. Wolf born May 5, 1853, is living in Lexington, Ky.
Mary L. Wolf, born Feb. 7, 1855, married Patrick Kelly Nov. 26, 1877 and died May 17, 1879. No heirs.

Zerelda A. Wolf, born Dec. 17, 1856, married J. C. Barlow Mar. 10, 1874, and died April 24, 1893. Leaves three heirs.
Levenia E. Wolf born Jan. 3, 1859, married Tom Deering Sept. 15, 1897.
Elizabeth J. V. Wolf born June 3, 1860 and married George Gardner Nov. 18, 1886, is now living.
Georgia A. Wolf, Jan. 23, 1865, married Thomas B. Smith. Feb. 26, 1889, living.
Elvira H. Wolf born Sept. 5, 1867, not married, is living in Lexington, Ky.

----

615 Sunnyside Avenue, Charlotte, N.C.
July 16, 1959

Mr. W. E. Brockman

It is a pleasure to acknowledge and answer your letter of July 13. Since our former correspondence, regulations made it necessary for me to retire from the staff of the library since I have just passed my 71st birthday.

The book that I published in 1950 concerned my mother's family only and the only Brockmanns therein are my father and the descendants of my parents. Therefore, this book would be of no interest to you tho I shall be glad to lend you a copy should you care to see it.

I am now working on a similar book on my father's family which I hope to have published by the first of next year. Unfortunately I can't go back very far with the Brockmann's but my grandmother was a "Raven" and on her line I can go back to 1500.

The introduction of the forthcoming book will read something like this "This book covers the ancestry and descendants, as far as can be found, of August Julius Brockmann and his wife Bertha Euphronzine Margaretha Raven, who were married in Osnabruck, Province of Hanover, Germany in November, 1852. They arrived in America in January 1853, and settled in Randolph County, North Carolina where they resided until 1860, removing then to Greensboro, N. C., where they resided the remainder of their lives."

I am writing from memmory from an office which I have established to write a local history for the Chamber of Commerce- hence the following dates are only approximate. August Julius Brockmann was born about 1821, son of Johann Ludolph Brockmann and his wife Matilda HanHeide. Johann Ludolph Brockmann was born about 1780 and died about 1825. That is as far back as I can go with the Brockmann line. My grandfather had one brother to come to America. His name was Edward and he settled in Sacramento, California. This was about 1853. He was heard from for a few years after going West and is presumed to have died and been buried at Sacramento. I know exactly where all descendants of my grandparents are and none seem to tie in with the names you mention. Sorry I can not be more helpful.

Sincerely,
Charles Raven Brockmann

TRIBBLE - GORDON - BURRIS

Data from William Richard Gordon
University of Pennsylvania, Philadelphia

ROGER TANDY
B. circa 1690
D. circa 1757
M. Sarah Quarles according to M. W. Hiden
TO: MISS COLBY, Descendant of EDWARD COLBY
B. London
D. Jamestown, Va., 1620
Original subscriber to stock in the Virginia Co., 1607, and later one of largest land-owners of Virginia.

FRANCES TANDY

B.

D. 1816 - Will Christian Co., Ky.

M.

TO:

THOMAS BURRIS (BURRAS, BURRUS, BURROUGHS - Many Spellings)

B. 1700, Jamestown, Va.

D. 1 Mar., 1789, Orange Co., Va.

Soldier in French and Indian War. In capt. Geo. Mercer's Co. of Va. Regt., Col. Geo. Washington. At Braddock's defeat, 1755. Served also at Yorktown, et cet., in Revolution. For complete history, see "Register of Kentucky Historical Society Magazine", May, 1926, Vol. 24, No. 71, Pp. 182-190 at Historical Society of Penna. (Comment: Thomas Burrus is said to have lost an arm for which he received a pistol from Gen. Washington, in memory of his service in the French and Indian Wars and that Thomas Junior served in Rev. War. At any rate there is some confusion here. - W.E.B.)

SARAH ANN BURRIS

B. 13 Sept., 1753

D. 15 Dec., 1830

M. 1768

To:

REV. ANDREW TRIBBLE (See Line)

B. 15 Mar., 1741, Caroline Co., Va.

D. 22 Dec., 1822, Clark Co., Ky.

Chaplain in the Virginia line "and also carried a gun". Old Ironsides Baptist Minister. For complete history, see account re. Burris in "Register of Kentucky Historical Society Magazine", above.

(For much data, see also "The Brockman Scrapbook", 1952, by William Everett Brockman, Midland National Bank, Minneapolis, Minnesota.)

From "Orange County Virginia Families" by W. E. Brockman, Published by Burgess Publishing Co., Minneapolis 15, Minneapolis 15, Minnesota:

P. 137/9: Orange County Public Service Claims, Revolutionary War:

P. 137 "At a court held by the Justices of Orange County Court, at the Courthouse, on the first, second, third, fifteenth, sixteenth, twenty-sixth and twenty-seventh days of April, 1782. For adjusting the claims made to the said Court, agreeable to an Act made and passed the last session of Assembly, Intitled an Act 'For adjusting claims for property impressed or taken for public service'. The following claims were allowed to be just and reasonable.'

P. 166 Will of Thomas Burrus, 2 Oct., 1788, of county of Orange and Parish of St. Thomas. Mentions Grandson Thomas Burrus, son of Thomas Burrus; gives and bequeaths to his daughter, Sarah Tribble one negro girl named Agnes, et cet.; mentions his daughter Francis Tandy Bush; and to his beloved wife Francis (Tandy) leaves his estate real and personal. This will was presented in Court in Orange County on Monday, 23 Mar., 1789, by Francis Burrus, Henry Tandy and Thomas Burrus, executors.

P. 161 Will of Jacob Burras ("I, Jacob Burroughs", but signed "Jacob Burras" in presence of wife "Mary Burrus") 20 March, 1742, of Parish of St. Margaret's and County of Caroline Va., mentions wife Mary, and son Thomas. Latter received 273 acres, part of 400 acres granted to Jacob Burras by letters patent 15 March, 1735, lying on North side of Hickory Creek in Hanover County. This will filed in suit in Louisa County in April-May, 1767, of Davis vs. Burrus.

Comment by W. E. Brockman: Dr. Gordon gives the above Jacob Burrus as father of Thomas Burrus, who married Frances Tanday. The Will of Joseph Martin, Louisa and property transfers indicate that Thomas, son of Jacob, married Sarah Martin. A deed 1759 at Louisa from Thomas Burrus and wife Sarah proves that his wife was Sarah and not Frances. More details on page 51, Brockman Scrapbook. W.E.B.

WM. TRIBBLE, SR. (TREBLE)(TRIBILL)
B. England
D. England
(William Treble, Sen. Yeo. Combe Flory. Sons - Sentence 1656 - Folio 255: From English Court Records)

WM. TRIBBLE, JR.
B. Yorkshire, England
D. England
Came from Wales, England, with William, Sr., but returned with him to England where both died.

PETER TRIBBLE
B. Yorkshire, England, came to America in 1680 and settled near Jamestown, Va. Made his Will in Essex Co., Va., 6 Apr., 1738.
D.
M.
To: ELIZABETH

GEORGE TRIBBLE, SR., A Virginia Constable
B.
D.
M.
To: BETSY (BETTY) CLARK
Daughter of Jonathan and Elizabeth Wilson Clark, and Aunt of George Rogers Clark of American Revolution.
George Tribble, Sr., furnished material assistance for the Revolutionary cause and is a patriot from whom descent will entitle one to membership in the S.A.R.**

REV. ANDREW TRIBBLE
B. 15 Mar., 1741, Caroline Co., Va.*
D. 22 Dec., 1822, Clark Co., Ky., Buried in family cemetery*
M. 1768
To: SARAH ANN BURRIS (See Line)
B. 13 Sept., 1753*
D. 15 Dec., 1830*
Early Baptist Ironsides Minister. Served in American Revolution in which "he carried a gun". Removed to Kentucky c. 1782. For extensive history, see "Register of Kentucky Historical Society Magazine", May, 1926, Vol. 24, No. 71, pp. 182-190, at Historical Society of Penna.

* In Tribble Family Bible.
**According to Prof. Walter W. Smith, University of Idaho.

Children of Rev. Andrew Tribble, per Tribble Family Bible:

Andrew Tribble	born March 15, 1741	died Dec. 30, 1822
Sally Tribble	born Sept. 13, 1753	died Dec. 15, 1830
	children	
Francis Tribble	born Nov. 1769	died Sept. 13, 1814
Samuel Tribble	born Dec. 31, 1771	

Peter Tribble	born Mar. 8, 1774
Thomas Tribble	born June 13, 1776
Nancy Tribble	born Nov. 6, 1778
Sallie B. Tribble	born Feb. 9, 1781
Silas Tribble	born June 3, 1783
Andrew Tribble	born Dec. 2, 1785
Mary Tribble	born Mar. 29, 1788
John Tribble	born Aug. 15, 1790
Martha Tribble	born Mar. 7, 1794
Dudley Tribble	born May 1, 1797

Marriages

Francis Tribble	married	M. Stoner
Samuel Tribble	married	P. Martin
Peter Tribble	married	M. Boone on Oct. 8, 1793
Thomas Tribble	married	Mary Phelps
Nancy Tribble	married	Chenault on Oct. 3, 1794
Sallie B. Tribble	married	Crews on March 17, 1799
Silas Tribble	married	B. White on Oct. 30, 1809
Andrew Tribble	married	L. Boone on Jan. 24, 1810
Mary Tribble	married	Stephenson on Dec. 23, 1826
John Tribble	married	M. White 1834
Martha Tribble	married	R. White on Oct. 5, 1802
Dudley Tribble	married	M. Tevis on Jan. 21, 1819

Samuel Tribble born Dec. 31, 1771
Polly Martin born Mar. 13, 1772

children

P. M. Tribble	born Nov. 22, 1792
Andrew Tribble	born Mar. 31, 1794
Orson Tribble	born July 4, 1795
Amelia Tribble	born Oct. 1, 1796
Malinda Tribble	born Jan. 11, 1798
Samuel Tribble	born Jan. 24, 1800
Mary Tribble	born Aug. 1, 1801
John H. Tribble	born Nov. 20, 1803
Rachel Tribble	born Dec. 5, 1805
Sarah B. Tribble	born Dec. 23, 1807
Alfred Tribble	born Jan. 11, 1811
Thos. M. Tribble	born Apr. 14, 1813

Note 1: For this line, see D.A.R. lineage of Mrs. Benjamin F. Buckley (Corday Leer Tribble Buckley), Lexington, Ky., who has numerous Tribble Bibles, et cet.

Note 2: Peter Burrus Tribble, son of Rev. Andrew Tribble. Married Mary Boone, dau. of Geo. Boone, younger brother of Daniel, the Kentucky Pioneer, and his wife Ann Linville: See Hazel A. Spraker's "Boone Family" for this and further Tribble data.

ORANGE 100 YEARS AGO

From "THE ORANGE REVIEW", Orange, Virginia
Thursday, March 24, 1949

MEMOIRS ("Recollections") of Mrs. Fanny Walker Aglionby. Mrs. Aglionby was an aunt of Mrs. Henry Hill (nee Page Walker) and a first cousin of the late Robt. S. Walker, founder of Woodberry Forest School. All of Mrs. Aglionby's descendants - five grandchildren and sex great-grandchildren - live in England.

--

I was born on March 25, 1821, in Madison County on the Rapidan River at "Edgewood" (bought in 1948 by E. N. Nesmith), the home of my grandparents, John Walker and Fanny Alcock Walker. The house in which I was born, said to be the oldest in the county, was built by Thomas Scott for his daughter Bettie, who married Joseph Wood. A son of this Thomas Scott, Thomas Scott, Jr., lived two miles up the river at "Scottsville" (bought in 1946 by Frank S. Walker). When this was being written in 1902, neither of these original dwellings was standing. My half-brother, Reuben Walker, now lives at Scottsville" in a modern house, situated about a half a mile from the site of the old one.

My F ther and Mother, James Wood Walker and Martha Porter Walker, lived a few miles distant at "Retreat" (later owned by Mrs. Jane Walker Walters). There were so many of us children, seven in all, and Mother's health was so poor that three of us and our colored nurse Amy were moved to the home of our Walker grandparents. They had left "Edgewood" and were now living at a new home, "Woodlawn" (of this house, situated on a hill just west of Walker's Chapel, only a few traces are discernible). So "Woodlawn" became my home until I was married on May 28, 1844, to Charles Aglionby, a British subject.

The first important event of my childhood that I clearly remember was the marriage in 1824 of Aunt Sally Ware Walker to Dr. Alexander Spotswood Taliaferro, a grandson of Governor Alexander Spotswood, of the "Knights of the Golden Horseshoe" fame. Dr. Taliaferro was a graduate of Princeton and an M. D. of the University of Pennsylvania. Miss Kitty Madison, a daughter of a neighbor, Francis Madison, and the neice of President James Madison, attended the wedding. My Aunt Sally died in 1834, leaving five children. Within five months after his wife's death, in a ceremony performed in the hotel parlor at Orange Court House, Dr. Taliaferro married Kitty Madison. She proved to be a devoted wife and loving stepmother. Her husband never practiced his profession seriously, but wasted his time and money in frivolities. Grandfather helped to support the family.

The Francis Madison family lived at "Prospect Hill" on the Orange-Madison road and near a hill on the Rapidan that was built in 1795 and jointly owned by four Madisons - James Madison, Sr., and three of his sons, James, Jr., William and Francis. "Prospect Hill" was later owned by Dr. Lee Taliaferro, who married my niece, Virginia Walker (whose granddaughter now shares in the ownership of this property.)

Fanny Madison, another daughter of Mr. and Mrs. Francis Madison, married a Mr. Thompson Shepherd. For their wedding trip Grandfather lent them his carriage. They went first to Montpelier for a stay of several days with Fanny's Uncle James and Aunt Dolly. They then drove down the Fredericksburg road to Verdiersville, where Mr. Thompson kept a place of entertainment, or tavern. Our household was without a carriage for more than a week and when going to distant places had to travel on horseback. But bad roads and lack of vehicles had accustomed us to this mode of travel. When attending Hampden-Sydney College, distant more than a 100 miles, Grandfather had always made the trips to-and-fro on horseback, accompanied regularly by a Negro servant who carried his baggage and brought home his horse.

General William Madison, a brother of Francis, lived a mile down the river at Woodberry Forest. Mr. and Mrs. Madison had eight daughters and several sons. The children of these sisters and brothers were my contemporaries.

As a child I went occasionally to the village of Madison with my parents or grandparents to visit a great-aunt (by marriage), "Aunt Molly," the widow of John Walker, known as "Lawyer Walker" ti distinguish him from a nephew, John Walker, Jr., who was called "Clerk Walker." When Madison County was formed from Culpeper in 1792, John Walker, 62 years old, became its first commonwealth's attorney, and John Walker, Jr., 23, its first County Clerk, an office that he filled for many years. To avoid confusion, my Grandfather, a third John Walker, was generally called "Jack" Walker. He was four years younger than "Clerk Walker." James Walker, an older brother of "Lawyer Walker" and my great-grandmother, was a member of the House of Burgesses for ten years, 1761-1771. Aunt Molly was a daughter of Capt. Prettyman Merry, owner of the "Haxall Place" in Orange County (now "Rocklands," home of Mr. and Mrs. C. T. Neale.)

A childhood disappointment long remembered was occasioned by the visit of the Marquis de Lafayette to Orange Court House in 1825. Older members of the family rode off to Orange, six miles distant, to attend the big reception and banquet in the Marquis' honor, leaving me behind in the care of faithful "Aunt" Charlotte, a colored nurse. A life-long lover of liberty, Lafayette came to America at the age of 20 to offer his services to this country. He became a general in Washington's army and was of great help in the struggle for independence. Following the American Revolution he returned to France and became a political and military leader during the most turbulent period in that country's checkered history. He would probably have been guillotined in the Reign of Terror had he not at time been in prison in Belgium. Now at the age of 68, as a guest of the United States, he was traveling by carriage, frequently over terrible roads, from one state to another to attend ceremonies. And all of this he survived to take active part in another French revolution, that of 1830.

At the age of seven I went to "Retreat," the home of Father and Mother, in order to be near (distant two miles) a one-room, old-field school. The teacher was Mr. Rhodes, a lame man who frequently resorted to corporal punishment to make his pupils more diligent. I attended this school two years.

My mother's health began to fail in the winter of 1829-30, and I was kept at home to be with her. Propped up in bed, she taught me to cut out dresses for the servants and to sew. She made me read aloud the Bible to her and to join with her in singing hymns. My Mother had a sweet voice and was fond of singing. I inherited from her a delight in singing. My Mother was a devout Christian and liked to attend church services but opportunities to do so were infrequent. Sometimes she rode on horseback with me behind her to the "Providence Methodist Church," where service was held once a month. She would have joined the Presbyterian Church, only there was none nearer than Fredericksburg. Mother died on July 19, 1830, only a few days after she had reached her 30th birthday. She left seven children to be cared for by their father and grandparents. Mother was born in Orange County, two miles above Raccoon Ford, at the home of her parents, Camp and Martha Porter.

In January, 1831, I was sent away to school. In those days schools began on Jan. 15th and closed the middle of December, with the month of August as a vacation. My grandmother's sister, Mrs. Patsy Johnson, who lived in Orange County near the Louisa line and not far from the Pamunky River, had engaged as a teacher for her children a Miss Davenport, who had been educated in Charlottesville. Miss Davenport was an excellent teacher and in order that I might get the benefit of her instruction my Father decided to place me in the Johnson home. Father and I made the 16-mile trip to the Johnsons' on horseback, he on one horse and I on another, with a carpet bag on the pommel of my saddle. I was only ten years old and completely exhausted after an all-day ride on roads so soft and muddy that we had to walk the horses much of the distance. Every detail of that trip continues a vivid memory. My year in the Johnson household was happy and beneficial.

Major Ambrose Madison lived at "Cleveland" (now owned by the Misses Clark), directly across the Rapidan from Woodlawn and four miles distant. Major Madison was a son of William Madison and a nephew of Ambrose Madison who lived at "Woodley" on the Orange-Gordonsville road (now the property of F. H. Walton). In January of 1832 Major Madison engaged Miss Davenport as governess for his daughter and took into his home as boarding pupils four girls: Lucy Welsh, Mat Booton, Mary Ella Chapman and me. One girl, Conwayella Macon, came daily from "Somerset" (where Mr. and Mrs. A. H. Jones now live), the home of her grandparents, Mr. and Mrs. Thomas Macon. Mrs. Macon, born at Montpelier, was a sister of the four Madison brothers previously mentioned. The commodious "Somerset" house was built in 1803 by Mr. Macon.

So Miss Davenport had as pupils six little girls, ranging in age from ten to thirteen, and a happy lot we were. Lucy Welsh married Reuben Newman, of Orange County. Mat Booton never married and continued her life at her Madison home. Four of us married husbands who lived in other states. Occasionally I took one or two of my school mates to my home for a week-end. Father brought us back to school one day and while at Cleveland became engaged in an excited conversation with Major Madison about a recent marvelous achievement - a railroad had been built from Boston to Lowell, Mass. They had grave doubts about its proving a success.

In 1833 Major Madison moved his family and little school to Orange for the winter months. We lived in a house across the road from where an Episcopal Church was being built. Orange had at the time only about two hundred and fifty inhabitants ans was without a church. Religious services were held in the Court House or in the ball room of the hotel. The stage coach from Gordonsville came right by our school. Frequently we girls would run to meet it and if we saw vacant seats, would ask for a ride. One evening we had gone to the top of the next hill to meet the stage. When it came along, we called, "Give us a ride!" A venevolent looking old gentleman with long white hair opened the door and said, "Good Evening, young ladies." It was General Andrew Jackson, President of the United States. He was on his way to Washington from his home in Tennessee. The President was given a banquet at the hotel that night. The speech of Welcome was made by the Hon. William C. Rives. When my Father told me that Congressman Rives' mother was a Walker and a relative, I felt very proud.

ORANGE COUNTY MILITARY COMMISSIONS

For Service in State Militia. From the Order Book on page as indicated.

PAGE	NAME	DATE	RANK
197	Anderson, William	Aug. 1742	Ensign
345	Anderson, George	Feb. 1742	Captain
394	Ashby, Thomas	Mch. 1742	Captain of Foot.
82	Bryant, Morgan	June 1736	
330	Bell, William	Mch. 1741	Cornet
54	Beverley, William	Nov. 1741	Lieutenant of Orange and Augusta
102	Bush, Phillip	Feb. 1741	Ensign
160	Buchannon, John	June 1742	Captain
347	Breckenridge, Robert	Mch. 1742	Captain
462	Brown, John	June 1743	Lieu. Co. of Foot.
499	Ball, Samuel	June 1743	Captain
198	Borden, Benj.	Aug. 1744	Capt. of Foot.
269	Bird, Andrew	Feb. 1744	Lieut. of Foot.
279	Bell, William	Mch. 1745	Lieutenant
328	Baylor, John (of Carolic Co.)	Apr. 1745	Major
199	Baylor, John	July 1749	Lieutenant
440	Baylor, John	May 1753	Lieutenant
156	Bell, William	July 1755	Captain
364	Barbour, Richard	Feb. 1758	Captain
396	Burnley, Zack	Oct. 1766	Major
67	Bell, John	May 1770	Captain
360	Bruce, Charles	June 1772	Captain
61	Brockman, John	Feb. 1777	Lieutenant
74	Burton, May, Jr.	Aug. 1777	Ensign
75	Burton, Ambrose	Sept. 1777	Ensign
75	Buckner, William	Sept. 1777	2nd Lieut.
90	Burnley, Zack	May 1778	County Lieut.
90	Barbour, Thomas	May 1778	Major
90	Burton, May, Jr.	May 1778	1st Lieut.
90	Buckner, William	May 1778	Captain
111	Burton, May, Jr.	May 1779	1st Lieut.
138	Burton, May, Jr.	May 1780	Captain
138	Burton, William	May 1780	2nd Lieut.
138	Beadles, John	May 1780	2nd Lieut.
152	Burton, James	July 1781	2nd Lieut.
152	Burton, William	July 1781	Ensign
161	Barbour, Thomas	July 1781	Colonel
161	Bell', Mary	July 1781	Jailor of Co.
229	Burnley, Garland	Feb. 1783	Captain
299	Barbour, Thomas	Oct. 1784	Co. Lieutenant
366	Bell, Thomas	July 1786	Ensign
	Burnley, Hardin	July 1787	Major
	Burton, May	July 1787	Captain
	Beadles, John	July 1787	Captain
	Bell, Thomas	July 1787	Lieut.
	Bell, James	July 1787	Lieut.
	Beckham, James	July 1787	Ensign
	Burnley, James	July 1787	Ensign

	Burton, William	Sept. 1787	Lieut.
	Burnley, Hardin	Sept. 1790	Colonel
	Bell, Thomas	Sept. 1790	Captain
	Bledsoe, Miller	Sept. 1790	Ensign
	Beadles, John	April 1793	Captain
	Bell, Thomas	April 1793	Captain
38	Cave, Benj.	Nov. 1735	Capt. of troop of Hrs.
63	Chew, Thomas	Mch. 1735	Major
351	Chew, Thomas	July 1738	
70	Cave, Robert	July 1738	Capt. Troop of Horse
99	Chew, Thomas	Feb. 1741	Col. of County
113	Curtis, Charles	Feb. 1741	Captain
160	Cathey, James	June 1742	Captain
160	Christian, John	June 1742	Captain
185	Clayton, Phillip	July 1742	Lieutenant
345	Campbell, Andrew	Feb. 1742	Captain
345	Carter, Joseph	Feb. 1742	Lieutenant
425	Coulton, Joseph	May 1743	Captain
506	Craven, Robert	July 1743	Capt. of Horse
1	Carpenter, William	Aug. 1743	
152	Clayton, Phillip	May 1748	Captain
157	Covington, Thomas	Nov. 1748	Lieut. of Foot.
71	Craig, Toliver	Feb. 1777	Captain
71	Conway, C tlett	July 1777	Captain
76	Chambers, Thomas	Oct. 1777	Ensign
101	Chambers, Thomas	Nov. 1778	2nd Lieut.
108	Cave, Belfield	April 1779	2nd Lieut.
137	Cave, Belfield	May 1780	1st Lieut.
137	Chambers, Thomas	May 1780	1st Lieut.
161	Cave, Belfield	July 1781	Captain
366	Coleman, James	July 1786	Ensign
	Cave, Belfield	July 1787	Captain
	Coleman, James	July 1787	Lieutenant
	Coleman, James, Jr.	July 1787	Ensign
	Coleman, Thomas	July 1787	Ensign
	Chapman, Joseph	Sept. 1787	Ensign
	Campbell, William	Sept. 1790	Lieut. Col. of Co.
	Cave, Belfield	Sept. 1790	Major
	Chapman, Joseph	Sept. 1790	Lieut.
	Coleman, James	April 1793	Capt.
	Chapman, Joseph	April 1793	Capt.
	Campbell, William	June 1793	Lieut. Col.
	Conner, Timothy	May 1780	1st Lieut.
330	Downs, Henry	March 1741	Capt. Troop Horse
110	Doggett, George	Feb. 1741	Lieut.
200	Dewitt, Charles	Aug. 1742	Lieut.
200	Duncan, William	Aug. 1742	Ensign
345	Denton, John	Feb. 1742	Capt.
1	Dunlap, Alexander	Aug. 1743	Capt. of Horse
56	Dobbin, John	Feb. 1742	Lieutenant of Horse
207	Daniel, Reuben	March 1755	Captain
558	Daniel, Reuben	May 1761	Captain
61	Daniel, Vivian	Sept. 1774	Captain
74	Daniel, Robert	Aug. 1777	2nd Lieut.

163	Dawson, John	Sept. 1781	Ensign
163	Deering, James	Sept. 1781	Ensign
280	Davis, John	May 1784	Ensign
280	Daniel, John	May 1784	1st Lieut.
298	Davis, Thomas	Sept. 1784	Ensign
	Daniel, John	July 1787	Captain
	Daniel, William	July 1787	Lieutenant
	Davis, John	July 1787	Ensign
	Dawson, John	April 1793	Captain
160	Evans William	June 1742	Lieutenant
200	Eastham, Robert	Aug. 1742	Captain
163	Early, James	Sept. 1781	Ensign
	Early, Joseph	July 1787	Ensign
137	Emgram, William	May 1780	Ensign
63	Finlason, John	March 1735	Captain
102	Finlason, John	Feb. 1741	Major
163	Field, Henry	June 1742	Captain
201	Farguson, Samuel	Aug. 1742	Ensign
394	Funk, John	March 1742	Lieut.
138	Fortson, Thomas	May 1780	1st Lieut.
342	Goodall, John	June 1757	Lieutenant
185	Green, Robert	July 1742	Captain
197	Gill, James	Aug. 1742	Captain
104	Guy, Henry	May 1742	Lieut. of Foot.
160	Guy, Samuel	Aug. 1742	Captain
270	Carnett, Anthony	Feb. 1744	Capt. of Foot.
47	Gibbs, Zachary	Aug. 1737	Lieut. of Foot.
76	Graves, Richard	Cot. 1777	2nd Lieut.
92	Graves, Richard	July 1778	Captain
280	Gaines, Richard	May 1784	2nd Lieut.
366	Gibson, John	July 1786	Lieut.
	Gaines, Richard	July 1787	Lieut.
	Gaines, Richard	Sept. 1790	Captain
	Gaines, Richard	Apr. 1793	Captain 1st Reg.
	Gaines, Reuben	Aug. 1793	Captain 2nd Reg.
4	Grymes, Ludwell	May 1769	Captain
260	Howard, John	Feb. 1737	Capt. Troop
197	Holt, Peter	Aug. 1742	Captain
345	Hite, John	Feb. 1742	Captain
345	Hobson, George	Feb. 1742	Lieut.
345	Hite, Jacob	Feb. 1742	Lieut.
345	Harrison, John	Feb. 1742	Lieut.
506	Harrison, Daniel	July 1743	Capt. of Horse
412	Hays, Andrew 5	Aug.	Lieut. of Foot
361	Hudson, Rush	Nov. 1757	Lieut.
	Head, Benj.	1777	Captain
73	Head, James	Aug. 1777	Ensign
74	Hansford, Benoni	Aug. 1777	2nd Lieut.
92	Hansford, Benoni	Aug. 1777	2nd Lieut.
74	Hawkins, James	Aug. 1777	2nd Lieut.
77	Hawkins, James	Oct. 1777	1st Lieut.
	Hawkins, James	Mch. 1777	Captain
	Hansford, Ben	Sept. 1786	Lieut.
	Hawkins, James	July 1787	Captain

	Hansford, Benj.	July 1787	Captain
92	Herndon, Zach	July 1778	Captain
238	Jones, Thomas	Sept. 1742	Lieutenant
346	Jones, Robt.	Feb. 1742	Ensign
327	Jameson, William	April 1745	Captain
490	Jones, Thomas	June 1736	Captain
207	Jones, John	March 1755	Captain
315	Jameson, Thomas	Jan. 1757	Captain
235	Jameson, Thomas	Feb. 1773	Ensign
75	Johnson, Robt.	Sept. 1777	2nd Lieut.
108	Johnson, Robert	April 1779	1st Lieut.
137	Jameson, James	May 1780	Captain
138	Johnson, Martin	May 1780	Ensign
161	Johnson, Benjamin	July 1781	Lieut.
	Johnson, Benjamin	April 1787	Lieut. Col.
	Johnson, Benjamin	Sept. 1790	Co. Lieut.
104	Jameson, Wm.	March 1779	Ensign
104	Karr, John	May 1744	Captain of troop of horse
53	Lightfoot, Goodrich	Feb. 1735	Commission
431	Lewis, John	Feb. 1738	Commission
247	Lightfoot, Goodrich	Sept. 1740	Captain of troop
99	Lightfoot, Goodrich	Feb. 1741	Captain
345	Lewis, John	Feb. 1742	Colonel
345	Low, Thomas	Feb. 1742	Captain
77	Lindsay, Caleb	Oct. 1777	1st Lieut.
149	Lindsay, Caleb	Nov. 1780	Captain
	Lindsay, Caleb	July 1787	Captain
53	Morgan, Morgan	Feb. 1735	Commission
163	Morton, George	May 1740	Commission
209	McCrackin, James	July 1740	Commission
247	Michael, Francis	Sept. 1740	Cornet
102	Michael, Francis	Feb. 1741	Ensign
160	Moffett, John	June 1742	Lieut.
163	Morton, George	June 1742	Ensign
163	Moore, Frans	June 1742	Ensign
197	McDowell, John	Aug. 1742	Captain
345	Morgan, Morgan	Feb. 1742	Major
345	Morris, Samuel	Feb. 1742	Lieut.
346	Morgan, Richard	Feb. 1742	Captain
462	McMure, Daniel	June 1743	Captain
462	Matthews, John	June 1743	Captain
293	Michael, Francis	March 1745	Lieut. of Foot
383	Moore, Francis	June 1745	Lieut. of Foot
489	Mallory, John	June 1736	Ensign
342	Moore, Francis	June 1757	Major
174	Morton, Jeremiah	July 1755	Capt.
218	Moore, Francis	Aug. 1749	Captain
552	Moore, Francis	April 1761	Major
447	Madison, James	July 1767	Co. Lieut.
447	Moore, Francis	July 1767	Lieut. Col.
480	Moore, William	March 1768	Captain
514	Moore, William	July 1768	Captain
514	Merry, Thomas	July 1768	Lieut.
4	NcNeal, Patrick	May 1769	Ensign

61	Mills, Nath.	Feb. 1777	Captain (Rec. to Governor)
90, 74	Miller, Robt.	Aug. 1777	2nd. Lieut.
90	Martin, Robt. Jr.	May 1778	Ensign
104	Moore, Reuben	March 1779	Lieut.
111	Miller, Robert	May 1779	Capt.
137	Morris, Reuben	May 1780	1st Lieut.
148	Merry, Prettyman	Oct. 1780	2nd Lieut.
161	Madison, James, Jr.	July 1781	Co. Lieut.
161	Madison, Ambrose	July 1781	Major
280	Merry, Prettyman	May 1784	Captain
298	Miner, Jere	Sept. 1784	Captain
	Miller, John	July, 1787	Captain
	Miller, John	April 1793	Captain
61	Mallory, Uriel (resigned)	Feb. 1777	Captain
345	Neil, Lewis	Feb. 1742	Captain
137	Newman, Alex	May 1780	Ensign
360	Patton, James	Feb. 1742	Col. horse & foot.
154	Patton, James	May 1742	Col. of Augusta
345	Pickins, John	Feb. 1742	Captain
345	Pennington, Isaac	Feb. 1742	Captain
24	Peyton, William	Nov. 24 1743	Lieut. of foot
315	Pendleton, Jno.	Jan. 1757	Ensign
33	Pearce, Jeremiah	Aug. 1763	Lieut.
33	Pearson, Henry	Aug. 1763	Ensign
61	Parish, Joseph	Feb. 1777	Ensign
75	Proctor, John	Sept. 1777	Ensign
92	Porter, John	July 1778	2nd Lieut.
104	Porter, Abner, Jr.	March 1779	Lieut.
104	Price, Richard	March 1779	Lieut.
110	Porter, Charles	March 1779	Lieut.
111	Price, Rich. Moore	March 1779	Ensign
137	Payne, Richard	May 1780	2nd Lieut.
137	Pannill, John	May 1780	2nd Lieut.
337	Quin, John	Jan. 1742	Lieut.
163	Rucker, John	May 1740	Capt. for County
99	Russell, Wm.	Feb. 1741	Captain
185	Roberts, John	July 1742	Ensign
197	Robinson, George	Aug. 1742	Captain
200	Roberts, Benj.	Aug. 1742	Lieut.
30 - (D.B.9)	Roberts, Benj.	Aug. 1746	Captain
24	Russell, Peter	Nov. 1743	Ensign
440	Roy, Mungo	May 1753	Colonel
137	Riddle, Lewis	May 1780	1st Lieut.
137	Rucker, Jno.	May 1780	Ensign
137	Robinson, John	May 1780	Ensign
366	Row, Thomas	July 1786	Lieut.
	Row, Thomas	July 1787	Captain
	Riddle, Lewis	July 1787	Ensign
	Row, Thomas	Sept. 1790	Captain
	Riddle, Lewis	Sept. 1790	Captain
	Row, Thomas	Apr. 1793	Captain

345	Rutherford, Thos.	Feb. 1742	Captain
	Smith, John	June 1739	Commission
163	Spencer, Edward	May 1740	Capt. for Orange Co.
247	Sisson, Bryan	Sept. 1740	Lieut.
268	Slaughter, Robert	Sept. 1740	Major
99	Slaughter, Robert	Feb. 1741	Lieut. Col. of Co.
160	Smith, John	June 1742	Captain
163	Spencer, Edward	June 1742	Captain
168	Smith, Just Phonica	June 1742	Lieut.
197	Scott, Robert	Aug. 1742	Lieut.
197	Scott, George	Aug. 1742	Ensign
346	Swearinham, Thomas	Feb. 1742	1st Lieut.
394	Smith, Jeremiah	March 1742	Capt. of Foot
26	Scott, Robt.	Nov. 1743	Capt. of Foot
104	Smith, Wm.	Aug. 1744	Capt. of Foot
103	Scott, Saml.	May 1744	Ensign
152	Slaughter, Thomas	May 1748	Lieut.
199	Spencer, Edward	July 1749	Major
364	Scott, Johnny	Feb. 1758	Lieut.
618	Suggett, James	March 1762	Lieut.
	Scott, Johnny	Nov. 1767	Captain
502	Smith Joseph	June 1768	Ensign
4	Smith	May 1769	Lieut.
4	Stevens, John	May 1769	Ensign
72	Singleton, Manoah	July 1777	2nd Lieut.
73	Smith, Wm.	Aug. 1777	2nd Lieut.
76	Stubblefield, Goe.	Oct. 1777	1st Lieut.
77	Shackelford, Zachy.	Oct. 1777	2nd Lieut.
90	Smith, Geo.	May 1778	(resigned as Captain)
104	Sisson, Caleb	March 1779	Ensign
109	Scott, John	April 1779	Ensign
137	Shackleford, Edmond	May 1780	Captain
137	Scott, John, Jr.	May 1780	1st Lieut.
137	Sanders, James	May 1780	2nd Lieut.
149	Shackleford, Zach	Nov. 1780	1st Lieut.
149	Stevens, James	Nov. 1780	1st Lieut.
160	Stubblefield, Robert	July 1780	Captain
163	Sleet, James	Sept. 1781	Ensign
366	Smith, Absalom	July 1786	Lieut.
	Shackleford, Edward	July 1787	Captain
	Shepherd, Geo.	July 1787	Captain
	Smith, Absalom	Sept. 1790	Lieut.
197	Thomson, Hugh	Aug. 1742	Captain
337	Tayloe, George	Jan. 1742	Captain
268	Thompson, William	Feb. 1744	Company of Foot.
160	Taylor, George	Feb. 1748	Major
181	Taylor, George	June 1749	Lieut. Col.
156	Taylor, George	July 1755	Col.
156	Thomas, Rowland	July 1755	Captain
156	Thomas, Richard	July 1755	Captain
315	Thomas, Robert	Jan. 1757	Lieut.
334	Taylor, George	May 1757	Co. Lieut.
552	Taylor, George	April 1761	Col.
334	Taliaferro, William	May 1757	Col.

552	Thomas, Richard	April 1761	Lieut.
552	Thomas, Rowland	April 1761	Lieut.
555	Thomas, Robert	April 1761	Lieut.
669	Thomas, Robert	April 1762	Captain
33	Taylor, James	Aug. 1763	Captain
	Thomas, Robert	Nov. 1767	Captain
	Taylor, James	March 1768	Captain
	Taylor, Zackary	March 1768	Lieut.
514	Taliaferro, Lawrence	July 1768	Captain
514	Taliaferro, Hay	July 1768	Lieut.
4	Taylor, James, Jr.	May 1769	Captain
4	Taylor, Zackary	May 1769	Lieut.
19	Taylor, Zacky	Sept. 1774	Captain
19	Taylor, Jonathon	Sept. 1774	Lieutenant
76	Thomas, Robert	Oct. 1777	Captain
90	Taliaferro, Lawrence	May 1778	Lieut. Col.
139	Thomas, Rowland, Jr.	May 1780	Lieut.
149	Thomas, Robert (resigned)	Nov. 1780	Captain
149	Thomas, William	Nov. 1780	2nd Lieut.
163	Thomas, Chs.	Sept. 1781	Ensign
298	Thomas, Jos. Jr.	Sept. 1784	Lieut.
	Taylor, Reuben	Sept. 1786	Captain
	Thomas, Joseph	July 1787	Captain
425	Valance, David	May 1743	Lieut.
38	Willis, Henry	Nov. 1735	Lieut. for Co.
345	Wood, James	Feb. 1742	Col. of Horse & foot
345	Walter, Edward	Feb. 1742	Lieutenant
56q	Watts, John	Feb. 1743	Ensign
201	Wilson, John	Aug. 1744	Captain
174	Walker, James	July 1755	Lieut.
552	Walker, James	April 1761	Lieut.
630	Walker, James	April 1762	Captain
61	Webb, Richard Crittenden	Feb. 1777	Lieut.
74	Wright, Wm.	Aug. 1777	Ensign
77	Waugh, George	Oct. 1777	2nd Lieut.
90	White, Benj.	May 1778	Captain
90	White, Richard	May 1778	Ensign
104	Waugh, Geo.	March 1779	Lieut.
111	White, Richard	May 1779	2nd Lieut.
137	Waugh, Geo.	May 1780	Captain
137	Willis, Lewis	May 1780	2nd Lieut.
137	Willis, Moses	May 1780	2nd Lieut.
137	Webb, Richard Crittenden	May 1780	Captain
138	White, Thos.	May 1780	Ensign
160	Wright, John	July 1781	Ensign
217	Welsh, James	July 1782	Lieut.
280	Wood, Joseph, Jr.	May 1784	Captain
	Webb, Rich?	July 1787	Captain
	White, Rich.	Sept. 1787	Captain
	Wright, John	April 1793	Captain
110	Winslow, Richard	Feb. 1741	Captain
238	Yarbrough, Richard	Sept. 1742	Ensign
247	Zimmeman, Christopher	Sept. 1740	Lieutenant
197	Zimmeman, Christopher	Aug. 1742	Lieutenant

NOTE: See Volume II, Orange County Families, for other Colonial and Revolutionary Soldiers. (W.E.B.)

MARSHALL-DURRETT

Relationships between these two families and their connection with the Brockmans is established by inference and partly by documents. We will start with Jael Johnson who was a daughter of Charles Taliaferro and she married Richard Johnson after having been married first to a Williams. She left a Will at Spottsylvania 1773, naming son Richard Tutt, who gets property known as "Elizabeth Tutt's Chest" and I assume a son-in-law, son James Williams, William Williams, daughter Betty Marshall, Sarah Cavenaugh, Jael and Philomen Cavanaugh. Without making a direct statement evidence seems to point out that Betty, daughter of Jael Johnson, married a Marshall, and son John married Elizabeth Markham and had a daughter that married a Brockman, son William married Elizabeth Williams, Sarah, married Richard Durrett, Patty married Thomas Jones. The Culpeper Marshalls are not mentioned in the Paxton Chart of the Marshall family. Elizabeth Marshall of Culpeper Will April 17, 1779, widow of John, named a son Markham and it would appear that her maiden name was Markham. Thomas Marshall left a Will at Culpeper May 3, 1793, naming wife Zanna and children, John, Elizabeth Petty, Mary Davenport, Lucy Ropon or Ripon, Thomas and Sarah. John Marshall, son of Thomas and Zanna was the John who sold 11 acres to Thomas Sims, Jr., July 21, 1800. Another Grandson of Elizabeth Markham Marshall and her husband John was Enoch, who died Culpeper, 1805, leaving an orphan, Margaret. She married Henry Sims of Culpeper who had a son, Henry C. Sims of Putnam, W. Va., and he was attorney for the C & O Railway and he said that his grandmother Margaret Simms was a niece of Humphrey Marshall, first cousin to Chief Justice Marshall, and Humphrey married Mary, sister of the Chief Justice. Elizabeth Marshall, Will at Culpeper, April 17, 1779, named children Thomas, William, John, Mary McClanahan, Markham, Margaret Snelling and grandchildren Thomas Smith and William Lovell.

There were two brothers in Spottsylvania, Robert and Richard Durrett, and it is believed that Bartholomew of Caroline and father of Joel whose daughter Nancy married Samuel Brockman, was a brother, certainly of the same family. Robert whose wife was Elizabeth Goodloe, left a Will at Spottsylvania Nov. 5, 1763, proved July 1, 1765, named son George, Robert, daughter Elizabeth, daughter Leah, daughter Katherine, wife Elizabeth and my "seven children", George, Robert, Mary Ann Hoskins, Diana Chapman, Elizabeth, Leah, and Katherine.

Richard Durrett, his brother, Will Spottsylvania, July 28, 1763, Bond July 4, 1768, ex-wife Sarah (Marshall), land in Caroline County and Spottsylvania to be divided among my boys. Any Estate I receive from Elizabeth Marshall or anyone else to be so divided. My daughters and younger children to be supported till they marry or come of age. Sept. 4, 1769, William Marshall, guardian to Ann, Richard, Marshall, James, and Sally Durrett, orphans of Richard Durrett. Richard Durrett had been named guardian of William, Mary, Joel, children of Bartholomew Durrett in 1763. Then in 1764, after Richard died, Benjamin Winn was named guardian of Dorothy, daughter of Bartholomew Durrett. It appears that Richard Durrett of Caroline, married Sarah Hampton, dau. of George, and he went to Albemarle and left will there 1784. Also Marshall Durrett settled in Albemarle. Richard, son of Richard of Albemarle, married Elizabeth, dau. of Isaac Davis and his family is covered in the Brockman Scrapbook. Was Richard of Spottsylvania father of Richard, of Caroline? That is not proven, however, connection with the family is definite. Dec. 21, 1775, Richard Durrett of Caroline transferred 116 acres which he "received from his father's estate in Spottsylvania" to William Durrett bounded by the lines of Elizabeth, George, Marshall and James Durrett, who were the children of Richard, Will 1763. John, another brother of Robert Durrett married Katherine, daughter of Henry Goodloe who left a Will at Spottsylvania and she was a sister to Elizabeth, wife of brother Robert.

No attempt is being made to give a documented line of the Marshalls or Durretts. This data is to help some one in the future. Captain O. T. Wills, who is descended from a marriage of Frances Durrett and William Wills, and whose address is in care of the Finance Corps, U.S. Army, 37A Benjamin Harrison Village, Indianapolis 16, In ana, has done some work on the Durrett Line. Will of Richard Durrett, Albemarle, Oct. 18, 1784, proved December the same year mentions son Richard, daughters, Elizabeth Watts, Ann Sanford, Frances Wills, Agatha Flynt, Nancy Sanford, Grandson Austin Smith, Reuben Sanford, daughter Mildred Williams, Sarah Flynt, deceased, granddaughters, Sarah Flynt and Susannah Burrus, and son-in-laws, Stephen Smith and also William Flynt. From this and other research his children seems to have been:

Richard, Jr., married Elizabeth Davis.
Elizabeth, m. Jacob Watts.
Ann, m. Robert Sanford.
Frances, m. Frederick William Wills
Mildred, m. Williams, 2nd, Stephen Smith
Agatha, m. Flynt.
Sarah, m. Flynt.
Ann, m. Thomas Burrus.

Albemarle Co., Va., Records

D. B. 6, p. 474, May 28, 1775 -

This Indenture made this 28th day of May in the year of Our Lord Christ one thousand seven hundred and seventy-five between Thomas Jones and Patty his wife Richard Durrett and William Brockman of Albemarle county of the one part and Jason Bacok of the county of said of the other part witnesses that the said Thomas Jones and Patty his wife, Richard Durrett and William Brockman for and in consideration of the sum of one hundred and sixty-five pounds current money of Virginia to them in hand paid by the said Jason Bacock the xxxxxxxxx whereof we xxx the xxxxxxxx acknowledge and thereof doth acquit and discharge the said Jason Bacock his heir executors and administrators and for diverse good cause and consideration then there unto moving that granted Bargained sold alien enfeoffed, confirmed be these present doth grant bargain sell alien enfeoff and confirmed unto the said Jason Bacock his heirs and xxxxxxxxx one track or parcel of land containing by estimation 370 acres lying on the Branched of Pretus Creek in the County of Albemarle and is bound as followith to wit: Beginning at a white oak-saplin and pine in Richard Durretts corner south 69 degrees East one hundred poles thence along the said line to two small hiccorys north 61 degrees East 23 poles hence a xx to a white oak 69 degrees East 18 poles hence along sd. line to a Black gum saplin South 86 degrees E st 12 poles thence to a white hiccory South 59 degrees East 22 poles hence along to a white oak on the road south 28 degrees West 20 poles thence to a pine and past oak south 69 degrees East 63 poles thence to great pine in Thos. Garths line south 23 and half degrees West 294 poles thence along the line to three pines North 39 and half degrees west 71 poles then down the Branch to the fork to a hiccory saplin 36 degrees west 21 poles then to two hiccory Bushes 23 degree west 18 poles thence north 19 poles there to several saplins north 13 degrees west 27 poles thence to a great white oak North 9 degrees west 21 poles to a tall pine North 23 degrees west 14 poles thence to a red oak on Brockman line north 5 degrees West 54 poles thence to a hickory and dogwood north 1 degree East 26 poles to hiccories north 49 degrees East 32 poles north 54 degrees west 10 poles north 26 degrees East 72 poles to the beginning to have and to hold the said land premises with the appertenance and every part thereof unto the said Jason Bacock his heirs and assign forever to the only pr per us of Enfeoff of him the sd. Jason Bacock his heirs and assigns forever now the sd. Thos. Jones and Patty his wife of Orange County and Rich'd.

Durrett and William Brockman of Albemarle County their heirs the sd. mentioned and granted premises with the appertenance unto said Jason Bacock his heirs and assigns shall and will warrant and forever defend against all persons whatever pretending to claim any light in xxxxxxx to the same on any part or parts thereof for this we the sd. Thos. Jones and Patty his wife, Richard Durrett, and William Brockman doth oblige ourselves to make the said Jason Bacock and his heirs what for the deeds he on they shall have fully advise devise or xxxxxxxxx. In witness hereof the sd. Thos. Jones and Patty his wife, Richard Durrett and William Brockman hath set own hand and find our seal the year and day above written.

Signed, sealed and Delivered
in present of us.

Thomas Jones
Patty Jones
William Brockman

MEMORANDUM

Xxxxxx xxxxxxx xxxxxx xxxxxxxx xxxxxxxxxxxx and sign of the within mentioned land and premises was had and taken by the within named Jason Bacock of and from the within named Thos. Jones and his wife Patty, Rich'd Durrett and William Brockman according to the form and affect of the within written deed on the day and year within written.

IN Present of Us.

Thos. Jones
Patty Jones
William Brockman

At Albemarle Court, Oct. 1775, this indenture was acknowledged by Thomas Jones, William Brockman party thereto and ordered to be recorded. Patty Jones personally appeared in Court and after being privately examined as Law directs, voluntarially relinquished her rights of dower in the land conveyed by the said Indenture.

TESTE: John Nicholas CLK.

Albemarle Co., Virginia Records

D.B. 4, page 112, Aug. 7, 1765.

Richard Durrett to Stephen Jones Jr., 200 A. for twenty pounds - On Preties Creek beginning at John Majors lower line - to Rogers Dicksons line - to Roger Quarles patent line - which land is a tract that was granted Roger Quarles in 1741.

Wit: Net Jackson
Richard Durrett, Jr.
Mary Wilson

Richard Durrett
Sarah Durrett

D.B. 4, page 468, Dec. 9, 1767.

John Major of King and Queen Co., to Thomas Jones 320 A. for seventy-two pounds. Branches of Pritties Creek - beginning at John Reds corner - to Hnery Haynes to Thos. Moremans - to Wm. Hoomes - to John Dowell - to John Rieds.

D.B. 4, page 234, 1766

Know all men by these present that we, John Durrett of Spotsvania Co., and Richard Durrett of Albemarle Co., divers and good cause do hereby give to George Martin of the said county of Albemarle, one negro girl named Dalphine and her increase which he is to xxxxxxxx and enjoy during his natural life and after his decease, we give the said negro girl and her increase to be divided Sally and Susannah Martin, daughter of George Martin by his last wife, Molly. Given under our hand this 20th day of Feb., 1766.

Wit: Mary Wilson
Wm. Wilson
Sarah Durrett

John Durrett
Rich'd Durrett

Compiled by Mildred Marshall.

Data of William and Richard Marshall of Albemarle Co., Va. Records of will, deeds and marriages recorded in Albemarle Co., Va. Also the line of W. Gordon Marshall.

Richard Marshall Will Book 4, p. 22, dated Oct. 1. 1798, probated April, 1799. Names wife Mary, Brother Wm. Marshall as executor. Witnesses: James Seims, Michael Catterton, Geo. Bingham and Matthew Boswell.

1. James Boswell Marshall m. Milly Hensley, 1795. No record of him in Albemarle Co., Va., after 1832.
2. Polly (Mary) m. Richard Sullivan, 1800, moved to Stokes Co., N.C.
3. Joseph Marshall m. Mary Boswell, 1810. (Moved to Ky.)
4. Henry Marshall m. 1st, Eliz. Walton, 1810; 2nd, Doretha Shiffet before 1830.
5. Richard Marshall m. Eliz. (Sally) Rodes, 1809, (moved to Saline Co., Mo., 1822.).
6. Betsey (Eliz.) m. Sullivan (moved to Stokes Co., N.C.).
7. Wm. Marshall m. Mary Connerly, 1792 (moved to Saline Co., Mo.).
8. Thomas Marshall m. Nancy Ancell, 1803, and or Patsy Marshall, 1819. (His wife or wives a matter of speculation).

NOTE: Richard Marshall Sr., was granted a pension by the State of Legislature of Va., in 1790, because he had been wounded in Camden while in the army, rendering him unable to support himself by labor. Twenty pounds in advance and twelve pounds annually for life.

(The above information by Dr. J. R. Smith, now deceased, and is proven by deeds recorded in Albemarle County, Virginia) M. Marshall.

MARSHALL FAMILY

William Marshall W. B. VIII, page 118, 1822, Albemarle County, Virginia, names wife Elender. Children:

1. Mary, not married when will made.
2. William Marshall m. Mildred (Estes): (My husbands line)
3. Henry Marshall m. 1st, Eleanor Wood; 2nd, Nancy Gibson, dates 1804 and 1849.
4. Nancy Marshall m. John Dorsey, 1816.
5. Rebecca Marshall m. James Wood, 1819.
6. Granddaughter, Frances Collier m. Martin Collier, 1818.
7. Richard Marshall m. Tabatha Cofer, 1793.
8. Thomas Marshall m. Susanna Rodes, 1792.
9. Samuel Marshall m. Polly Hersley, 1799.
10. Elizabetha Marshall m. William Howard, 1789.
11. Margaret Marshall m. William Boswell, 1794.
12. Lotty Marshall m. Levy Wells, 1806.

(Several of the above children's descendents are known.)

William Marshall, (son of William Marshall, W. B. 8, p. 118, 1822) will is recorded in Albemarle County, Virginia, W. B. XVII, page 485, 1847, names wife, Mildred. Children:

1. Jinny Marshall (see James Brockman to Jane Marshall license date June 3, 1 1833, Alb. Co., Va. records)
2. Mildred Rhoads married Robt. P. Rodes, Feb. 20, 1824, Albemarle Co.
3. Brice Marshall (executor) m. 1st, Elizabeth Martin, 1830; 2nd, Ruthie Harris 1846.

4. Nancy Marshall Howard m. Eli Howard, May 22, 1834, by Rev. Jno Gibson, Albemarle Co., Va.
5. Blueford Marshall m. L.A.S. Crenshaw, June 8, 1837, Albemarle Co., Va.
6. Sidney Marshall Harris m. Jno. M. Harris Jan. 19, 1837, by Rev. Goss, Albemarle Co., Va.

(It may be William Marshall was married a second time and Mildred was his second wife. Recorded in Albemarle Co., Va., a marriage - Wm. Marshall to Mildred Martin, Nov. 13, 1833, by Rev. John Goss. None of the above children, however, according to marriage, could be descended from Mildred Martin. Recorded in Madison Co., Virginia. Wm. Marshall to Margaret Bryant, Aug. 19, 1798, by Hamilton Goss, Nov. 8, 1798. No proof this is same Mr. Wm. Marshall.)

Brice Marshall (son of Wm. Marshall will, 1847) born Sept. 27, 1805, and his 1st wife Elizabeth Martin born Oct. 27, 1808. Ruthie Harris, Brice Marshall's second wife born Oct. 27, 1814.

Brice Marshall and Elizabeth Martin were married Jan. 31, 1830. Both of Albemarle Co., Va. by Rev. Goss.

Brice Marshall and Ruthie Harris were married March 13, 1845. Recorded in Green Co., Va. Children: (Brice Marshall died Feb. 20, 1876.)

1. Susan H. Marshall m. James M. Norfold, 1866.
2. Benjamin Marshall (b. Jan. 14, 1847, d. Nov. 23, 1938) married Susie Thomas (b. Sept. 1, 1849, d. Jan. 9, 1927) March 21, 1867.

Benjamin and Susie Thomas Marshall's children:

1. Alice Marshall
2. Ada Marshall
3. Rice Marshall
4. Emmet Marshall
5. Elma Marshall
6. Laurel Marshall
7. Bennett Marshall
8. Woodie Marshall b. July 11, 1884, d. Oct. 5, 1953.
9. Mary Lou Marshall
10. Zebby Marshall
    (All children marriages and descendants known)

Bible Record of Walter Woodie Marshall, b. July 11, 1884, d. Oct. 5, 1953, son of Benjamin and Susie Marshall.

Mamie Lee Johnson, b. May 26, 1891, daughter of Robert E. Johnson and Martha Jane Smith Johnson.

Walter Woodie Marshall m. Mamie Lee Johnson, June 2, 1908, in Pelham, N.C. Children:

1. Orvall Hansford Marshall, b. Oct. 5, 1809, married Dorothy Harbottle, Nov. 10, 1931.
2. Marvin Keith Marshall, b. June 25, 1912, married Ruby Coleman, Aug. 23rd, 1937
3. Woodie Gordon Marshall, b. Feb. 1, 1915, married Mildred C. Miller, Nov. 28, 1935.
4. Edith Mornie Marshall b. April 23, 1917, m. Daniel Taylor, July 25, 1936.

5. Wallace Jian Marshall b. May 12, 1920, d. March 22, 1943, in Scotland.
6. Selma Hortense Marshall b. Feb. 19, 1928, married Robert D. Brandt, June 30, 1949.

Grandchildren:

Sylvia Lee Marshall b. June 22, 1940
Joanne Coleman Marshall b. Dec. 24, 1942
Cynthia Lou Marshall b. Dec. 24, 1946
Walter David Marshall b. Jan. 7, 1937
Adele Louise Marshall b. Sept. 21, 1950
Betty Jane Taylor b. Oct. 13, 1939
Daniel Merideth Taylor b. Sept. 6, 1944
Eric Marshall Brandt b. Jan. 27, 1956
Robb Duncan Brandt b. Nov. 11, 1958.

(Bible in possession of Mrs. Mamie Johnson Marshall, widow of Walter Woodie M Marshall and mother of W. Gordon Marshall.)

Record of Robert E. Johnson's Bible.

Robert E. Johnson and M. J. Smith were married Dec. 22, 1881.
A.G. Campell and C. T. Johnson were married July 26, 1903.
J. M. Davis and A. M. Johnson were married Dec. 23, 1903.
Joseph Rogers Detton and Emma Jones Johnson were married May 24, 1920.
D. Clinton Hammon and Emma Johnson Detton were married June 14, 1930.

R. E. Johnson was born Oct. 2, 1859.
M. J. Johnson was born Feb. 9, 1860.
Alice M. Johnson born June 2, 1884.
Carrie T. Johnson born Sept. 10, 1886.
Walter D. Johnson born Dec. 17, 1888.
Mamie L. Johnson born May 26, 1891.
Early P. Johnson born Dec. 20, 1894.
Emma J. Johnson born June 29, 1900
Luccille McCartney Detton born Aug. 11, 1921.

Robert Johnson died April 23, 1901.
Emly S. Childress died May 20, 1910.
Robert Edward Johnson died May 16, 1934.
Joseph Rogers Detton died Sept. 2, 1922.
Martha Jane Johnson died Jan. 5, 1945

(Bible in possession of Mac Clinton Hammon, Charlottesville, Virginia)

Bible of John Vaughan Miller, dated 1828, (now in possession of Mrs. Rosa Carpenter, Orange, Va.) ancestor of Mildren Miller Marshall.

John Vaughan Miller and Elizabeth was married Monday, 24th February, 1823. (my line)
John H. Miller and Mildred Ware was married Wednesday, 20th December, 1848.
Andrew I. Miller and Sarah Ann Anderson was married 18th Jan., 1849.
W. F. C8nningham and Julia Miller, daughter of J. V. Miller was married Dec. 20, 1868.
Andrew Jackson Cunningham and Custis Lee Cunningham were born Aug. 15, 1878.
George W. M. Miller and Mary C. Ware was married 1848-9.

Mary C. Miller wife of George W. M. Miller departed this life Friday morning about day break, 15th Feb., 1850.

Walter Scott Cunningham was born May 15, 1883.
Amanda Blanch Cunningham was born May the 9th, 1886.
John V. Miller son of William and Ann Miller was born Wed, 14 Oct., 1795.
Elizabeth Southworth daughter of George and Elizabeth Southworth was born 13th March, 1805.
George William Meriweather Miller, son of John and Elizabeth, was born Wed., 20th of Oct., 1824 - 15 minutes of 12 morning.
John Henry Miller, son of John and Elizabeth was born Monday, 9th of Oct., 1826 - 15 minutes of 11 morning.
Andrew Jackson Miller, son of John and Elizabeth was born 1st March, 1829 - 20 minutes of 6 in the morning.
Elizabeth Ann Ware Miller, daughter of John and Elizabeth Miller was born Sat. morning 11th day of Feb., 1832 - 7 minutes after 10 o'clock.
Sarah Malvina Miller, daughter of John and Elizabeth was born Friday, 28th Aug., 1835 15 minutes after 8 in the evening.
Mary Mereweather Miller, daughter of John and Elizabeth Miller, was born on Sunday night, 20th of June, one o'clock, 1841.
Julia Scott Miller, daughter of John and Elizabeth Miller was born on Monday morning 18th Jan, 1847 - 15 minutes after 6 in the morning.
Adellan Florance, daughter of John H. Miller and Mildred, was born 14 day of Dec., 1850.
John Edgar, son of John H. Miller and Mildred was born Sat. morning, 5th of Feb., - 15 minutes of 7 in the morning, 1853.
Andrew Jackson Miller, son of John N. Haden and Elizabeth Ann, his wife, was born 1st of Sept., 1853.
Son of John N. Haden and Elizabeth Ann, his wife, was born Monday night, 30th Dec., 1855.
George Henry Miller, son of Andrew I. Miller was born ?Sunday morning, 16 Sept., 1849.
xxxxxxxxxxx E. Ware, son of Richard A. H. Ware and Mary Edna was born Tuesday evening 4th Sept., 1849.
John Thomas Miller, son of Andrew I. Miller and Sarah, was born the 1st day of Jan., 1853.
Meriweather Alonza Miller, son of John and Mildred Miller, was born 7th day ? 1861.
Ada Lee Miller, daughter of John and Mildred Miller, was born 7th day of March, 1864.
Elizabeth Cunningham was born Oct. 6, 1869.
Thomas H. Cunningham was born March 22, 1872.
Willie Cunningham was born May 25, 1874.
John E. Cunningham was born ? 10th, 1876.

George Southworth was born ? 1760, departed this life after a short illness of ? even days Wednesday night about seven o'clock in xxxx 79 years of his age, 13th of Nov., 1839.

Mrs. Elizabeth Southworth wife of George Southworth departed this life on Sunday morning about 6 o'clock, 18th of Oct., 1846, in her 83rd year.

George William Miller, son of John V. and Elizabeth Miller departed this life on the 25the day of Dec., 1854, in Warren Co., state of Tennessee, the 30th year of his age 2 months and five days.

John H. Miller died 15th Jan., 1844, in the 46 year of his age in Hanover Co., Virginia

William Miller, Clerk, the father of John V. Miller, was born 1st Dec., 1766, and departed this life about 4 o'clock in the morning of Sat. the 28th March, 1846, age 79 years, 3 months and 27 days.

John V. Miller was born Wed, 14th Oct., 1795, and departed this life the 9th of May, 1860.

Elizabeth Miller, wife of John V. Miller was born the 13th March, 1805, and departed this life the 23rd of Jan., 1864, age 58 years, 10 months, and 10 days.

Adala F. Miller, daughter of John and Mildred Miller was the 14th day of Dec., 1850, and departed this life the 15th day of March, 1870, age 19 years, 3 months and 1 day.

Mildred L. M. Miller, the wife of John H. Miller, departed this life on Wednesday morning about 11 o'clock - 3rd of April, 43 years, 7 months, this lacking one day, 1872.

"Old Va. Clerks" by J. Johnson, page 189, Goochland Co., Va., formed 1728 from Henrico
William Miller, Clerk 1791-1846 - 55 years

Wood Bible (now in possession of Mrs. Nannie Miller Herndon, Gordonsville, Virginia.)

William G. Wood and Catherine A. C. Wood married 23 Dec., 1852.
William G. Wood, born 6th of March, 1825.
Catherine A. C. Wood, his wife, was born 4th June, 1832.

Ages of Our Children:
James Allen Wood born 7th of March 1854.
Joseph Benjamin Wood, b. 26th June, 1855.
Isabella Marion Wood, born 30th day of Dec., 1856, and died 1947 (two different writtings)
John Robert Wood born 17th March, 1859.
Nannie Rouzee Wood, born 4th Nov., 1861.
Johnson Barbour Wood, born 2nd of May, 1864.
V. B. Wood, born 29th day April, 1868.
(On back of Bible:)
Holland Orsborne born Dec., 18, 1811.

Catherine A. C. Wood was the daughter of Benjamin Mitchell and Isabella Chapman Mitchell and the granddaughter of Henry Mitchell and Mary Lucas Mitchell. (Proven by deed and wills in Orange County, Virginia.)

William Garland Wood was son of (John?) Wood and Sarah Thompson Wood and grandson of ----- Wood and Nancy Griffin Wood of Maryland. (That information from a letter written by Catherine Michell Wood in 1906 to son John in Missouri).

Orange Co., Va. records
Isabella Marion Wood married John Edgar Miller, Dec. 14, 1876.

Miller and Wood Bible (now in possession of Mrs. Nannie Miller Herndon, Gordonville, Va.).
Charles Lee Miller born Jan. 4, 1878.
Ches Lee Miller born Aug. 29, 1879.
Leslie Glen Miller born June 10, 1882.
Joseph Benj. Miller born April 10, 1886.
Nannie Lee Miller born Sept. 19, 1889.
David Johnson Miller born April 24, 1892. (my line)

Everett Lenwood Miller born Jan 26, 1895.
William Jennings Bryant Miller born Sept. 9, 1896.
James Eric Miller, born Nov. 5, 1898.
John Robert Miller born Nov. 1, 1900.

John R. Wood died Feb. 14, 1906.
Ches L. Miller died May 16, 1941.
Volney B. Wood died Oct. 19, 1908
Leslie Miller died May 23, 1918.
J. Edgar Miller died Sept. 5, 1918. (my line)
Catherine Wood died Oct. 28, 1921.
Isabella Marion Miller died April 18, 1947. (my line)
Charles L. Miller died Nov. 7, 1950.

Mildred Catherine Miller b. April 17, 1918.
Sophia Herndon born Sept. 8, 1918.
France Marion Osborne born Feb. 5, 1836, died June 12, 1865.
Sarah Lee Miller born 29th Oct., 1922.
Ernest Morris Ford m. Sophia Miller Herndon Jan. 28, 1939.
Morris Herndon Ford born Oct. 25, 1939.
James Wood died March 24, 1885.

New York American Bible Society, 1856.

(All the above records from Mildred Marshall, 1441 Oxford Road, Charlottesville, Va.)

DURRETT-MARSHALL

In 1744 William Marshall of Caroline transferred for nominal consideration of five pounds, 400 acres in Spottsylvania to Richard Durrett of Orange. The county lines were then not definite and the area above and North of the Rivanna was Hanover, later Fredericksville Parish, Louisa, and finally Albemarle. However Spottsylvania extended into this area and in 1734 Orange was formed but there were many years before the line was clearly drawn. It is likely that the 370 acres sold in 1775 by William Brockman, Richard Durrett and Thomas Jones is a part of the 400 acres transferred by William Marshall. Richard Durrett and wife Elizabeth of Caroline in 1775 transferred 116 acres to William Durrett and if he was the son of Richard, who died 1784, then he moved into Albemarle, and was the son of Richard Durrett and wife Sarah Hampton. The deed of Charles Taliaferro in 1729 to Jael Johnson, his daughter and her son James Williams (son by first marriage of Jael) is proof that she was his daughter. Betty Marshall, daughter of Jael Johnson, was apparently wife of William Marshall, and she was a Williams and William was the son of Elizabeth Marshall referred to in the Will of Richard Durrett 1763-68. This suggests that William Brockman, Thomas Jones as well as Richard Durrett were legatees of Elizabeth Marshall, but whether William was legatee thru his wife or mother, who could have been a Marshall is not known at this writing. My conclusion that William Brockman married Elizabeth Mason seems sound but the name Mason in the family could have come from William's mother. At any rate one of them William or Samuel, married a Mason and one a Marshall. One William Marshall married Elizabeth Williams, and John, who married Elizabeth Markham (Will Culpeper) was then likely William's father and, William was son of Thomas Marshall, spouse of Elizabeth who passed on the Marshall land to the Durretts and other heirs.

FURTHER DISCUSSION OF TWO MAJOR BROCKMANS

Yanceyville, N.C.
Oct. 24, 1959.

Dear Mr. Brockman:

There were only 19 Brockman deeds; one was a Brock deed. Therefore I am searching the marriage and Will Index to take the place of the one I miscounted.

There are no Brockman marriages shown in the index for men or women.

Book B, page 20. On Sept. 2, 1782, John Brockman of Caswell County, N.C. sold 150 acres of land on Little Wolf Island Creek to Major Brockman, of Caswell. The adjoining owners were John Brockman; there were no witnesses.

Book B, page 331. On Oct. 13, 1783, John Brockman got a State Land Grant for a money consideration, the land being on Little Wolf Island Creek and joined Isaac Durham.

Book C, page 135. On Sept. 19, 1785, John Brockman and wife Amelia Brockman of South Carolina sold 172 acres on Little Wolf Island Creek to Andrew Arnett, it joins Bastian and Brockman. The witnesses were Isaac Durham, John and Thos. Arnett.

Book C, page 136. On Sept. 19, 1785, John and Amelia Brockman of South Carolina, his wife, sold 400 acres on Little Wolf Island Creek to Andrew Arnett, joining Geo. Harvey, Isaac Durham. The witnesses were Isaac Durham, John and Thos. Arnett.

Book C, page 137. On Sept. 19, 1785, John and Amelia Brockman of South Carolina sold 100 acres on Little Wolf Island Creek to Isaac Durham, joins Andrew Arnett. The witnesses were Andrew, John and Thomas Arnett.

Book M, page 53. On March 2, 1801, Major Brockman of Caswell Co., sold 150 acres land on Little Wolf Island Creek to John Crouch, joins John Brockman. The witnesses were Joseph Arnett, James Gabson and Thomas Duncan.

Book M, page 205. On Dec. 24, 1801, Obediah Tucker of Caswell sold 109 acres on North side of Hogan Creek to James Brockman of Caswell Co., joins Strader. The witnesses were Thomas Duncan, Turner Patterson, James Powell.

Book N, page 21. On April 23, 1801, John and Susanna Crouch of Caswell sold 150 acres to Major Brockman, on Little Wolf Island Creek. Witnesses were Turner Patterson, James Brockman, Peter Williams, and Obadiah Tucker.

Book P, page 141. On Jan. 2, 1808, James Brockman of Caswell sold 109 acres on Hogan Creek to Turner Patterson, joins Strador. The witnesses were Levi Ford, Major Brockman and John Arnett.

Book S, page 232. On Dec. 9, 1817, Thomas Patterson and Major Brockman, both of Rockingham Co., N.C. sold land to Obadiah Nunnally, it being the Obadiah Tucker land. Obadiah Tucker had one child, a daughter, Polly, who married Turner Patterson and she had children named Thomas, Betsey, Bartlett and Polley. Major Brockman married Betsey Patterson. This was the Obadiah Tucker estate. The witnesses were Elijah Withers, -------Barbour and Elijah Withers, Jr.

Book S, page 263. On April 17, 1818, Major Brockman of Caswell sold 4 acres to John W. Grant. The witnesses were John Barton, Thomas Barton and Archibald Grant.

Book S, page 127. On April 13, 1818, Daniel S. Farley of Caswell sold 22 acres to Major Brockman, Jr. of Caswell, land being on Wolf Island Creek and joined Major Brockman, Senr., John Grant. The witnesses were J. W. Grant, Edwin Rainey.

Book U, page 341. On Oct. 18, 1823, Major Brockman of Caswell sold 15 acres on Pumpkin Cr. to Chas. P. Harrison. Witnesses were J. W. Grant and Wm. W. Price.

Book V, page 231. On Jan. 8, 1821, Elizabeth Brockman, daughter of Turner Patterson, of Rockingham Co., sold land on Hogan Creek to Obadiah Nunnally. Witness was B. Yancey.

Book V, page 233. On July 9, 1821, Major Brockman, Sr., sold 139 acres on Fish Pond Creek to Major Brockman, Jr., both of Caswell, the consideration was money. Joins Daniel S. Farley, John Baldwin. Witnesses were John Keesal, Wm. H. Nunnally.

Book W, page 187. On July 3, 1825, Major Brockman, Sr., of Caswell, sold 200 acres in Caswell and Rockingham Counties and on Big Wolf Island Creek, to John W. Grant. Major Brockman, Sr., was Trustee for Allen Nichols and John W. Grant. Land joined Durham, Morehead, Field Nichols, Allen Nichols, Jesse Wilson. Witnesses were Elijah Yates and Thomas Henderson.

Book W, page 355. On May 11, 1826, John Brockman of Rockingham Co., sold 193 acres on Pumpkin Creek to Wm. W. Price. Land joins Joseph Obrian, Wm. Patterson - this being land left to him by his father Major Brockman deceased. The witnesses were James A. Durham, Absalon Watt.

Book X, page 222. On Oct. 24, 1827, John Brockman sold land to Thomas Archer and John Cahol, it being land willed to him by his father Major Brockman, joining Major Brockman, Jr., deceased. Witnesses were James Rawley, and Wm. Patterson.

Book GG, page 429 On March 21, 1843, John Holt, Attorney in Fact for Barney Brockman of Rutherford Co., Tennessee, sold 100 acres on Little Wolf Island Creek to Wm. W. Price, joins Mathew Miles or Mills, Grief C. Mason, and the land came to Barney Brockman from his Father, Major Brockman, deceased, by will.

I do not have any cemetery inscription for any Brockman.

WILLS

In Will Book K, page 100, is recorded the Will of Major Brockman of Caswell Co., N. C., written on Sept. 21, 1825, and probated in October, 1825, in which he named his wife, Elizabeth Brockman and he willed his son John some property; also he willed property to his wife for her lifetime and then to his three youngest children named Barney, Susanna and Mary Brockman. His son John, was appointed Executor and the witnesses were James and Yelverton D. Rawley.

This was the only Brockman will that we found.

I hope this information will be of help to you in your book.

Sincerely yours,

J. B. Blaylock
Register of Deeds

In 1945, I began recording miscellaneous personal records here in the Office and so far I have recorded about 550 Bibles, several family histories; church histories, old letters; newspaper clippings, several thousand cemetery inscriptions and many other items not recorded elsewhere. People migrated in the old days as well as now, therefore, I take records from anywhere in the U.S.A. If you have any Bible records, and Cemetery inscriptions of people from the eastern seaboard states of the U.S.A., I would like to record them here without charge.

J. B. B.

Major Brockman, referred to in Revolutionary War Records as Major B. Brockman, and later recorded as Major Brockman, Senior in the records of Caswell County, North Carolina, was son of John and Mary Collins Brockman and was born October 13, 1755, subsequently moving to Guilford County, North Carolina, and living there when he sold his land in Louisa County, Va., in 1776. Just when he married his first wife, presumed to be Jessie Jones, is not known but we know that at the time he made his Will in Caswell County, 1825, his wife was Elizabeth Patterson, or Betsy Patterson Brockman daughter of Turner and Polly Patterson and granddaughter of Obidah Tucker, the latter being deceased in 1817, when some of the Tucker land was sold by Thomas Patterson and Major Brockman. The Will of Major Brockman named wife Elizabeth and four children as legatees, and the fact that son John received more than half of the estate suggests that he was the eldest son and by the first marriage of his father. John Brockman disposed of two large parcels of his land received by the Will of his father, Major, in 1826, and in 1827, and it is believed that he then left the state and located in Tennessee. Just why Elizabeth and the three younger children did not stay and farm their substantial holdings is not known, but it is apparent that they soon left and finally located in Tennessee. Stephen H. Brockman, son of Barney, and grandson of Major, Senior, passed down to me thru his daughter Emma Augusta Brockman Lebo this statement: "Major Brockman, my grandfather was born in Virginia and buried in S. C. (Note he lived in N. C. but may have been buried in S. C.) My grandmother took children Barney and Mary in an oxcart to Illinois subsequently returning to Tennessee, where my father Barney was farmed out as an apprentice to Andrew Johnson, tailor, till age 21. I have a coat pattern cut out of a Nashville newspaper, 1865, for a coat made for Andrew Johnson. Major Brockman was born in 1755 and Barney was born October 10, 1819." No reference is made to children John and Susannah, and it is assumed that Susannah stayed with her mother, or she may have married young.

In March 21, 1843, Barney Brockman, then 24, and giving his address as Rutherford Co., Tennessee, sold land in Caswell which he inherited from his father, and si since he had an interest only after the death of his mother Elizabeth, it is presumed that she died about that time. John, son of Major Senior is presumed to have been the father of Barney B. Brockman, Senior, who was born in Tennessee May 13, 1856, and married Mary S. Clotes at Goodlettesville, December 7, 1880. The family moved to Colorado, then to Oklahoma, Missouri and then back to Tennessee, where Barney Brockman, Junior, lived and this data comes from Mrs. Barney B. Brockman, Jr., 207 Newell Drive, Ferguson, Missouri. Barney, Jr., had six brothers and one sister, and it is regretted that she did not supply the names which she states are in the Barney Brockman, Senior, Bible in her husband's possession. Children of Major B. Brockman, known as Senior and wife Elizabeth Patterson Brockman and perhaps a first wife:

1. John, moved to Tennessee, probably father of Barney Sr., who was born 1856; son Barney, Jr., of Ferguson, Missouri.

2. Barney, sold his land in 1843 and then lived in Tenn; mar. Telitha Landrum. He was born 1819 and his wife Jan. 16, 1821, in Tenn. They broke up over the war between the States as Telitha was sympathetic to the North. He died at Orange, Texas, and she died 1898 at Bryan, Texas. Children: Martha, Mollie, Minnie, Sallie, Nora, Tom R., Jim W., and Stephen Harlan Brockman. The children of Stephen and wife Mattie Ann Conway have been given in the Brockman Scrapbook. Emma Augusta, the sixth child married Miles B. Lebo and they live in Arlington, Texas.
3. Mary.
4. Susanna.

Major Brockman, Junior, son of John and Amelia Martin Brockman, born December 18, 1760, served in Revolutionary War and married in 1779 Mary Patterson, daughter of Turner and Susannah Patterson. He lived in Caswell where his father had moved about 1780 and where his Uncle Major B. Brockman, Senior, has come to from Guilford. The first reference to his name as Major, Jr., was in 1818 when he bought land in Caswell and in 1821, when Major Senior sold land to Major Brockman, Junior. The next reference is in 1826 when John Brockman sold land that he received from his father Major, deceased by Will, "next to Major Brockman, Junior, deceased." Just why John Brockman, father of this Major did not mention him in his Will, 1800, is not known but it is assumed that he had already provided for him by gifts and grandson James was adequately provided for by his marriage to Susannah Brockman, daughter of Henry and granddaughter of John. The Will of James Brockman appears in this record. So far as we know, Major Jr., had only two children, James and Mary, and there is no record of the death of his wife Mary Patterson Brockman.

Children of Henry Brockman and wife Susannah Patterson: Will - Greenville, S.C., July 19, 1834, Proved April 20, 1835.

1. Amelia Brockman, married Thomas Campbell.
2. Mary, married Theophilus Cannon
3. Anna, married Hammett.
4. Frances, married James Peden.
5. Lucy, married James Brockman, son of Major and wife Mary Patterson.
6. Elizabeth, married John Dawson Smith.
7. Thomas Patterson, married Mary Kilgore.
8. Joel D., married Harriet Terry.
9. John, named in grandfather's will, deceased by 1825.

THE LINES OF HIRAM LEROY AND JOHN BELTON BROCKMAN

Major Brockman, wife Mary Patterson

James Brockman, wife Lucy Brockman

William Thomas Brockman, wife Elizabeth Bennett

James Hiram Brockman and wife Frances Ursula Hoy. Their Children:

* 1. Myron Ernest, born October 31, 1879
* 2. William Thomas, born October 11, 1881
* 3. Albert Hoy, born September 18, 1883
4. Hiram LeRoy, born February 16, 1886 (more later)
* 5. Earle Wingo, born November 11, 1888
6. John Belton, born October 21, 1891 (more later)
* 7. Frances Dean, born November 11, 1895, died 1896
* 8. Lucy Olivia, born February 21, 1897

*Descendants given in the Brockman Scrapbook.

FAMILY RECORDS OF DR. HIRAM LeROY BROCKMAN, SR.
AND HIS WIFE, FLORA GRACE WITT BROCKMAN.
* * * * * * * * * * * *

HIRAM LeROY BROCKMAN, SENIOR, B. S. 1918, M. D. 1920, University of Oklahoma, was born in Spartanburg County, South Carolina, February 16, 1886, died Greer, S.C., April 28, 1942. He was the fourth son of James Hiram Brockman (February 9, 1854 - February 7, 1931) and Frances Ursula Hoy Brockman, (July 15, 1858 - June 11, 1932). He was married December 24, 1918, at Norman, Oklahoma, to Flora Grace Witt, born October 16, 1887, in Lee County, Virginia. Their children:

1. Hiram LeRoy Brockman, Jr., born May 24, 1921.
2. David Dean Brockman, born August 4, 1922.
3. Betty Lou Brockman, born January 11, 1925, died January 19, 1928.

I. Hiram LeRoy Brockman, II, B.S. cum laude, Furman University, Greenville, S.C.; M.D., Medical College of Charleston, S.C., 1944; Diplomate American Board of Surgery, Fellow American College of Surgeons. Born Greer, S.C., May 24, 1921; in private practice General and Thoracic Surgery, The Medical Towers, Houston, Texas. Former Research Fellow Cardio-vascular, Baylor Univ. Coll. of Med., Instructor in Surgery, Baylor; Chief, Experimental Surgery Section, University of Texas, M.D. Anderson Hospital and Tumor Clinic; married June 12, 1954, to Marilyn Spruill Hooks, born July 7, 1932, Greenwood, Mississippi. B.S. Delta State Teacher's College, Cleveland, Mississippi, and University of Houston. Graduate M.D. Anderson, School of Technology, Houston; daughter of John Dewitt Hooks, born October 16, 1904, realtor of Winona, Mississippi, and Mary Spruill Hooks, born February 22, 1906. They have one son:

(1) Hiram LeRoy Brockman, III, b. April 24, 1957, in Spartanburg, S.C.

II. David Dean Brockman, B.S., Furman University, M.D., Medical College of S.C., Charleston, S.C., Diplomate American Board of Psychiatry and Neurology, Clinical Assistant Professor of Psychiatry University of Illinois, Member American Psychiatric Association, Candidate Chicago Institute for Psychoanalysis; in private practice of psychiatry, Chicago, Illinois. He married June 28, 1950, Martha Ann Rinebolt, born May 3, 1922, B.A. degree from Art Institute of Chicago, Certificate from William & Mary College, Williamsburg, Va., in Occupational Therapy, daughter of Clarence Allen Rinebolt (10-20-1883 to 11-10-1956), a prominent and successful fruit farmer of Ludington, Michigan, and his wife, Mary Ellen Boucher Rinebolt, born January 7, 1884. Dr. and Mrs. David Dean Brockman have two daughters:

(1) Pamela Ann, born July 10, 1952, in Chicago Lying-in Hospital.
(2) Sherrill Ruth, born October 14, 1955, in Chicago Lying-in Hospital.

Flora Grace Witt Brockman, born Lee County, Virginia, is the daughter of Ambrose Powell Witt, born Lee County, Virginia, June 19, 1854, died October 31, 1926, and his wife Allie Octavia Davis, born Lee County, Virginia June 19, 1864, married June 2, 1880, died August 26, 1941.

Ambrose Powell Witt was son of Martin Harrington Witt, born Lee County, Virginia, circa 1810, died Lee County, Virginia, February 22, 1906; Martin Harrington Witt was son of Anthony Witt, born in North Carolina 1778, died Lee County, Virginia, January 22, 1862, married Stokes County, N.C., to Elizabeth Mace on August 9, 1806. Anthony Witt was son of Edmund Witt and wife, Anna________.

Allie Octavia Davis Witt, mother of Flora Grace Witt, was daughter of Eli Davis, Junior, born Claiborne County, Tennessee, July 6, 1823, died Lee County, Virginia, May 24, 1917, married December 26, 1845, to Nancy Jones, born Lee County, Virginia, June 7, 1829, died Lee County, Virginia, March 15, 1902.

Eli Davis, Jr., was son of Eli Davis, Sr., born Stafford County, Virginia, August 11, 1779, died Hancock County, Tennessee, January 23, 1861, married April 3, 1806, in Grayson County, Virginia, to Martha (Patsy) Baker, born Wilkes County, N.C., October 27, 1791, died Hancock County, Tennessee, November 21, 1869.

The above Martha (Patsy) Baker was the daughter of Reverend Andrew Baker, born 1749, died Lee County, Virginia, September 24, 1815, married circa 1769 to Elizabeth Avant, born (it is believed) October 12, 1752.

Rev. Andrew Baker was an early Baptist preacher in Virginia and North Carolina; he was a soldier and chaplain in the Revolutionary War (History of Kentucky, Collins, pg. 13); his place of residence during the Revolution was Montgomery County, Virginia. Semples History of the "Rise and Progress of the Baptists in Virginia", mentions Rev. Baker several times, as pastor of St. Clair's Bottom Baptist Church, Symthe County, Virginia. Fox Creek Baptist Church, Grayson County, Virginia, and "History of North Carolina Baptists" - Paschall, and "A History of the Ashe County, N.C., and New River, Virginia Baptist Associations" by J. F. Fletcher, name a number of churches of which Rev. Andrew Baker was pastor or organizer. The following is quoted from "History of North Carolina Baptists" - Paschall, Volume II, page 138:

> "The actual date of its constitution (Eaton's Church) as shown by the minutes of Eaton's Church was December 16, 1790; the ministers who assisted were Rev. William Petty and REV. ANDREW BAKER, the latter one of the ablest, wisest and most successful ministers in Wilkes County and the adjacent parts of Virginia, and already one of the leaders of the Yadkin Association."

Rev. Baker's last pastorate was "Thompson's Settlement Baptist Church" the oldest Baptist church in Lee County, Virginia, the minutes of which show that Rev. Baker and wife, Elizabeth, joined that church by letter on "October third Saturday, A.D. 1811." Under date April 23, 1815, the minutes of this church read:

> "On the sabbath, the 23rd day of April, A.D. 1815, a remarkable occurrence was transacted

> by Elder Andrew Baker, who baptized James Gilbert - in the Loan Branch, a tributary of Wallings' Creek. James Gilbert was the last male he baptized in his lifetime."

And another item in said minutes reads:

> "Sabbath the 24th day of September, A.D. 1815 was a remarkable day in the memory of several persons, for on this day old Father Andrew Baker expired after some days of sickness, aged 66 years. He lived 22 weeks after he baptized James Gilbert and Matilda Randolph, who is the wife of William Randolph. His remains were buried in the Robert Clark's Cemetery, 7 miles SW from Jonesville, Lee County, Virginia."

Semple's "Rise and Progress of the Baptists in Virginia" states: "Among Elder Baker's last public service was the baptism in 1816 (1815) of Rev. James Gilbert."

Children of Rev. Andrew Baker and wife, Elizabeth Avant:

1. Solomon, born April 13, 1770
2. Henry, born August 14, 1774
3. Andrew, born February 18, 1777
4. Joseph, born April 8, 1779
5. James, born January 27, 1782
6. John, born August 15, 1784
7. Nancy, born January 10, 1787
8. Elijah, born May 8, 1789
9. Martha (Patsy) born October 27, 1791, in Wilkes County, N.C.

Summer's "Annals of Southwest Virginia", page 1257, gives a long list of early marriages performed in Washington County, Virginia, by the Rev. Andrew Baker.

From a great deal of research done by Grace Witt Brockman, the following lineage of Elizabeth Avant, wife of Rev. Andrew Baker, is believed to be correct, though not fully documented as yet:

Elizabeth Avant (Avent) born October 12, 1752, was daughter of Peter Avent, born Sussex County, N.C., died Northampton County, N.C., 1779, and his wife, Amy Massey (Joseph) of Brunswick County, Va. Peter Avent was son of Thomas Avent, born 1661, French Huguenot who came to Virginia 1698 and settled in Surrey County, Virginia, died October 31, 1757, married Margaret Elizabeth Gooch, daughter of Claiborne Gooch, son of William Gooch and Ursula Claiborne, daughter of Col. William Claiborne, first Secretary of the Colony of Virginia.

Nancy Jones, mentioned above, wife of Eli Davis, Jr., was the daughter of James Jones, born Henry County, Kentucky, October 20, 1805, died Lee County, Virginia, October 27, 1854, son of Samuel and Nancy ______ of Henry County, Kentucky.

James Jones married August 12, 1828, Lorinda Warren, born Lee County, Virginia, November 4, 1806, died Lee County, Virginia, July 14, 1862.

Lorinda Warren was the daughter of Thomas Warren, born Stafford County, Virginia September 20, 1773, died Lee County, Virginia, September 18, 1860, son of John and Charity Warren of Stafford County, Virginia; Thomas Warren married circa 1796, Clarkey Hyden, born Stafford County, Virginia, 1771, died Lee County, Virginia, July 12, 1844.

Clarkey Hyden was the daughter of Henry Hyden, born December 2, 1735, died circa 1794, Stafford County, Virginia, married circa 1760, Lydia _______ (said to be a Miss Hoskins from Wales).

Henry Hyden was a son of William, born circa 1705, died intestate Stafford County, Virginia, about 1748, married Mary ______. Henry Hyden was a patriot in the Revolutionary War, furnishing supplies for the Continental Army, being too old for active duty.

The following are quotations from letters written to Mrs. Grace Witt Brockman (Mrs. Hiram LeRoy), by an elderly Methodist minister of Inman, Virginia, in 1938:

"Inman, Virginia
March 10, 1938

My Dear Mrs. Brockman: The maiden name of Thos. Warren's wife was Hyden. She was Clarkie Hyden of Stafford County, Virginia, and the sister of Mary Hyden Woodward, my great grandmother and of William Hyden who served as a Revolutionary soldier throughout the war. Their daughter Lorinda married James Jones; their daughter Nancy married Eli Davis; their daughter Octavia married Ambrose Witt. Cousin Octavia and Ambrose lived in our home during a four week normal school in the long, long ago 1881 - fifty-seven years ago, when I was a boy of fifteen. I remember them as well as yesterday.

I have no documentary data as to the maiden name of Lydia, wife of Henry Hyden of Stafford County, Virginia. Someone in the family claimed to have learned it was 'Hoskins.'

Thos. Warren is said to have been a first cousin of Anna McPherson of Stafford County who married Robert Ely. The Elys came to Lee County in 1798. The Warrens came in 1804. The Woodwards came in 1809.

Children of Henry and Lydia Hyden of Stafford County, Virginia:

1. William, born February 4, 1761, died December 24, 1858, married 1st to Elizabeth Eaton, 2nd to Martha Baldwin, was a revolutionary soldier. Placed on pension roll February 19, 1834, was living in McMinn Co., Tennessee at the time of death.
2. Jennie, married James Woodward, Stafford County, Virginia.
3. Mary, married Jesse Woodward, Stafford County, Virginia, was born May 12, 1765, died August 10, 1855, in Lee County.
4. Lydia, born 1767, died May 1, 1859, was not married.
5. Sallie, married a Mr. Latham.
6. Clarkie, married Thomas Warren. Thomas Warren came from Stafford Co., Va., bought 130 acres of land April 24, 1804, on North side of Powell's River, near Jonesville, Va. Children of Thomas and Clarkie Hyden Warren were: Harrison, Matthew, Rodney, Lorinda, Miriam and Teresa.

(Signed) E. N. Woodward."

NOTE: In addition to the above children of Thomas Warren, his will names, daughter Adie Schofield, daughter Sooky Smith, and daughter Narcissa B. Blakemore. (Will Book No. 3. page 192, Lee County, Va.) (Prepared and submitted by Grace W. Brockman) (Mrs. Hiram LeRoy Brockman, PO Box 622, Greer, South Carolina.)

FAMILY OF JOHN BELTON BROCKMAN

* * * * * * *

John Belton Brockman, sixth son of James Hiram and Frances Ursula Hoy Brockman, was born in Spartanburg County, South Carolina, October 21, 1892; he was educated at Reidville High School and Clemson College, South Carolina; he is a farmer and orchardist, owning and living on several hundred acres of land which originally was owned by his ancestors, the Brockmans and Deans. In 1948, he was elected Supervisor of Spartanburg County for a term of four years, re-elected in 1952 and in 1956 for four year terms, and will be a candidate in 1960 for his fourth term of four years. Under his supervision are the building and maintenance of all County roads (3500 miles), both dirt and surfaced, including the Road Paving Department, Bridge Department, Patching and Repair Department; he is also supervisor of five prison camps with a total average of two hundred prisoners. In eleven years of service he has supervised the building of 775 miles of newly paved roads, five new Prison Camps, new office, warehouse and maintenance shop buildings.

On November 7, 1917, John Belton Brockman was married to Mamie Catherine Bearden, born December 12, 1894, daughter of John Albert Bearden, born May 17, 1850, married November 14, 1878, Mary Lucinda Watson, born March 27, 1858, granddaughter of Lecil Bearden, born 1816, and his wife, Eleanor Nichols, born 1813, and of James Watson of Laurens County, S.C., who was killed in the War-Between-the States and lies buried in the War Memorial Cemetery in Knoxville, Tennessee, whose wife was Mahala Catherine Toland.

John Belton Brockman and Mamie Catherine Bearden Brockman have three children:

1. Mary Kathleen, born October 7, 1918.
2. John Belton, born May 19, 1922.
3. Wendell Kent, born October 31, 1925.

Mary Kathleen Brockman married December 7, 1939, Daniel Leon Kimbrell, born February 6, 1916, and they have two children:

1. Daniel Leon, Jr., born October 15, 1940.
2. Mary Candace, born November 15, 1947.

John Belton Brockman, Jr., married January 26, 1946, Joselyn Louise Cox of Tabor City, North Carolina, born September 21, 1923, and they have had five children:

1. Catherine Joselyn, born March 22, 1947.
2. Barbara Diane, born March 14, 1950.
3. Jerry Keith, born August 19, 1951, died August 19, 1951.
4. John Belton, III, born September 29, 1952.
5. Miriam Louise, born February 8, 1954.

Wendell Kent Brockman married August 20, 1949, Ruth Jones of Spartanburg, S.C., born December 29, 1929, and they have three children:

1. Ruth Elaine, born November 26, 1950.
2. Debbie Jane, born January 14, 1954.
3. Wendell Kent, Jr., born July 29, 1957.

John Belton Brockman, Senior, is descended, on his maternal line, from Joel Dean, a Revolutionary soldier. On the plantation on which John Belton Brockman, Sr., now lives is an old family cemetery, enclosed with a rock wall built by the slaves, and in which are buried the above Joel Dean and his wife, Mary Brockman Dean, their son, Alford Dean and wife, Jane Bobo Dean, and Frances Caroline Hoy Dean, grandmother of John Belton Brockman. It is believed also that Ursula Marchbanks Dean, mother of Joel Dean, the Revolutionary soldier, is also buried in this old cemetery, as she died at age 98 at the home of her son, Joel Dean.

DEATHS

GREENVILLE PIEDMONT (newspaper)
November 10, 1959
Greenville, S.C.

JOHN V. MASON

John V. (Jay) Mason, 90, retired teacher of 117 Manly St., died Monday at 8:25 p.m.

Mr. Mason was born and reared in Greer, a son of the late John Perry Mason and Lucy Ann Brockman Mason.

He attended Furman University and for a number of years taught in the city schools of Charleston. For 24 years he was principal of Bryan-Stratton Business College at Providence, R. I. He retired in 1951 and had lived in Greenville since that time.

He was a member of the First Baptist Church of Greer. His wife was the late Bertha Cummings Mason.

Surviving are a son, William V. Mason of Key West, Florida; four grandchildren and six great-grandchildren.

Funeral services will be conducted Thursday at 3:30 p.m. at the Wood Mortuary by Dr. Joseph C. Clapp. Burial will be in Abner Creek Baptist Church Cemetery.

The following have been asked to meet at the mortuary Thursday at 3:15 p.m. to serve as active pallbearers: Jack, Bernard, Kent, Ralph and Bill Brockman, and Tommy Tzouvelekas.

The body will remain at the mortuary. The family is at the home of Thomas H. Brockman, 117 Manly St., Greenville.

INDEX to
Orange County, VA. FAMILIES - Vol. #3

INDEX to
Orange County, VA. FAMILIES - Vol. #3

INDEX to
Orange County, VA. FAMILIES - Vol. #3

INDEX to
Orange County, VA. FAMILIES - Vol. #3

INDEX to
Orange County, VA. FAMILIES - Vol. #3

INDEX to
Orange County, VA. FAMILIES - Vol. #3

INDEX to
Orange County, VA. FAMILIES - Vol. #3

INDEX to
Orange County, VA. FAMILIES - Vol. #3

INDEX to
Orange County, VA. FAMILIES - Vol. #3

INDEX to
Orange County, VA. FAMILIES - Vol. #3

INDEX to
Orange County, VA. FAMILIES - Vol. #3

INDEX to
Orange County, VA. FAMILIES - Vol. #3

INDEX to
Orange County, VA. FAMILIES - Vol. #3

INDEX to
Orange County, VA. FAMILIES - Vol. #3

INDEX to
Orange County, VA. FAMILIES - Vol. #3

INDEX to
Orange County, VA. FAMILIES - Vol. #3

INDEX to
Orange County, VA. FAMILIES - Vol. #3

INDEX to
Orange County, VA. FAMILIES - Vol. #3

INDEX to
Orange County, VA. FAMILIES - Vol. #3

INDEX to
Orange County, VA. FAMILIES - Vol. #3

INDEX to
Orange County, VA. FAMILIES - Vol. #3

INDEX to
Orange County, VA. FAMILIES - Vol. #3

INDEX to
Orange County, VA. FAMILIES - Vol. #3

INDEX to
Orange County, VA. FAMILIES - Vol. #3

INDEX to
Orange County, VA. FAMILIES - Vol. #3

INDEX to
Orange County, VA. FAMILIES - Vol. #3

INDEX to
Orange County, VA. FAMILIES - Vol. #3

INDEX to
Orange County, VA. FAMILIES - Vol. #3

INDEX to
Orange County, VA. FAMILIES - Vol. #3

INDEX to
Orange County, VA. FAMILIES - Vol. #3

INDEX to
Orange County, VA. FAMILIES - Vol. #3

INDEX to
Orange County, VA. FAMILIES - Vol. #3

INDEX to
Orange County, VA. FAMILIES - Vol. #3

INDEX to
Orange County, VA. FAMILIES - Vol. #3

INDEX to
Orange County, VA. FAMILIES - Vol. #3

INDEX to
Orange County, VA. FAMILIES - Vol. #3

INDEX to
Orange County, VA. FAMILIES - Vol. #3

INDEX to
Orange County, VA. FAMILIES - Vol. #3

INDEX to
Orange County, VA. FAMILIES - Vol. #3

INDEX to
Orange County, VA. FAMILIES - Vol. #3

INDEX to
Orange County, VA. FAMILIES - Vol. #3

INDEX to
Orange County, VA. FAMILIES - Vol. #3

INDEX to
Orange County, VA. FAMILIES - Vol. #3

INDEX to
Orange County, VA. FAMILIES - Vol. #3

INDEX to
Orange County, VA. FAMILIES - Vol. #3

INDEX to
Orange County, VA. FAMILIES - Vol. #3

INDEX to
Orange County, VA. FAMILIES - Vol. #3

INDEX to
Orange County, VA. FAMILIES - Vol. #3

INDEX to
Orange County, VA. FAMILIES - Vol. #3

INDEX to
Orange County, VA. FAMILIES - Vol. #3

INDEX to
Orange County, VA. FAMILIES - Vol. #3

INDEX to
Orange County, VA. FAMILIES - Vol. #3

INDEX to
Orange County, VA. FAMILIES - Vol. #3

INDEX to
Orange County, VA. FAMILIES - Vol. #3

INDEX to
Orange County, VA. FAMILIES - Vol. #3

INDEX to
Orange County, VA. FAMILIES - Vol. #3

INDEX to
Orange County, VA. FAMILIES - Vol. #3

www.ingramcontent.com/pod-product-compliance
Lightning Source LLC
Chambersburg PA
CBHW021901020426
42334CB00013B/428

* 9 7 8 0 8 9 3 0 8 7 9 5 1 *